FEATURE FILMS AS HISTORY

Feature Films as History

EDITED BY K.R.M. SHORT

CROOM HELM   LONDON

© 1981 K.R.M. Short
Croom Helm Ltd, 2-10 St John's Road, London SW11

British Library Cataloguing in Publication Data

Feature films as history.
   1. Moving pictures in historiography
   I. Short, K R M
   907
   ISBN 0-7099-0459-2

Printed and bound in Great Britain
by Billing and Sons Limited
Guildford, London, Oxford, Worcester

To
Reinhart Koselleck, Professor of History and former Director
of the Zentrum für interdisziplinäre Forschung in the University
of Bielefeld, Federal Republic of Germany

CONTENTS

PREFACE

Today there are historians whose interest *is* the movies; increasingly there are also historians interested *in* the movies. Historians whose interest *is* the movies are committed to researching an important international industry which has aspects which are economic, technological, social, psychological and aesthetical. In this final respect its artistic implications tend to make it unusual in comparison with other international institutions with basically economic motives. Whether or not the historian takes an international or national perspective on the movies, or whether the concern is on any one or a combination of its aspects, depends largely upon which area he or she finds most fascinating and potentially productive for scholarship.

The historian who is interested *in* the movies is motivated by the question of whether the central line of research can be supported or illuminated by evidence drawn from the world of the movies. One can easily imagine the intellectual historian turning to the movies after having exhausted novels, short stories, autobiographies, school textbooks, political speeches and other literary sources in search of evidence relating to that great American tradition that anyone can become a millionaire or President of the United States, if not both. It was, however, the political historian who was the first to venture into feature films in search of evidence to support research on propaganda, particularly in Nazi Germany. Lenin was well remembered for having claimed that 'Of all the arts . . . for us the cinema is most important'. Dr Joseph Goebbels would not have disagreed. The Fatherland and the Motherland were both to be re-educated through the use of newsreel, feature film and documentary. The reason that Eisenstein's *Battleship Potemkin* (1927) met censorship in the Western democracies was because it was feared that the film would contribute to the popularity of Communism and encourage revolution. Could the reconstruction of that episode in the 1905 Revolution produce such an effect amongst the audiences of that day?

Although it is almost impossible to measure the ideological effect of *Potemkin* on its audiences either in Russia or in the West, D.J. Wenden has provided a carefully documented study of how the film was made in *'Battleship Potemkin* – Film and Reality' (Chapter 2). Wenden traces the various influences which shaped Eisenstein's conception of the events, while comparing the final product with what appears to have actually happened based upon limited documentary evidence.

Does the propaganda role of the feature film extend beyond the totalitarian state, for example to Great Britain or the United States, two major film producers? Here the question is not of the direct control by a 'propaganda ministry' as in the cases of Russia or Nazi Germany but of censorship, administered either by the state or by the motion picture industry itself. Tony Aldgate in his 'Ideological Consensus in British Feature Films, 1935-1947' (Chapter 5) raises the question of why, during a period of economic and social turmoil, followed by a world war, there was so little indication in feature films that Britain had social and political ills, curable or otherwise? Why were there so few efforts to offer a lead forward by the British motion picture industry? Aldgate carefully documents the films which indicated some glimmering of social and political concern, while Nicholas Pronay's 'The First Reality: Film Censorship in Liberal England' (Chapter 6) offers a simple answer for the almost total silence — censorship.

Britain's self-censorship by its film industry through the British Board of Film Censors dated back to 1913. Over the years the industry's self-censorship more and more served as informal government censorship through the appointment, as president of the Board, of prominent politicians who were in close contact with the government through the Home Secretary. Pronay's study illustrates the importance of documentary evidence in determining the mechanisms which led to the production and release of unexceptional films, entertainment which, during the 1930s, like the newsreels, would not disturb the political, social and economic *status quo* which favoured the National Government's continued dominance.

The situation in the United States during the 1930s was not dissimilar as Hollywood maintained a scrupulous silence about the Nazi menace and its virulent anti-Semitism. The Motion Picture Producers Association's so-called Hays Code saw to it that what flowed out of the movie town factories were dreams to occupy the minds of the millions and not revolutionary propaganda threatening the American way of life despite its shortcomings. Hollywood's conservatism and censorship were thawed by the Second World War. One indication of these significant changes were that the unwritten law that there were no Jews in Hollywood or in Hollywood films was suddenly suspended. As outlined by Kenneth Short in 'Hollywood

Fights Anti-Semitism, 1945-1947' (Chapter 8), the Jewish GI became a standard figure in war movies. When America returned to peace this development was extended to the production of such untypical movies as *Crossfire* and *Gentleman's Agreement*, the latter made by Darryl F. Zanuck, who had first taken on anti-Semitism in 1935 in his production of *The House of Rothschild* for 20th Century Fox. Hollywood had now begun a crusade on behalf of the American Jew.

The American black was also being treated differently in Hollywood both in front of and behind the cameras. Although he was not allowed to take his place next to the now common Jewish GI, the black man was beginning to be taken seriously in a movie industry which had long promoted the Black Sambo image for the predictable laughter it produced. Thomas Cripps, already noted for his splendid history of the Negro in American film up to 1942 (*Slow Fade to Black*, Oxford University Press, New York, 1977), now looks at the impact of what he calls 'conscience liberalism' upon three specific film projects during the war years (Chapter 7, '*Casablanca, Tennessee Johnson* and *The Negro Soldier* — Hollywood Liberals and World War II'). Utilising the documents of the NAACP and other relevant sources, Cripps suggests that the conscience-liberal movies of the 1940s may have been the 'ideological pre-conditions of the modern civil rights movement'.

The articles by Wenden, Cripps, Aldgate, Pronay and Short will not strike the traditionally trained historian as being so dissimilar from his own documentary approach to contemporary history; only the subjects might seem novel. The other two articles in this collection represent a somewhat different matter for they use the feature film for extracting a very different sort of evidence. Monaco and Strebel are traditionally trained historians who have moved beyond the boundaries of accepted historical methodology to gain access to evidence which the usual tools fail to uncover.

In Monaco's study of 'Movies and National Consciousness: Germany and France in the 1920s' (Chapter 3) he is particularly concerned with the visual impact and symbolism of silent films. He sees in the symbolism of time and space, represented by the films of these two traditional competitors for European dominance, significant differences which he assigns to a 'reflection of a state of consciousness'. The argument is fascinating, the proposals challenging.

A bridge between the methodological extremes represented in this collection of articles is offered by Elizabeth Strebel's 'Jean

Renoir and the Popular Front' (Chapter 4) in which she uses the documents common to the one side and the visual and psychological analysis of the other. Certainly with a cinematic genius like Renoir such an approach is wholly appropriate for there was an *auteur* capable of conscious self-expression linking the artistic with the political. Strebel argues convincingly that Renoir's camera technique is wholly consistent with his concurrent Popular Front commitment and experience.

Historians until now have taken too literally the disclaimer added to the credits of feature films that 'any resemblance to persons living or dead is purely coincidental'. Movies cannot simply be dismissed as entertainment. Despite Louis B. Mayer's advice that if one wanted to send a message one should use Western Union and not a Hollywood movie, movies did have messages, at least some of them did. It is the responsibility of historians to determine which movies had a message, who was sending the message, what the message was and, finally, if any of the audiences understood the message.

The origin of this book can be traced back to the autumn of 1977 when three of its contributors attended a conference on 'Film and History' at the University of Bielefeld's Zentrum für interdisziplinäre Forschung (ZiF). A second conference, organised by the editor and again sponsored by the ZiF, was held two years later and entitled 'Historical Realities and the Feature Film', drawing scholars from Denmark, West Germany, France, the Netherlands, Great Britain and the United States. The editor and his fellow contributors acknowledge their debt to the ZiF and especially to Professor Reinhart Koselleck, who sponsored the conference and acted as its most generous host. Other participants of the conference whose contributions do not appear in the volume also merit our thanks for their critical contributions to this set of articles: Professor Pierre Sorlin ('Cinema and the Unconscious: A New Field for Historical Research?'), Professor Arthur Marwick ('Images of Class in the Feature Film'), Karsten Fledelius ('Protectors of the Homeland — *Alexander Nevsky* and *Der Grosse König*'), Wilhelm van Kampen ('Der historische Spielfilm als geschichtlich Quelle'), Eric Swiatek ('*The Only Way*: The Escape of the Danish Jews to Sweden in October 1943 — Film and Historical Reality'), as well as Karl Stamm, John Jansen, Ursula Sporman-Lorenz, Lucian Hölscher and Joseph Agassi.

Although it is not possible to mention all of the individuals and institutions that have aided the contributors to this volume, the editor would like to acknowledge his personal debt to the following: amongst the archivists and archives, Charles Silver, Museum of Modern Art, New York; David Francis and Elaine Burrows, National Film Archive, London; Barbara Humphrys, Motion Picture, Broadcasting and Recorded Sound Division, The Library of Congress, Washington, DC; and Clive Coultass and Anne Fleming, Imperial War Museum, London. Assistance was also given by Antony Slide, Academy of Motion Picture Arts and Science, Hollywood, and Elizabeth Oliver of the British Universities Film Council, London. A major debt is owed to Professor William K. Everson for both invaluable advice and the use of films from his private collection. Help and information were also given by Professor Thorold Dickinson and Professor Sergie Drobashenko. Mary Jane Short ably assisted in the editing of sections of the manuscript.

Research work in the United States was facilitated by the generous help of Rabbi Solomon Bernards of the Anti-Defamation League of B'nai B'rith, and the ADL's former National Programme Director, Oscar Cohen. Mr Cohen unselfishly opened his files on the Jew in the movies, as well as sharing many of his personal insights, soon hopefully to be incorporated into his book on American Jewry. Joel Ollander, National Co-ordinator of the National Jewish Community Relations Advisory Council, was also unstinting in his help. The unrivalled hospitality of Thomas and Alma Cripps and Martin and Jonie Jackson made the often lonely business of research far less trying.

The editor should like to thank his contributors for their co-operation, the secretarial staff of the ZiF for their help at various stages of the preparations of the conference papers, the librarians of the ZiF and the University of Bielefeld, Adelheid Baker (translator), the ever-willing Herr Hecht of ZiF's reprographics department, and finally Christine Trinder for her secretarial skills. Paul Smith of the University of Southampton is owed a special debt of gratitude for his inestimable help in bringing this project to fruition: I am also pleased to acknowledge the help and encouragement of Peter Sowden of Croom Helm.

Finally, I should like to thank my wife and my two sons for coping with the innumerable strains imposed upon them during my sabbatical year at the University of Bielefeld's ZiF.

Kidlington, Oxford

1 INTRODUCTION: FEATURE FILMS AS HISTORY

K.R.M. Short

Feature films can be used by historians in two ways. Firstly, historians can use film as evidence in their study of political, economic or social history. Secondly, historians can study films and the film industry as a topic worthy of historical interest in the same way as they study 'The First World War' or 'The Great Depression'. Twentieth-century historians increasingly use film as evidence. In particular, films provide much interesting evidence on how the Nazi and Soviet propaganda machines worked. Only recently, however, have historians begun to accept that films and the film industry are subjects worthy of historical study in their own right. This essay takes the view that this important development is well worth while and should be given every encouragement. It surveys the special problems which historians of films have to face in gaining access to, and handling, their source material, and points to some of the interesting themes that emerge in studying films.

The political, social and economic impact of mass communications, first upon the nations of Europe and North America and later upon the rest of the world, is undoubtedly one of the most significant aspects of twentieth-century history. The invention, technical perfection and marketing for mass consumption of photography, sound recording, movies and radio had revolutionised public entertainment and the communication of current events as far back as the late 1920s, coming to a fuller realisation with the birth of public television in the middle years of the next decade. The new media offered a set of new tools, in addition to the press, with which governments, political parties and pressure groups could attempt to shape public opinion and use its potential force either to secure or to retain political, social or economic power. This revolution in communications brought with it the possibility of 'thought' control which Orwell's novel *1984* took to its frighteningly logical end. Historians, not unexpectedly, were attracted to this particular aspect of the communications revolution.[1]

Propaganda fitted relatively easily into the traditional historical focus on political history; cinema also offered a source — the newsreel — which seemed, amongst the various varieties of film sources, to be akin to history's traditional written and published sources. The newsreel offered 'camera-eye-witness' records and a commentary which initially appeared as something like an original source, if not an unimpeachable witness. Over the last decade, the experience of using the newsreel material of Germany, the United States and Great Britain has taught the historian caution. Newsreels have proven to have been highly susceptible to the significant limitation of partial coverage, and to the manipulation of content and presentation for economic and political reasons, as well as to being used as 'advertisements' of the feature film's production company. The important work of Raymond Fielding, Nicholas Pronay, Tony Aldgate, and Göttingen's Institut für den Wissenschaftlichen Film, has made it possible to recognise the manner in which the power elite in various countries sought to use the newsreel to achieve their own ends. *Die Deutsche Wochenschau* of Dr Goebbels' Nazi Propaganda Ministry provided a remarkable example of attempted thought control as part of a comprehensive programme which dealt with every possible source of information. Generally speaking, historians have learned that the newsreels show us today what their producers thought yesterday's audiences wanted to see as entertainment; the newsreel is also a primary source for what the controlling elite, whether through formal censorship or through informal influence, wanted the movie audiences — the popular masses — to know or believe. The continued historical study of this aspect of the history of the movies is extremely important providing as it does a unique record of the period say, in the United States running roughly from 1911 (when Pathe began commercial production of newsreels) until 1967 when Hearst Movietone and Universal Newsreels finally ended production.[2]

The political content of the semi-weekly or weekly newsreel constituted only a small part of the seven to ten minutes ('one reelers') of the typical issue containing from six to ten 'stories'. The sport, fashion, human interest, catastrophies and other typically topical ingredients have not found any particular usage except, it might seem, for the insatiable appetite of television documentaries to recreate the past to feed audience nostalgia. The political content of the newsreel was a small part of the whole and even then the newsreel did not attempt to show events in depth nor to demonstrate their relationships over an extended period of time. It was entertainment and not education that motivated the newsreel makers. Out of the two or two and a half hours of entertainment, the newsreel was almost insignificant. On the other hand, movie historians have not as yet found much use for the marvellous cartoons or visually intoxicating travelogues and features which fleshed out the 'Full Supporting Programme (Great Britain)' or the 'Selected Short Subjects (USA)'. The greatest proportion of production investment and audience interest was committed to the feature film; it is towards this source that historians have now begun to focus their energy.

Any historian interested in the movies must initially come to terms with the industry's notoriously unreliable literature, the record of over eighty years of legend, fact, rumour and misremembered detail. Much of this information is based upon tales generated by the studio press agents intent on promoting their stars and thus their films by feeding the tremendous audience appetite for gossip via the fan magazines and newspaper columns, such as those of the famous adversaries, Louella Parsons and Heda Hopper. Until recently, with few exceptions, movie history has tended to be an extention of the 'dreams' which Hortense Powdermaker referred to when she labelled Hollywood the 'dream factory'. Certainly Hollywood and other movie production centres had something in common with Detroit, but, whereas its assembly lines simply produced black Model T. Fords, Hollywood produced similarly packaged formula feature films bedevilled by mountains of misinformation generated by studio publicity agents. The memories-in-print of actors, actresses, directors, producers, studio owners *ad nauseam* has produced even more substantial evidence of that acknowledged fact that some Hollywood people believed in the dream world in which they lived. The literature of the dream factories is the first hurdle that the historian will cross – a highly enjoyable but mostly barren waste.[3]

History became part of the great Hollywood lie – lies which were perpetuated by the five hundred or so journalists encamped about Hollywood. The actor David Niven was briefly a correspondent for London's *Sunday Express* and thus found himself on the studio mailing list. He was tremendously amused by the press releases (inadvertently sent to him by his own studio, Samuel Goldwyn) describing his life in terms that could only be fantasy. An excellent example of the problem of using movie memories, even at their best, is provided by Niven's immensely entertaining *Bring on the Empty Horses* (New York, 1975, p.182). He makes no pretence of writing history but the book is a likely source for information on contacts between Hollywood's English colony and the propagandists seeking to get American support for Britain during 1938 to 1940. One of the most curious of American pro-British responses had been Alice Duer Miller's narrative poem *The*

White Cliffs, published in August 1940 after having difficulty at first in finding a publisher. Unexpectedly the poem became a best seller; a dramatisation was broadcast coast to coast by NBC with Alfred Lunt introducing the programme featuring his wife, Lynn Fontaine, reading the poem (both were British subjects). The famous song 'There'll be blue birds over the White Cliffs of Dover' was inspired by the poem. The poem also became a best seller in Nazi-besieged Britain and the BBC broadcast a dramatisation featuring Constance Cummings. Naturally there was interest in turning the story into a movie. Niven recounts (in a chapter on Ronald Colman) how the notoriously foul-mouthed Harry Cohn, president of Columbia Pictures, enlisted Colman's help in convincing Mrs Miller, a New York socialite, to allow him to produce the movie. Colman was told:

> 'Tell the old bag how goddamned tasteful I am,' said Cohn. 'Shit! I'm making "The Lost Fucking Horizon" ain't I?'
> Colman dutifully did his best and Alice Duer Miller was visibly weakening during luncheon in his dressing-room. Afterwards he took her on a tour of the rabbit warren of a studio, avoiding the seamier parts of it.
> He thought she might be impressed by a walk through the writers' building because on the doors were the titles of forthcoming productions and the well-known names of those slaving over the screenplays within. The place, smelling of coffee, was impressive with its air of quiet concentration and the steady 'clacking' of typewriters underlined the industry of Harry Cohn's employees.
> 'This picture will be going into production soon,' said Colman, pointing to a door on which was written —
> 'TOM BROWN'S SCHOOLDAYS'
> Writers — TOWNE AND BAKER
> Alice Duer Miller was genuinely delighted — 'Why that's just wonderful! . . . they are going to make a film of *that* . . . what a charming idea . . .!'
> At that moment the door flew open and out rushed the diminuitive Gene Towne. He grabbed Colman by the lapels of his jacket, he was glassy-eyed with excitement.
> 'Hey, I've got it! Goddammit, I've *got it*!! It wasn't the *boys* who did it . . . the sons of bitches!! . . . It was the *masters, the bastards!*'

This is a typical Hollywood story which offered to provide some background information to the process which lay behind the production by MGM of *The White Cliffs of Dover*, released in June 1944. Is the story reliable?

1. The poem was not completed until August 1940. The trip to the Columbia lot could not have taken place earlier than the autumn of that year but Cohn claimed to be 'making' *Lost Horizon* which, although starring Colman, had appeared three years before. It may simply be that the proper tense of the verb was lost in 'oral transmission'.
2. Colman was reportedly making a film (apparently *Lost Horizon*) at the time for Columbia, but the only film he made for Cohn in this period was made in 1942. During 1940 he made films for Paramount and RKO.
3. If the date was 1942 (*The Talk of the Town*), what of the anachronism of the scriptwriters of *Tom Brown's Schooldays* released in 1940?
4. Finally, since Niven had rejoined the British Army at the outbreak of war, he would most probably not have heard the story until after his return to Hollywood in 1945 and does not retell the story for twenty years.

It is quite possible that Colman did take Mrs Miller on a tour of Columbia Pictures; Colman did at some time own the film rights to the story and he may have had an offer from Cohn to produce it. Having failed to find adequate finance, Colman did sell the rights to the MGM director Clarence Brown, who in turn sold it to MGM with the proviso that he direct the film. Brown, having worked with Mrs Miller for a fortnight on the story, received an outline from her in early June (the 'treatment' is dated 25 May 1942). Two years later, Mrs Miller having died in the meantime, *The White Cliffs of Dover* finally reached the screen. What of Niven's story? Internal inconsistencies provide problems but, in general, the story seems to be 'almost true'.

  Pursuing 'memoir' evidence of Hollywood involvement in pro-British propaganda leads to the autobiography of that splendid British actor Sir Cedric Hardwicke (*A Victorian in Orbit*, London, 1961). He provided the story of how he failed to rejoin the British Army Reserve; the War Office had cancelled his commission because he was over-age. This was followed by the potentially important record of a meeting (undated) in Washington between the British Ambassador and a group of similarly over-age British actors, including Hardwicke. Lord Lothian told the group that they were more valuable to the war effort keeping

up the British image in Hollywood than wearing a uniform at a desk
in London. While documenting his various efforts to do just this,
Hardwicke mentioned an amusing incident at an unnamed studio on
the set of an unnamed film. Several British actors including himself
and C. Aubrey Smith were to act the parts of the Japanese War
Cabinet. When Smith delivered the opening lines with his unmistakable
English accent, the producers immediately decided to replace the
British actors with White Russian émigrés.[4] This use of either English
or White Russian actors for Asian parts is unusual since there did not
seem to be any shortage of Chinese-American actors, led by the
ubiquitous Richard Loo, for such parts, as *The Purple Heart* (1944)
about the Doolittle bomber raid on Tokyo in 1942 provides ample
evidence. Thus far it has not been possible to locate a film with a White
Russian Japanese War Cabinet. Does such a problem have the effect
of casting doubt about the accuracy of Hardwicke's reporting of the
meetings with Lord Lothian? The answer is 'yes' but only to the
extent that it reminds the historian (who should need no such
reminder) of the necessity of corroborative evidence, particularly for
memoirs which are by definition written long after the events described.
It is necessary to search Lord Lothian's public and private papers. Are
there additional memoranda concerning the manner in which
Hollywood's anglophiles, like MGM's Sidney Franklin, could help the
war effort? Hardwicke provides the historian with a starting-point for
research whereas the tendency in the past was for 'historians' of the
cinema to be satisfied simply with retelling such a story as
unquestionable fact. Authors such as Hardwicke and Niven were gifted
men who had made their life's work the playing of roles, the telling of
tales, the creation of fascination with words. It would be most unlikely
if these accomplished thespians had memories which preferred accuracy
over effect; where history is concerned they are probably closer to
Shakespeare than to von Ranke.

The same sort of caution must be urged in the use of 'oral history'
or interviews. Such evidence can be valuable but great care must be
taken to verify such memories from other sources. There is perhaps no
film historian with more experience in interviewing movie people than
Thomas Cripps, whose documentation for the article in this volume
indicates a substantial and critical use of such material.

It is easy enough to say that historians must have documentary
evidence if the history of the movies is to be properly written. How
often does the historian run up against a brick wall in trying to get
contemporary documents about a film or a group of films? Looking

at the documentation of the various authors represented in the recent (1979) *American History/American Film*, edited by John O'Connor and Martin Jackson, the answer seems to be more often than not. This is not to say that the documentation does not exist. One of the tasks of the movie historian is to locate material long forgotten in the dust-covered cartons stored in the director's attic. Fortunately, it is increasingly recognised that the history of the industry is central to the American experience and not simply the ephemera of entertainment. One example which bears upon the Anglo-American theme seems typical. During a search for information on *The White Cliffs of Dover* (MGM, 1944)[5] it was discovered that its director, Clarence Brown, now too elderly to be interviewed, had given his personal papers to the University of Tennessee. The story treatment by Alice Duer Miller (the poem's authoress) was uncovered but nothing else of significance was found concerning the film. Nor did correspondence with the two surviving writers of the screenplay produce a shooting script. One of the writers simply said that it would be impossible for him to find a script in his basement where material had been accumulating since 1938. He had, however, bequeathed the material to Brandeis University. It would appear to be imperative that a central directory be established which would provide locations for such material spread between university libraries and Hollywood basements. The recording of 'oral history' through interviewing such people is also an essential task for today. There must be a vigorous campaign to get cinema people to commit to posterity not only television interviews but their letters, diaries and documents. It is upon such material and the files of the world's film studios that the next generation of movie historians will write the 'new' history. It is important to remember that the films themselves are also in danger unless they are safely stored and restored. There have been three major fires in recent years, two in North American and one in France, destroying millions of feet of nitrate film from the pre-1950 period. Studio documentation is also important.

The studios have no particular reason to open their files going back fifty years or so to historians. Fortunately they are releasing them to university libraries but often with highly restrictive provisions. An example of this is provided by Warner Brothers, the documentary records of which are divided between Princeton University and the University of Southern California. Major cinema collections of 'paper' documents are also being developed at the University of Wyoming and Brigham Young University. It will become increasingly important

for the various repositories of such material to communicate the nature
and extent of their collections, particularly those libraries the holdings
of which are comparatively small in this area of movie history and
might go unnoticed by the historian.

Another important source is the record of the censorship process as
applied before and after film production. The British Board of Film
Censors script files from 1930 to 1940 are housed in the library of
the British Film Institute in London. They provide a mine of
information on the content control of British films, as well as offering
useful insights into Hollywood filmscripts which were also submitted
for comment. Britain was an important market for the American film
industry, which did not want to find its products frozen out for
making a rude comment about the Duke of something or other which
was not essential to the story line. How did the Board react to the
proposed production of historical romance, for example Gaumont's
Jew Süss in 1933-34, when by implication it was a criticism of the
emerging anti-Semitism of Nazi Germany? This was the moment when
the Foreign Office was putting pressure on the BBC to moderate its
reporting of events in the Third Reich. Surely the cinema was not
immune to such pressure? Another example would be the production
of *Father Takes a Walk*, as it was titled in the United States, but made
in England as *Mr Cohen Takes a Walk*. This film, produced in 1935
by Warner Brothers at Teddington, starred the German Jewish
refugee, Paul Graetz (he had also played in *Jew Süss*). Was the British
Board worried about the implications of a story of a successful
London Jew for the contemporary British scene; if not, did it approve
this script as an antidote for the anti-Semitic brutalities currently
being administered by the master race or as a bit of harmless ethnic
comedy? The answer lies in the script reports. What the reports will
tell historians about films which were produced and distributed may
not be as important nor as interesting as what they tell about the
projects which were still-born because of their failure to gain the
approval of the Board.[6]

Hollywood laboured under a similar sort of restrictiveness with the
Motion Picture Producers of America (MPPA)'s Production Code
with its four thousand words of moral and political 'thou shalt nots'.
Raymond Morley's *The Hays Office* (New York, 1945), based upon
the MPPA's records, says relatively little about the application of
the rules to the making of individual movies, since the book's purpose
was to assure America, and particularly the government, that its
self-policing policy was a great success and that no federal legislation

was necessary. In order to determine how 'successful' the MPPA was, a full scholarly reassessment of those records is required in conjunction with the records of the various production companies. Film archives preserve a proportion of the world's film production (often in truncated if not battered versions of the originals, 'censored' by both wear and distributors, in addition to committees); it is the records of the censors and the film studios which will tell us what the audiences were not fit to see. The film-making process produced various sorts of documentation, such as memoranda, but the chances of gaining access to it at the moment are slender but improving. What is more likely to be available to the researcher is the film script, an important historical document which can provide valuable insights into the intentions, if not the achievement, of the film makers.

There is a steadily increasing number of scripts being published these days, the Lorrimer series being perhaps the most prominent. John Gassner and Dudley Nichols published three valuable collections of *Best Film Plays* in 1943, 1944 and 1945. There was also *The Citizen Kane Book* (Secker and Warburg, 1971) containing the shooting script and Pauline Kael's essay 'Raising Kane'. The University of Wisconsin Press has published the filmscript, *Mission to Moscow: The Feature Film as Official Propaganda* (Madison, 1979), edited by David Culbert, one of America's best-known film historians, while Thomas Cripps has edited *Green Pastures* in this Wisconsin/Warner Brothers Screenplay Series. There were also Ernest Betts's editions of *The Private Life of Henry VIII* 1934) and *Jew Süss* (1935). A published movie script provides (London, important preliminary insights into the structure and verbal content of the film. Such scripts can be misleading if they are based upon the script used in the film's production ('shooting script') rather than reconstructed from the soundtrack dialogue, the final product. Soundtrack dialogue can be tape-recorded during the viewing of the film and later transcribed in order to ensure accuracy.

The shooting script, on the other hand, contains valuable information on the film-making process. Film archives and institutes, like the British Film Institute, do hold copies of shooting scripts (over 6,000 in this instance). A circular letter to the various repositories will often turn up the required script but the scholar is usually prohibited from ordering a copy since the material is protected by the studio's copyright.

One small example of the importance of the shooting script for historical research is offered by *The White Cliffs of Dover*. Study of the script indicated that additional scenes were shot after the completion of the film, obviously in response to criticisms at the previews about its reconstruction of the Dieppe Raid. While the Canadians had provided the majority of the troops that went ashore, the movie showed only American Rangers and British Commandos. The new scenes included clearly identifiable Canadian bodies. Omitting to make such concession to historial accuracy might have contributed to the film's economic failure in Canada, much as Warner Brothers' failure to provide an adequate British Army presence in *Operation Burma* (1945) led to its withdrawal from British distribution.

Shooting scripts are daily work sheets for the film makers with prepared dialogue and directions which are constantly being modified in the process of shooting the film. In one sense the 'final' script is the one which is frozen on to the film's edited soundtrack, the final version of the film ready for distribution. Memories, contemporary documents and scripts are the stuff of which movie history is only partly made, whether they testify to the movie-making process before, during or after. The most important document still remains the film itself for, whatever people intended the film to be, it is the final product which represents the realisation of the creative effort.

Television's appetite for movies as an inexpensive way of filling air-time is immense. One can apparently settle into a chair in front of a New York television set and watch movies from the several channels virtually non-stop 24 hours a day. With the advent of cable television, even the South Carolina viewer armed with the *TV Guide* covering the stations linked by satellite to the cable company will be able to do the same thing. This is without doubt the cheapest way for historians to see the movies on their research list, especially if they do so in conjunction with a video recorder for replay. There are over 12,000 movies available for showing on American television and a book like Leonard Maltin's *TV Movies 1979-80* (Signet, New York, 1978) provides a quick run-down on basics — director, cast and plot details, and running time. The traditional mode of film study is viewing at one of the forty or so major world film archives. This is normally cheaper than hiring a film for study through one of the major 16 mm film distributors, such as Film Inc. in the USA or Harris Films Ltd in the United Kingdom. Print quality will also be better at the archive; most archives charge for the service, one exception being the Motion Picture Division of the Library of Congress. (The current price of viewing a feature film at the National Film Archive in London is £3.45, including value-added tax, roughly twice as much as going to see a film at the cinema.)

As a document the film has special problems associated with its being a very long strip of sprocketed nitro-cellulose or triacetate film stock which is easily broken and just as easily mended. Scenes can be removed for reasons of conscious censorship or inadvertent damage to the film or as a means of shortening the timing on a cinema programme. Copies were made for foreign markets and are different in detail from that released for domestic consumption; the history of the particular copy being studied has a great deal to do with the 'completeness' of the film as a document. A film can, however, be 'complete' in two different forms. The original version of Renoir's *La Grande Illusion* contained the passage in which the French soldier and the German farm woman lived together, complete in the sense that that is how Renior cut the final print for distribution. There is also a 'complete' print without this compromising passage, being the version which its audiences saw. If one is considering the impact of the message of this film for before 1958 (when the passage was restored), it has to be the edited version that is focused upon in historical research. D. W. Griffith's *The Birth of a Nation* has three editions and one can be certain that each of the uncounted prints in distribution will be marginally different simply because of wear and tear. One document in several forms provides special problems for the historian. In order provisionally to establish the 'completeness' of a print it is usual to check the running time as reported in the trade press of the various countries. One of the interesting things that emerges in the extremely valuable *Monthly Film Bulletin* of the British Film Institute is the running length of American films which subsequently have their time shortened, suggesting censorship of some material.

Film timing is also important for the historian when it comes to writing about the film. After a careful description of a particular scene, it should be 'located' in feet/metres or minutes from the beginning of the film. Such information makes it easier for someone else seeking access to that particular material. Where do the calculations begin from? The usual method is to begin the timing from the first impression on the film, whether it is the image of the credits or soundtrack material providing perhaps an overture for the film. In order to establish the running time of the copy of the film being used, the archivist can provide length noted on the index or registry card (to which researchers do not always have access). It is not easy accurately to time the material on the

Steenbeck (or Moviola) editing table because of the necessity of having
to change reels (when using the 35mm copy) eight, nine or ten times
depending upon the film's length. A stop watch is indispensable and in
many ways minutes are preferable to locating via length measurements,
although footage/metreage counters are usually fixed to the machine.[7]

Film archives seldom possess printed catalogues and it is necessary
to send circular letters to establish the location of particular films.
Great Britain's National Film Archive has a catalogue of its viewing
copies which is invaluable. The average film archive holds far more
films than it can afford to provide viewing copies of for research. Films
are thus held for preservation and if a viewing copy of a particular film
does not exist then lobbying by the researcher is required for the
archive to produce a viewing copy from its preservation material. The
archive also has tremendous difficulties associated with the highly
inflammable and chemically unstable nitrate films which were
produced before 1951-2 when safety triacetate film was generally
introduced. To view a film or a group of films it is necessary to make
an appointment to allow for the films to be transported from the
storage vaults and for the use of the Steenbeck viewer; moreover,
if the material is nitrate it must be seen in a fireproof viewing room.
Although the historian is not used to having to pay for research
facilities it is a necessary fact of life when using film materials.

Generally the historian finds himself undertaking content analysis
concerning what characters in the film say and do. His concern will
also be with symbols either pictorial or musical (tunes evoke particular
responses from the audience, as does the texture of the music). Seldom
will he, unlike his colleagues who study film from the aesthetics side or
that of semiotics, be terribly concerned about how long, in minutes
or frames, something takes to happen. He is not going to do a shot-by-
shot analysis of the film which could take weeks; few archives
encourage such detailed study. At times the counting of the number
of frames (the individual 'pictures' of the movie) may be the only way
to understand an important filmic device.

Sidney Lumet's film, *The Pawnbroker* (1964), makes a special
use of cinematic devic, the flashback, to convey its meaning. The
film tells the story of a Jewish concentration camp survivor who is
a New York pawnbroker in Black Harlem. Although he has over the
years managed to suppress the memories of the death of his wife
and children he still has flashes of fragmentary memory. These very
small bits of 'flashback' are in the beginning almost subliminal,
taking up 6 frames or about 15 seconds each. Flashes recall German

guards and savage dogs, wedding bands stripped from women's fingers, a man hanging on the barbed wire. These snippets of memory are psychological reminders of the upcoming anniversary of his wife's death — one sees them much as the central character does and the viewer is frustrated by not being able to capture the content or meaning of these random fragments of the past. The flashbacks become longer and longer until they become of almost intolerable lengths in the mind of Sol Nazerman as he moves towards a nervous breakdown. There is no doubt that this mechanism of the flashback, used in a manner analogous to the psychological processes of the mind, is central to the film's record of the horrifying legacy of the Holocaust. Lumet's structure, produced by editing, is an integral part of the message and, as in the instance of Renoir's technique discussed in Elizabeth Strebel's article on 'Jean Renoir and the Popular Front', needs to be taken very seriously.

The message of a film or group of films is contained therefore not only in the dialogue but also in the visual symbols that present themselves to the viewer. Often these symbols are so deeply part of a particular social and historical context that the 'foreign observer' may be unaware of their emotive value. A film which stands out in this respect is *Since You Went Away* (1944), the first film produced by Selznick after *Gone With the Wind.* This film about the courage of home front America has highly evocative music tunes of both patriotic and sentimental types, all of which would have 'triggered' emotional responses unconsciously in an American audience, but might pass generally unnoticed in any other. These aural symbols are extremely important in creating the appropriate emotional response or climate among the audience. Music is one of the most vital ingredients of the film maker's craft and must be carefully assessed and noted. Music provides one element of film communication, while the film maker also creates another in his effort to invent costumes and settings which seem to the viewer to be authentic, thus making it easier for a member of the audience to 'believe' in the action taking place on the screen.[8] Much of this authenticity is purely visual and not essential to the plot. In *Since You Went Away* there is an important tracking shot from outside a 'typical' Hollywood version of an American suburban home at evening, pointing towards the lighted window. The camera lingers as it passes 'through' the window in which hangs a small satin flag with a star on it. Then the camera moves on into the house and the family. In America the symbol of the flag and star did not need to be explained; most people in the audience had one hanging in their front window indicating the number of sons, daughters or husbands they had in the armed forces. If it was a gold star it meant that one of them had died in service. Where this particular film is concerned, it is only the first of a long list of symbols which evoked response without need of comment or explanation. The film researcher must learn to look beyond the action to the posters on the wall in a wartime canteen in order to understand the importance of creating the believable context. Where the movie is about contemporary events there is also an important degree of reflection of the current society even if it has the sort of larger-than-life magnification of Hollywood in the 1940s. Films shot on location have the added advantage of being a record of, say, Hollywood in the 1920s, when films like the *Mack Sennett Keystone Kops* were shot in its streets.

The message of a film can be communicated through skilful direction as in the case of Renoir, it can be communicated through the evocative symbolism of both ear and eye, but primarily it will be communicated through the content of its dialogue, especially since the advent of sound. It is interesting to see that, in the various articles in this collection, only one, 'Hollywood Fights Anti-Semitism, 1945-1947', heavily stresses the content of the dialogue. The conversations about anti-Semitism provide the message of the film which has relatively little action. Certainly the dramatisation of the provocations suffered by either the Jew Dave Goldman or his journalist friend posing as a Jew has a powerful emotional impact but the dialogue carries the essential message. Even the silent film had titles which must be taken seriously for they were not simply tacked on; titles were considered to be essential to and part of the total conception of the film.

After the historian has seen the film, studied its background music, its dialogue (for silent films, the titles), the visual symbolism, and the edited structure, he begins to have some idea of what the film means to him. The extent to which this might also be valid for the person in 1944 who saw the same film depends upon how effectively the researcher is able to immerse himself in the period historically and culturally. This is essential for the historian for he is not attempting to assess the film artistically but rather to understand how it reflects its time and produces evidence towards the solution of his historical problem. The film's box office popularity provides an important clue to the movie's impact, its artistic quality or lack of it notwithstanding.

Forty or fifty years after a move is made, how does the historian gain a valid impression of the effect of the film upon its audiences?

Clearly the researcher is not a 'person of the period' to the extent that he looks at the film with eyes unclouded by his knowledge of the events which have taken place since the film's production. Is it possible to judge contemporary understanding and response retrospectively? The most obvious answer is the unsatisfactory but essential one of turning to the film reviewers in the national and local press of the various nations where the film was distributed. When doing this it is important to remember that a film reviewer is hardly a typical member of the audience but rather a professional film watcher with all of the prejudices of his caste.

Film archives such as the Museum of Modern Art in New York and the British Film Institute in London maintain 'clippings files' which are newspaper cuttings on individual films, mixed in with press books (studio public relations booklets with press releases, placard examples, still photographs for the local newspaper, etc.; in general material to help the local theatre manager 'sell' the film). These clippings files can be in scrapbooks, file folders, and increasingly on microforms, microfiche being the most popular. Using a reader-printer, the researcher can photocopy directly from the microfiche, thus aiding his collection of material. A total reliance upon such files is a mistake for one must search the widest range possible for comments upon the films which are being researched. The popularity of a film can be partially judged through information printed in trade journals such as the American *Variety*. Photographs can be obtained from the archive/ institute 'Stills Collection' but be warned that these are usually publicity photographs taken during the film's production. Pictures which accurately reflect the audience-eye-view must be taken directly from the film itself — these so-called 'frame shots' photographed from the relevant frame in the film.

The preface to this volume suggested that there are two basic approaches that historians might take towards feature films. On the one hand there are those historians who study the movie industry and its products, especially the newsreel and the feature film. Joining this expanding group of historians, particularly in America, are those, such as intellectual, political or social historians, who see the feature film as a potentially important source of information to add to their traditional sources. While the notes to this chapter (notes 1 and 3) mention several interesting articles on the methodology of film scholarship or 'why historians should bother about feature films at all', the approach of this volume has been committed to the pragmatic rather than the theoretical. The articles in this collection provide examples of traditionally trained historians using the materials of the cinema to illuminate important historical areas. If the conclusions of these examples are credible then one might reasonably expect the case for using feature films in historical research to be proven.

Before attempting to use feature films and their allied 'paper' and oral sources, the historian must be prepared, however, to adopt the hypothesis that feature-length movies, despite being almost exclusively fictitious in nature, have the ability to reflect historical realities in a useful, if not unique, manner. Its corollary is that feature films have a significant and demonstrable impact upon their audiences either in confirming an existent value-system or in contributing to its modification with political, social or economic ramifications. At all times the feature film must be viewed as but part of the over-all pattern of mass media communications in a given society. Few films will have been based on original film scripts, which means that the themes which they exploit or explore are derived from best-selling novels and popular magazine short stories. In a similar manner extremely popular movies have regularly been dramatised for radio, using move stars as actors.

The historical realities reflected in British, American or French feature films are related to the very nature of the movie business. Put in its simplest form the movie producers give the audiences what they think will entertain or please them. The feedback on this production 'estimate' is measurable in box office success or failure, leading to the bankruptcy of the movie producer or a modification of his views as to 'what the public wanted' and subsequent alterations in the stars, situations and plots of his films. The public is not, however, a homogeneous entity and the national or international success of a particular film or genre may be less significant to the historian than its failure in a section of the United States, say the mid-west. An example of this can be found in the history of anti-Semitism in the United States (not surprisingly, there are unresolved problems associated with it). When 20th Century Fox undertook production of *Gentleman's Agreement* it had every reason to expect that it would 'flop' because it believed that movie audiences in America as a whole did not want to be lectured on whom they should love. It was also generally recognised that there was a significant level of anti-Semitism existing throughout the nation. One indication of this lack of brotherhood was the Office of War Information's confidential survey of 1942 indicating that, while only 2 per cent of the respondents in the rural mid-west expressed anti-Semitic grievances, the figure was

15 per cent in the rural south. The OWI initiated 'love your brothers' programmes to overcome or dampen down this anti-Semitism but its level of success is impossible to judge. Laura Z. Hobson's novel *Gentleman's Agreement* was, however, a best seller in 1946. Such a novel had a generally different consumer than the feature film, but 20th Century was prepared to take the risk because it was a proven 'property' and Darryl F. Zanuck was prepared to fight anti-Semitism through the fiction film, carrying his company and the New York bankers with him. His marketing department expected that the film would not do good business in the south because the section traditionally rejected 'message' pictures. Despite such expectations the film was extraordinarily successful in the south but failed to do business in the mid-west. Was the mid-west more anti-Semitic than the OWI surveys imagined; had there been a major shift in opinion in the south since 1942; or were these polls less indicative of public opinion sectionally than the box office performance of this particular movie? One way to extend the investigation would be to do a careful analysis of the sectional box office takings in association with a detailed analysis of local newspaper reviews for both *Gentleman's Agreement* and the crime-thriller *Crossfire*, appealing as it might to a different sort of audience. Before 1950 films dealing with such social issues are exceptional in portraying problems as they existed in a manner acceptable to a commercial audience. The portrayal may not be wholly realistic nor totally believable but it is a powerful document of how anti-Semitism was viewed in 1947.

The exceptional film, as are those of Jean Renoir discussed in Elizabeth Strebel's chapter, clearly offers one sort of evidence concerning political, social or economic problems (and in some cases solutions) but does that mean the common fare of the cinema has nothing to offer? Whereas the exceptional film will point to the soft spots of a society, the unexceptional run-of-the-mill movie testifies broadly to that society's political, social and economic consensus. Consensus is a difficult word requiring careful hedging for it means different things to different nations in different periods. The strict censorship which sought to control feature film output in Soviet Russia and Nazi Germany produced consensus films which were indicative of what the totalitarian regime wanted its population to believe, reinforcing acceptable latent convictions about other nationalities while supporting the basic ideals and policies of the governing elite. Soviet ideals are the very essence of Soviet cinema since movies were conceived of as an educative medium for a nation whose masses were illiterate. One of the important questions to be answered in the Soviet cinema is the extent to which developing Soviet historiography was paralleled by the presentation of the Russian past in feature films. The 'truth of the past' was to be communicated to the present so that Russia's people could be motivated by it, as in the case of Sergei Eisenstein's *Alexander Nevsky*. By uniting the people of the land with the city, the sickle with the hammer, Nevsky defeated the Teutonic knights (for which read Hitler's legions). The unexceptional film in a censor-controlled society was an important tool for education and reinforcement; exceptional films like the Nazi *Jew Süss* and the *Eternal Jew* were harbingers of a change of governmental policy – the Final Solution.[9] Exceptional and unexceptional films within totalitarian states, such as Nazi Germany and Soviet Russia, inform the historian as to what the state wanted its citizens to believe.

Historians may be ready to accept the evidential importance of feature movies produced in a totalitarian setting for measuring the intention, the concepts and the success of a national propaganda machine, but what of the unexceptional movies of the so-called democratic world of the period 1920-50. These films represent possibly 98 per cent of the total production; are they at all useful? This is the other aspect of consensus perception. While one knows, often specifically, who is trying to sell what in a Nazi film, what of the Hollywood product in which there is apparently no effort to impose a consensus, but rather the attempt is being made to reflect consensus as the best means of ensuring box office success? The popularity of the Horatio Alger success story throughout Hollywood's history points to how deeply embedded this concept was in the American consciousness and the almost infinite permutations which could be produced from this simple idea. The Hollywood western is a classic definition of Fredrick Jackson Turner's frontier thesis ascribing the uniqueness of American character and institutions to the existence of the ever-moving frontier; the gangster films of the 1930s were a not-too-inaccurate symptom of America's fascination with crime and violence in the Prohibition Era – one needs only to read the newspapers, magazines and 10¢ pulp novels of this era. If the historian wishes to 'see' what the white American consensus was concerning the black 10 per cent of the population he only has to look at the 'Uncle Tom' and 'Black Sambo' in Hollywood pre-1939 production. The former character was the loyal 'nigger' who goes back well beyond D. W. Griffith's *The Birth of a Nation*; the latter was superstitious, happy, ignorant, always dancing, and could have been viewed in 1905 at a local nickelodian.

While the consensus of the controlled state reflected the views of the governing elite, the movies of the 'free' state were not simply expressive of what the majority of the audience apparently wanted to see. As mentioned previously, censorship played an important role in the United States, Britain and France, reflecting government and elitist views on what the 'common people's' entertainment should be, consistent with the established norms of national morality. In the case of the United States the powerful religious pressure groups of White Anglo Saxon Protestants (WASPs) joined with the White/European Roman Catholics (WERCs) to cow Hollywood into the creation of the Hays Committee which was accepted by the industry as the morality watchdog to keep threatened federal censorship legislation outside the studio gates. After all, if the forces of the WASPs could force prohibition upon the nation's reluctant majority, how much more frightening was the WASP coalition with the Roman Catholic Church? Hollywood's films offer two conflicting views parading as consensus — one majority and one minority. The minority WASP/WERC norms kept married couples in twin beds, the gangster heroes in cement boots in the last reel, virtue always triumphing and swear words off the soundtrack. Hollywood, seeking to provide the unorganised paying majority with the sex, violence, immorality and adventure that they craved, imitated the genius of Cecil B. DeMille, which glorified the violence and sexual lust of the Old Testament so that it could be justly overcome in the final reel, thus making everybody happy. Violence, Sex and Retribution ensured box office success. Until the 1950s, when the censorship system of Hollywood collapsed along with the industry in general, the products of the dream factory represented a marriage of convenience. The story in Great Britain during this same period is different primarily in the extent to which the function of censorship was an informal expression of government operating through the British Board of Film Censors. Substantially it meant that, whereas the Hays concern was primarily moral, the BBFC also exercised an important brief relating to the protection of the nation's political and class institutions. Nevertheless, there are some exceptional films which eluded the semi-official government-imposed consensus on British film production. No one as yet has suggested the extent to which the projection of American democracy and economic levels of affluence as seen in Hollywood films might have influenced the changes which took place in the British nation after 1945. After all, imported

Hollywood films represented a very different view of politics and morality from that presented by British films under the direct control of the BBFC.[10]

Unlike methodological discourses upon historiography using traditional sources, the preceding discussion has little recourse to what research using feature film materials has proven. The use of such materials is comparatively recent and the development of its methodology is only in the early stages. What cannot be offered in terms of realisation is offered as reasonable expectations. The historian using feature film documentation must be prepared to use the films themselves. Only studying the films in detail will make it possible for historians to discern the important differences between the evidence of both exceptional and unexceptional films.

The historical record will be enriched by the additional documentation both of a nation's reflected values and ideas, particularly of history, and of the continuous struggle within the entertainment industry of the cinema between the democratic and totalitarian code makers attempting to impose their morality and political beliefs. The struggle for the control of the life of a nation is embedded in its feature film records, not unlike the history of life locked into the rock strata of geological time.

Notes

1. The following have important contributions to make to the literature on historical scholarship in the field of the movies: Michael T. Isenberg, 'Toward an Historical Methodology for Film Scholarship', *The Rocky Mountain Social Science Journal*, 12, no.1 (January 1975), pp.45-57; I.C. Jarvie, 'Seeing Through Movies', *Philosophy of the Social Sciences*, 8, no.4 (December 1978), pp.374-9; Karsten Fledelius, 'Strategies of Analysis of Narrative Films', in K.R.M. Short and Karsten Fledelius (eds), *Film and History: Methodology, Research and Education* (IAMHIST/Eventus, Copenhagen, 1980); Paul Smith (ed.), *The Historian and Film* (Cambridge, 1975); Pierre Sorlin, *The Film in History: Restaging the Past* (Oxford, 1980); John E. O'Connor and Martin Jackson (eds), *American History/American Film: Interpreting the Hollywood Image* (New York, 1979).

2. Oxford Microform Publications Ltd is currently preparing a microfiche edition of a unique record of the five major American newsreels between 1942 and 1945. *American Newsreels Record World War II* (edited by K.R.M. Short) is a 12,000-page record of analyses, script summaries and issue sheets made by the Library of Congress Film Project as part of the Office of War Information's intelligence operation which monitored opinion on the screen and then attempted its manipulation in order to improve America's home-front performance.

3. An excellent introduction to the literature of the movies is to be found in Daniel J. Leab's 'Film Books', in Jean Peters (ed.), *Collectable Books: Some New Paths* (Bowker, New York, 1979), pp.95-117.

4. In *Visions of Yesterday* (London, 1973, p.73), Jeffrey Richards identified the film as *The Purple Heart* but there are no White Russians to be seen and the Japanese parts are played by Chinese-American actors. It is possible that Richards is right but only evidence from the 'shooting script' indicating that such a War Cabinet scene was 'shot' and then scrapped (left on 'the cutting-room floor' is the common expression) can confirm the identification.

5. For a detailed study of *The White Cliffs of Dover* and its background see K.R.M. Short, 'Anglo-American Co-operation in World War II: The Dilemma and a Solution — *The White Cliffs of Dover*', in K.F. Reimers (ed), *Geschichte und Audiovisuelle Medien* (Politische Medienkunde, München, (1981).

6. Jeffrey Richards is currently studying these script reports and his 'Content Control: the British Board of Film Censors in the 1930s' will appear in the *Historical Journal of Film, Radio and Television* in 1981; also see N. Pronay and D. Spring (eds), *Propaganda, Politics and Film, 1918-1945* (Macmillan, London, 1981).

7. The problem of location is complicated by the fact that some archives will have the film in question on two 16mm spools, while another will have it on ten 35mm reels. Assuming that the researcher knows how many minutes into the film the scene in question is to be found, he should have little difficulty in selecting the appropriate reel, but this only works with 35 mm prints. It is better for the researcher to quote feet/metres when referring to a 16 mm print to enable the searcher to run on at high speed until the Steenbeck counter indicates the approximate location — approximate since there is a variation from one counter to another. It is also useful to have an equivalency table relating feet to metres (and minutes) in the event that the citation is in feet and the Steenbeck counter is in metres!

8. It is a curious fact that the movie maker's traditional settings and costumes for the Middle Ages are actually appropriate to the early sixteenth century's recreation of that period for themselves. If the film maker were to make an effort to reconstruct authentically the twelfth century, the audience would have great difficulty in relating to it because of their previous conditioning as to what the Middle Ages looked like. On the other hand, it is widely recognised that the movie which is staged in its contemporary period, e.g. a 1930s comedy, provides visual evidence of living styles, speech mannerisms, and even architectural details which are of interest. Such material may be deemed, however, of comparatively little use. The study of certain feature films of the 1920s and early 1930s has also produced some important insights into the integration of Eastern European Jews into American society. See K.R.M. Short, 'From Ghetto to Ghetto and Beyond: The Experience of Eastern Jewry in America as portrayed in the Cinema of the 1920s and 1930s', in Short and Fledelius (eds), *Film and History*.

9. Nazi films carried a far higher proportion of politically motivated material than they are generally given credit for. The 'hard' propaganda was carried in the long newsreels accompanying the unexceptional feature films which were essentially entertainment.

10. During World War II both the Ministry of Information in London and the American Office of War Information sought to control and manipulate the presentation of plot and character according to what these two organisations determined to be the war effort's interest. There is evidence that the United States government spent $1.5 million during the war to present the right image of American life on the movie screens of South and Central America. This was a counter-propaganda effort designed to oppose the effect of Nazi feature and documentary films circulating in the Americas.

2 *BATTLESHIP POTEMKIN* – FILM AND REALITY

D.J. Wenden

Battleship Potemkin is one of the best-known and most widely admired films of all time. But it is not only a landmark in the history of the cinema, it is for most people their main source of information about the mutiny of the *Potemkin*. This article will compare the story of the mutiny and the events in Odessa, as portrayed in the film, with that story in reality, as reconstructed by an historian, and will discuss possible reasons for the differences.

Making such comparisons is not easy. We can look at the film over and over again, study it shot by shot, and refer to David Mayer's published analysis.[1] We have no such detailed minute-by-minute, or even day-to-day, account of the events it portrays. The motion picture lasts for just over one hour; the mutineers controlled the ship for over eleven days. Unfortunately, no movie cameraman took pictures of the mutiny, of the arrival of the warship in Odessa, or of the battles between strikers and troops in the city. We cannot compare 1905 film with the 1925 reconstruction. Some photographs survived and several participants in the struggle have recorded their versions in newspapers, books and official reports.

This article is based on a variety of sources yielding information on the risings in Odessa and on the *Potemkin*, but as in all historical investigations many questions are left unanswered or are given ambiguous answers. Almost as many unsolved mysteries surround the making of the film, how much Eisenstein knew about the mutiny he portrayed, and why he presented it as he did. A note on the main sources is given at the end of the article. Much more, however, remains to be done.

Eisenstein's variation from the truth, or failure to tell the whole truth (as he knew it), are not necessarily sinister or reprehensible. He was making a feature film, not a work of history. He had been commissioned to produce a work commemorating the 1905 Revolution, but it was intended for general distribution, and was meant to be an entertainment as well as a revolutionary sermon. To achieve this, and to make a film that would appeal to unsophisticated Russian audiences, Eisenstein had to change and simplify the confused story of the mutiny.

37

The events he portrayed were only twenty years away, but those two decades had witnessed the 1917 Revolution and the creation of Bolshevik Russia. He had been asked to produce a picture about the 1905 Revolution that would justify the political system of 1925. The authorisation for the production came from the Official State Committee of the Presidium of the Central Executive Committee of the USSR set up to celebrate the year 1905. As Herbert Marshall explains in his recent book on *The Battleship Potemkin*, the film was made to 'social command' (*sotsial'nyyzakaz*), that is the command of the Communist Party of the Soviet Union.[2] The propaganda was blunt and direct, unlike Eisenstein's more equivocal treatment of Stalinist agricultural policy in *The General Line* (1928) where occasional hints of disaffection and jibes at the party bureaucracy can be detected. He underlined the contrast between the revolutionary sailors and their reactionary officers, and also by implication the vindictive soldiers on the steps, by falsifying as well as simplifying some of the events he portrayed, even though he assured the All Union Creative Conference of Workers in Soviet Cinematography in 1935 'that we tried to take the historial events just as they were and not to interfere in any shape, manner, or form with the process as it actually took place'.[3] Later he wrote of using 'the events first taken as unembellished facts themselves so arranged as to form a consecutive whole'.[4]

By 1945 he appeared to have had a change of heart. Discussing the controversial role of the tarpaulin in the attempted execution of the mutineers, he quoted Goethe approvingly: 'For the sake of truthfulness, one can afford to defy the truth.'[5] In the same article he admitted that his film ended in a false triumph, with the apparent rallying of the whole Black Sea Fleet to the side of the mutinous *Potemkin*, although in reality the revolt ended in ignominy. His excuse for this distortion was

> But we were justified in ending the film with the historical battleship victorious. Because the 1905 Revolution itself, though drowned in blood, has gone down in history as an objectively victorious episode, the harbinger of the triumph of the October Revolution.[6]

Success in 1917 justified drawing a veil over failure in 1905. However, in putting forward this justification he contradicted his earlier assertion that he did not 'interfere in any shape, manner, or form with the process as it actually took place'.

It is possible that Eisenstein by 1945 had become aware of facts about the 1905 struggle he had not appreciated ten years earlier. A more likely explanation of this change of ground is the change in the political climate and in the director's own status. In 1935 the first wave of the Stalinist purge trials had begun. Eisenstein's position was far from secure. He was unable to complete any film project. *Bezhin Meadow* was interrupted by his attack of smallpox and later abandoned owing to political difficulties in 1937. Few men at that time would have risked admitting in Moscow that they had falsified history, even in the cause of great revolutionary propaganda. Confessions of falsification of history were reserved for the Trotskyite criminals who were being destroyed by Vyshinsky and the NKVD in the most spectacular falsification of history of all time. Ten years later, although Stalin was still in power, the Soviet Union had triumphed in the Great Patriotic War. The regime, politicians and artists were more self-confident. Eisenstein himself had directed *Alexander Nevsky*, and was at work on *Ivan the Terrible*. Minor, harmless distortions of the truth in the revolutionary cause could perhaps be more readily revealed.

In his writings Eisenstein acknowledged only those few minor distortions. We will probably never know whether he was, or was not, aware of the more substantial departures from historical accuracy discussed later in this article. These have three main sources. Firstly, Eisenstein, like any writer of historical fiction, simplified and distorted the truth in order to make his story more dramatic. In some cases his reasons were political: the doctored version produced a film more likely to preach the message required by the Communist leaders and by Eisenstein himself. Although his enthusiasm for Stalin may have waned, he never lost his loyalty to the Soviet ideal. Thirdly, he was probably unaware of certain occasions when his version differed from the true course of events in 1905.

Eisenstein had been directed to make a film on the general theme of 1905. Several mysteries surround the process by which this directive was translated into the final production of a comparatively short (and at 5 reels, 1,850 metres (6,070 feet), *Battleship Potemkin* is short) feature film. The first is the substitution of the story of the revolt on the *Potemkin* and the unrest in Odessa for a general survey of the 1905 Revolution. The second is why two films (the lesser-known *Ninth of January*, directed by Viskovsky, was a sister film of *Battleship Potemkin*), intended to mark the twentieth anniversary of a revolution that erupted in January 1905, were not commissioned until the spring of 1925, and not shown until the last month of that year. The third is when and why Eisenstein, who on 2 July 1925 wrote to his mother that he had been given until August 1926 to complete the project,[7] was instructed to deliver a print before the end of the year. The fourth is how much of the grander *The Year 1905* project was begun and what happened to the abandoned material.

There is little information on the last point but the film library of the British Film Institute has a still photograph that is said to be from the unfinished *The Year 1905*. Whether Eisenstein's deadline was advanced from August 1926 to December 1925, or whether he mistakenly imagined that he had more time, is not clear. The project, like the finished film itself, seems to have come to an abrupt, foreshortened close. This, together with the belated commissioning of the work part way through the year, may explain the substitution of *Battleship Potemkin* for the whole of *The Year 1905*. We, the audience, probably have reason to be grateful since, as Bertolucci has demonstrated recently, it is not easy to make a successful film based on a whole year, and certainly not easy to make a successful short film on such a theme. In an article in the *Berliner Tageblatt* in June 1926 Eisenstein explains that he had only 'three months for production – even in Germany this might be considered a record production schedule. Two and a half weeks were left to me for the montage of the film, for the editing of 15,000 metres of film.'[8] It seems likely that lack of time compelled the change of plan from *The Year 1905* to *Battleship Potemkin* and that the brilliant use of the ship's revolt as a symbol for the whole revolutionary effort of the Russian people in 1905 was forced on Eisenstein.

Shooting began in July in Leningrad on a general script prepared by Nina Agadzhanova-Shutko. The end of the Baltic summer and a delay in the completion of the original script drove Eisenstein and his team south to Odessa to film the sequences planned on the naval mutiny. Once there they became the whole film, and the original scenario was replaced by a new outline usually attributed to Eisenstein himself. Here a fifth mystery appears. Did this scenario owe anything to Sergei Tret'yakov, the well-known Soviet dramatist? In an article published in 1977 Lars Kleberg[9] advances evidence that suggests strongly an association of ideas between Tret'yakov, a former associate of Eisenstein at the Proletkult Theatre, and the director of *Battleship Potemkin*. Kleberg's evidence can be summarised as follows.

In December 1925 and January 1926 within four weeks of each other the two colleagues from the Proletkult unveiled new works, *Battleship Potemkin* at the Bolshoi Theatre on 24 December, and a play by Tret'yakov, *China Roars*, on 23 January in Meyerhold's Theatre. *China Roars* is based on an event in June 1924 in a town on the Yang-tse River. An American trader was killed and the commander of a British gunboat threatened to bombard the town unless the murderers, or two hostages, were handed over for execution. The action of the play alternates between the harbour and the deck of the warship, with confrontations between the British captain and the Chinese coolies. Just as the execution is completed news comes that riots have started in Shanghai, and the 'Roar of China' is taken up by the local townspeople. The theme, and in particular the structure, of the play have many obvious similarities with *Battleship Potemkin*. In November or December 1924 Eisenstein had access to an early version of the play and may even have been asked to work on its production. When Tret'yakov returned from China in the summer of 1925 he was added to the advisory board of the studio producing *Battleship Potemkin*. From 1 September for some weeks he was with the crew in Odessa, and in November worked with Eisenstein in Moscow on the cutting and wrote some sub-titles. Kleberg suggests that these 'coincidences' may explain how Eisenstein was able to concentrate the theme of 1905 so rapidly and effectively into the story of the ship's mutiny and how Eisenstein arrived at the strict, terse dramaturgical structure that characterises *Battleship Potemkin* but was not developed in either the earlier film *Strike* or the scenario of *The Year 1905*. In the film credits the dramatist appears only as a joint author of the sub-titles!

The June mutiny on the *Potemkin* is not regarded as a major event by most historians of the 1905 Revolution. The crucial disturbances were the strikes and riots in St Petersburg and Moscow, the disaffection in some military units and the widespread peasant risings from August 1905 until April 1906. The Tsar's decisions to grant the concessions made in the October Manifesto and to hasten a revision of the land setttlement were prompted by widespread urban and rural revolts, not by the *Potemkin* sailors' abortive gesture (eleven days that did not shake the world) nor even by the strikes in Odessa, which were overshadowed in that city by the counter-revolutionary pogroms against the Jews in November.

The *Kniaz' Potemkin Tavrichesky* was a three-funnelled battleship of 12,600 tons, with four twelve-inch and sixteen six-inch guns.[10] Completed in 1903, she was a Russian version of the United States *Maine* class of warship, and was the last large Tsarist naval vessel based on a British or American prototype. Subsequent ships were built to French designs, with French or German equipment and armour. Fred T.

Jane, in *The Imperial Russian Navy*, published in 1904, deplored the disappearance of this market for British exports.

> I was told in Russia, not once but a dozen times, that the 'Strike Clause' was the stumbling block, Russia insisting on its absence, and British firms (knowing all too well what its absence might mean in these days of agitation) insisting on its maintenance. The agitator helped the British mechanic to kill his goose as far as Russia is concerned.[11]

The *Potemkin* was the most powerful unit in the Black Sea Fleet. Her speed, the weight and velocity of her armament, could not be matched by the five other, older battleships based on Sebastopol. This technical superiority explains the Tsarist Admiralty's alarm at her disaffection. She could outmanoeuvre and outshoot any unit, or almost any combination of units, likely to be sent against her. Moreover, after the Japanese had virtually eliminated the Russian Far Eastern Fleet and the ships of the Baltic Fleet sent to the Pacific the *Potemkin* was one of the few effective modern Tsarist battleships left afloat. A British consular report in May 1905 suggests that, together with other units of the Black Sea Fleet, she was being prepared for Asian waters.[12] This appears to have been only a rumour but it might help to explain the crew's readiness to mutiny. Certainly the attempts to draw drafts of men for service in ships from the Baltic Fleet that were sent to the Far East had occasioned unrest and resistance at Sebastopol, the base of the Black Sea Fleet.[13]

Well before the *Potemkin* uprising in June 1905 there had been agitation among the sailors. Mention is made of unrest in December 1904. Matyushenko, the ringleader of the *Potemkin* rising, had taken part in this action. Surprisingly Matyushenko, who was known to be an active Social Revolutionary, was not imprisoned but was one of the many political activists designated for service at sea.[14] It was assumed that, dispersed among the ships on manoeuvres, they would be less dangerous than if they were concentrated in the Crimean depot. A general rising of the fleet was planned, initially for early June off Tendra Island. This, however, did not take place since the bulk of the fleet was kept in harbour and the *Potemkin* sailed alone for firing practice near Tendra on 12 June. (All dates given are according to the old Russian calendar.) At this stage the rising seems to have been postponed until early August. The *Potemkin* mutiny in June was a premature outburst, roundly condemned by Kirill Orlov, one of the few Bolsheviks involved, as hasty action by 'the strong pressure of the Anarchist-Social Revolutionary element'.[15] Strangely enough, the ship's crew was deemed to be politically backward, but because of this, and because of her operational pre-eminence, it had been intended that the general uprising should start on the *Potemkin.*

With the mobilisation of the Black Sea Fleet the ship's crew had been brought up to its full complement of 731. Also on board were fifty or sixty technicians and workmen engaged in repair and refitting.[16] Such men might have been expected to include a high proportion of revolutionary elements. But they seem to have played little or no part in the subsequent troubles, and are mentioned only in a comment that no additional rations had been provided for them, and that this accentuated dissatisfaction with the food. These shipyard workers were eventually put ashore in Odessa.

On 12 June the ship sailed to the Tendra Strait to test the linings of her new guns. Captain E.N. Golikov was in command. The officers had little sea-going experience. Service in the Black Sea Fleet brought few opportunities for long cruises. The ratings were mainly peasants, conscripted for seven years' service. One account suggests that many were drawn from the Bessarabian provinces and this may partly explain their later willingness to seek refuge in Rumania.[17] They were poorly paid, harshly disciplined and forbidden to marry while on active service. Many of the company were raw recruits.

As the ship steamed out of Sebastopol, strikes and disturbances broke out in Odessa. Most Russian cities had experienced spasmodic outbreaks of political and industrial disorders since the massacre of the crowds marching behind Father Gapon to petition the Tsar in January. The country was weary of a despotic regime, the incompetence of which had been exposed by defeats at the hands of the Japanese. Odessa, the fourth-largest Russian city, housed a large commercial and industrial proletariat. Over a third of the population (at the 1897 census 139,984 or 34.65 per cent) were Jews. They dominated the grain export trade and the professions. Their presence had two political consequences. An oppressed minority, they included revolutionary elements who were very active politically: strong branches of the Jewish Bund and Russian Social Democratic Party flourished in Odessa. But the very prominence of the Jews in radical movements enabled the authorities to convert anti-semitic prejudices among peasants and workers into patriotic counter-revolutionary pogroms. The high proportion of Jews in Odessa made the city more politically conscious, but also made it possible to split the working-class movement and switch mob energy away from anti-government riots into attacks on Jewish shops and warehouses. This happened during the outburst while *Potemkin* lay in the harbour, and on a larger scale later in November.

The events portrayed in the film arose out of this political ferment in Odessa and on the ships of the Black Sea Fleet. In the opening sequences Eisenstein establishes the mood with shots of fierce waves breaking on a jetty, followed by examples of the harsh discipline and brooding unrest below decks. At midday the men protest at the maggoty meat being prepared for their dinner.

Such an outburst did occur on the ship. While the *Potemkin* waited to begin firing, her torpedo boat escort sailed off to Odessa to buy food and stores. Owing to the strikes in the city little fresh food was available. Ironically the carcasses that were to spark off the revolt came from Odessa, and their poor condition was due to earlier revolutionary action in the harbour. Their condition was not improved when on the return journey the torpedo boat ran down a small fishing vessel, and could not deliver the stores to the ship's galley until 4 a.m. Bad meat did not improve in the Crimean mid-summer heat. The next morning it was crawling with maggots. The ratings protested. Earlier complaints had been made in May. As in the film, the ship's surgeon Dr Smirnov pronounced it fit to eat, saying that it needed only to be washed with vinegar or brine. When the men refused the bortsch made from the putrid flesh Captain Golikov ordered a parade on deck.

Up to this point the film and the actual events, so far as I can reconstruct them, coincide, except that the film suggests that the mutiny was a spontaneous reaction to bad food and the repression of complaints about the food. The only variation from the truth comes early in the film when Matyushenko and Vakulenchuk are shown talking together, implying that they are fellow revolutionaries. In fact, Vakulenchuk, the martyr of the *Potemkin*, whose lying-in-state on the Odessa quay and subsequent burial formed an essential, almost the only, link between the ship and the townsfolk, seems, as I will show later, to have been an innocent martyr, shot by chance, and not, as the film implies, a leader of the revolt.

We return to the parade on the deck of the ship. In the film the Captain orders those satisfied with the bortsch to take two steps forward. A few move but the majority stay still. The captain threatens them with hanging, but summons instead a firing squad and proceeds to order the execution of a group of dissidents, who are first covered

by a tarpaulin. Vakulenchuk appeals to the guard who refuse to fire and
the mutiny erupts.

Eye witness accounts of the parade contradict each other at several
points. Some suggest that the captain, afraid and confused, dismissed
the men and walked away, saying that he would report the matter to
the Commander-in-Chief. As he left, the initiative was seized by the
sterner second-in-command Gilyarovsky who reformed the ranks and
proceeded with further threats and action. Others suggest that the
Captain stayed on deck and in command, ordering those satisfied with
the food to move behind him or to pass from port to starboard. All
these accounts surprisingly agree that the Captain asked those satisfied
to move. It would seem better tactics to ask those dissatisfied with the
soup to step forward, forcing them to take the initiative, and enabling
those who were uncertain to remain still and, by implication, content.
Again the accounts differ, some suggesting that most of the men
moved, others very few responded. Eventually a group of sailors, 12,
30, 50 or 60 (the film shows 19), were herded together in the stern.
The officers ordered a tarpaulin to be brought. (A tarpaulin, to be
placed over or under the men – this point is discussed later – was a
warning that a summary execution might take place.) The squad
refused to fire, restrained some say by Leading Torpedoman
Matyushenko, the chief Social Revolutionary Party member on board
and throughout the leading figure. In desperation Gilyarovsky seized
a rifle and shot at the petty officer commanding the firing squad whom
some say was Leading Seaman Vakulenchuk; others suggest that he aimed
at the petty officer but hit instead Vakulenchuk, one of the condemned
sailors. In all accounts Vakulenchuk appeared and was wounded almost
by chance. In the film he and Matyushenko are from the beginning
the two leading revolutionaries, shown conspiring in the film's opening
shots. Vakulenchuk is the sailor who reads the leaflet in the hammock
below decks and also the sailor who calls on the guard to ignore the
order to fire.

After the outburst Gilyarovsky was immediately shot dead by
Matyushenko. The other officers were hunted down. Dr Smirnov, the
ship's surgeon who dismissed the complaints about the rotten meat,
attempted to commit suicide with his lancet. Several, including Captain
Golikov, were killed on board or in the water as they attempted to swim to
the torpedo boat escort. One account, that of Kuzma Perelygin, a sailor
who was by his testimony opposed to the mutiny from the outset,
claims that even at this stage the crew was divided, and some sailors
who opposed the mutiny also jumped overboard and were fired on

as they swam away. No other version refers to such an early split in the ship's crew and it is possible that Perelygin's story was influenced by a desire to stand in well with the Russian authorities. His version was given to Melas, a Russian police agent in the Rumanian port of Constanza. It seems clear that the nine hostages were placed under arrest and that three officers unenthusiastically joined the rebels, remaining with them for most of the voyage. Within one hour the mutineers had taken over the ship.

This film conveys a different impression. The Captain remains a dominating figure, controlling events until he is seized by the rebels. Gilyarovsky does not shoot Vakulenchuk almost by chance, but hunts the unarmed ringleader around the ship until he shoots him down and the sailor's body falls first into a cradle formed by mast and ropes and finally into the sea. Scores of his comrades leap into the water and bring back the body. In fact Vakulenchuk did not die immediately: he may have fallen into the water, but certainly lay for several hours in the sick bay.

At several points in the film a sly, hypocritical priest appears, encouraging the execution, and later feigning death to avoid the attention of the rebels. A priest, Father Parmen, was on the ship. He was wounded on the head by Matyushenko during the uprising, but remained on board and was asked by the crew to accompany the body of Vakulenchuk to the military cemetery in Odessa. Even Matyushenko records that on the evening of the second day 'the drummers summoned the crew to prayers on deck'.[18] The religious beliefs of the peasant sailors survived the shock of insurrection. Eisenstein's account of the uprising ends abruptly with the death of Vakulenchuk and moves on immediately to the passage of his body from the ship to its first place of rest on the quay in Odessa, an event that took place 24 hours later.

The factual differences between the real mutiny and the film mutiny are comparatively marginal and can be justified by the need to maintain dramatic force and unity. Eisenstein's *Battleship Potemkin* is here more historically accurate than either of the two Hollywood versions of *The Mutiny on the Bounty* (MGM, 1935 and 1962).

Eisenstein does, however, strain the truth in his determination to portray a clear confrontation between the united forces of evil on one side and of virtue on the other. The real Captain Golikov acted much less despotically and decisively than did his film counterpart. He was eventually dragged half-dressed from his cabin, where he was contemplating an attempt to swim to safety. He was only killed after a debate among the crew. Eisenstein does not show his end but leaves us in little doubt about what the film mutineers would have done with this overbearing martinet. The officers in the film are united in their infamy. In fact several survived and three joined the insurgents, who appointed Lieutenant Alexeyev as commander of the ship. The ringleaders needed his technical skills and recognised that the bulk of the crew felt happier with an officer as master of the ship.

The crew, whom Eisenstein showed as united and single-minded, were in practice divided and hesitant. As mentioned earlier, one account asserts even that the initial revolt met with strong resistance. Matyushenko and his associates had to prod them into action, and later they had repeatedly to be kept up to scratch by the civilian revolutionaries who came aboard at Odessa. They eventually gave up the revolt, hunger and fear driving them to seek internment in Rumania. During their few days in Odessa harbour they refused to become directly associated with the town's strikes and riots. The hard-core naval revolutionaries who wanted to link up with the civilian disturbances were afraid to do so and leave the ship in the hands of the apathetic majority. (Eisenstein presented a black and white story matching his black and white pictures rather than the battleship grey reality.)

A trivial but intriguing confusion surrounds the attempted execution and the role of the tarpaulin. In the film the sailors selected for execution are herded in the prow, and a tarpaulin is slung over them, placing a barrier between the living and those about to die. But was it to be placed over or under the victims? Either position can be justified. A cover over the men would hide them from their ship-mates in the firing squad. Army mutineers on land would almost certainly have faced riflemen from a unit other than their own. A man-of-war at sea is often isolated, and there may be no opportunity to summon anonymous executioners. A naval or marine firing squad may be asked to kill men with whom they have broken bread that morning. A tarpaulin diminishes their anguish.

But Eisenstein in his essay on the film, *The Twelve Apostles* (1945),[19] claimed that in the Tsarist navy a tarpaulin would have been placed not over, but under, the victims, in order to protect the deck from bloodstains in the interests of a cleaner, neater execution. He writes that he deliberately threw the canvas over the men in order to create a spectacular image of 'a gigantic bandage covering the eyes of the condemned'. A former naval officer acting the role of Matyushenko protested at this falsification. 'We shall be ridiculed . . . This was never done.' But Eisenstein 'ordered the scene to be shot the way you see it in the film . . . The scene was left in the film as it was. It became part and parcel of the historical event.'

He used this invention to defend himself in a legal case brought by a survivor of the mutiny, claiming payment of a fee for his rights in the story. In a sketchy account of the action against the film makers, Eisenstein wrote that the plaintiff claimed to be one of the men 'under the tarpaulin during the shooting on the quarter deck', and the lawyers were demanding judgement in his favour 'when the whole noisy affair was blown sky high . . . For the simple reason that no one on the *Potemkin* had been covered with a tarpaulin . . . The scene was the director's invention.'

Investigation suggests that the story was a director's fabrication to win a legal battle, and not the reversal of naval tradition. Almost all the eye witness accounts written before the making of the film in 1925 refer to the appearance of a tarpaulin which was placed *over* and not *under* the ratings. The Acting British Consul in Galatz, Rumania, sent a report of the mutiny by Vasily Barkovsky, a gunner on the ship, to the Foreign Office on 12 July 1905.[20] The gunner explained that the firing squad was ordered to shoot the ringleaders, 'first covering them with a tarpaulin'. Perelygin[21] reports that the Captain ordered the guard to load their rifles, bring the tarpaulin, and cover these scoundrels'. Comparisons between fact and film become even more perplexing when the director claims as a fictional invention an action which seems actually to have taken place. The story becomes even more bizarre when we discover a report in the *New York Times* of 24 October 1926 of a law suit in which an unknown Dachenko sued the State Cinematograph Trust, which had paid him the equivalent of $750 for his part authorship of the scenario of *Battleship Potemkin*, but refused to give him a percentage of the picture's earnings. It was suggested that he had written only the scenario and that Eisenstein had introduced ideas and scenes of his own. The 'People's Court' decided that Dachenko and Eisenstein were joint authors, and awarded to each 1 per cent of the film's earnings. If this is the court case Eisenstein refers to in *The Twelve Apostles* one's faith in the director is further shaken. He not only distorts the story of the tarpaulin, but also claims to have won a case that was lost (unless it was subsequently won on appeal). If it is not the case in question, what is one to make of a total lack of reference to Dachenko and his association with the film in any of the credits or published material on the making of the film?[22]

The third and fourth sections of the film include more substantial deviations from historical truth. Eisenstein presented the citizens of

Odessa paying homage to Vakulenchuk's body in a tent on the quayside, while the battleship lay at anchor in the harbour. Sailing boats carry food and gifts to the crew. On the shore well-dressed crowds in a holiday spirit use the steps leading from the harbour up to the town centre as a grandstand from which they can wave to the ship. Suddenly at the top of the stairway a detachment of troops arrives to clear the crowds. They march down the steps, pausing to shoot at the civilians fleeing before their relentless advance. This brilliant film sequence ends with the destruction of the innocents by the sabres of mounted Cossacks at the foot of the staircase. The savagery of the troops is answered by the guns of the *Potemkin*, which bombard the Odessa Theatre, the garrison's military headquarters. Their shells are the only contribution from the revolutionaries at sea to help the revolutionaries in Odessa. Eisenstein portrays the townspeople as spectators of events on the ship and, by implication, the sailors as spectators of the massacre on the steps. Once the Cossacks have finished their sweep and the guns have answered, the city plays no further part in the film.

Eisenstein kept to the facts in refusing to exaggerate the connection between the two simultaneous revolts. But in some other respects he gave a false picture of events between 14 and 16 June in Odessa. The battleship arrived in the harbour at 8 p.m., seven hours after the fatal parade on deck. She dropped anchor and remained isolated for the night. The next morning was the second day of the general strike in the town, but the sailors made little response to the appeals for help. Apart from sending Vakulenchuk's body ashore, the crew concentrated on replenishing supplies of food, coal and water. The two latter items were essential if the ship was to remain mobile. The collapse of the adventure, ten days later in Rumania, was hastened by shortage of coal and the damage to the boilers caused by sailing hundreds of miles on sea water. However, on 15 June, they found coal in the harbour and spent most of the afternoon in the laborious and dirty task of transferring the fuel from a collier into their bunkers.

Provisions were bought in the town. The crew paid cash, using some of the 27,000 roubles (about £3,000) they found in the ship's treasury. The money was used sparingly throughout their brief period of independence. A large sum remained untouched to the end. Before they surrendered to the Rumanian authorities, the balance was split up among the crew, Gunner Barkovsky recording that he received 80 roubles. Sightseers as well as supplies came on board. Eisenstein shows a cheerful passage of food and livestock from small boats into .the *Potemkin*. In actual fact, far from welcoming this fraternisation, the sailors soon resented the swarm of undisciplined, tiresome visitors. They decided to 'clear out the landlubbers'. Some women, however, remained on board for several days, comforting the crew, but provoking arguments. The British Consul noted three days later the arrival of a party from the ship seeking bandages and medical supplies, since there had been fighting among the crew over the women.[23]

On 15 June the crew received representatives of the revolutionary parties in the port and sent delegates to land Vakulenchuk's body and to deliver a petition to the French Consul, but established no close contact with the strikers. They specifically rejected a request to send a large armed party ashore. The local Social Democrats hoped the sailors might persuade the soldiers to defy their officers, and repeat the *Potemkin* mutiny in the military garrison. But despite the repeated efforts of representatives of the Odessa political parties (including Feldmann, known as Ivan the Student, and Kirill Petrov) the mutineers made little response and treated the city and its military garrison as a potential threat, and the citizens and strikers as almost irrelevant onlookers of their own private concerns.

The film highlights two episodes, the devastating massacre on the steps and the battleship's brief, but seemingly effective, bombardment of the military headquarters on shore. The first is a brilliant invention by Eisenstein to represent the savagery of the forces of reaction; the second flatters the spirit and concern of the crew. Let us examine these two sections in some detail.

Eisenstein was understandably captivated by the cinematic possibilities provided by the Odessa steps. Completed to the design of a Sardinian architect, Boffo, in 1841, the stairway stretched up from the harbour front to the equestrian statue of the Duc de Richelieu and the fashionable shopping streets beyond. The Duke was a French Bourbon emigré, appointed Governor of Odessa by Alexander I during the Napoleonic Wars. The impression of height and distance was increased by the architect's skill in making the steps nearly twice as wide at the bottom as at the top. From the statue only the large square landings breaking up the descent were visible. From the bottom the landings could not be seen, and the eye saw only the steps in a continuous upward sweep.

Eisenstein recalls that

neither the original script nor the montage drafts provided for the

shooting scene on the Odessa steps. The idea flashed in my mind
when I saw the steps . . . Another source might have been the dim
recollection of an illustration I had seen in a 1905 magazine, showing
a horseman on the smoke enveloped steps.[24]

Marie Seton adds 'that in his researches Eisenstein found a series of
sketches by a French artist who had witnessed the massacre on the
Odessa stairway'.[25] Maxim Straukh specifically mentions pictures in
the French magazine *L'Illustration*[26] that brought back for Eisenstein
memories of the 1905 riots in Riga.

   L'Illustration for the summer of 1905 included three articles on the
Potemkin mutiny but no sketches of a massacre on the steps.[27]
Contemporary British accounts record no such massacre although the
Illustrated London News published a picture of 'where the mob and
the Cossacks met, the steps of St Nicholas Church'.[28] This church is
nearly two kilometres from Richelieu's statue. The Italian magazine
Via Nuovo has a picture of a crowd on the steps, but a peaceful
gathering almost exactly matching the opening shot of Eisenstein's
sequence.

   There was a massacre on the steps, but it occurred on the night of
15/16 June. Four of the five eye witness accounts left by those on
board the ship mention the outburst, but they express comparatively
little concern and no sense of involvement with this drama on shore.

   The massacre was not a slaughter of innocents but a desperate
brutal attempt to maintain order in a city in revolt. The strikes in
Odessa and other cities in Russia in 1905 were outbursts of primitive
anger by industrial workers and peasants. Once the veneer of control
exercised by Tsarist administration was broken, the crowds looted and
drank their way through shops and warehouses. By 14 June that veneer
of control had been lost in Odessa. Matyushenko's own account laid
the blame on the town authorities. He acuses them of provoking anti-
Jewish riots and leaving cases of vodka about to encourage disorder.

   After the end of the meeting near the body of Vakulenchuk, the
   crowd at the port consisted merely of curious middle-class elements
   and hoodlums. There were very few workers and all their attempts
   to hold back these people or to interfere with them were useless.[29]

The most that the army could hope to do (the Mayor had fled to
report on the situation to St Petersburg) was to try to contain the
riots in the harbour area and the industrial suburbs, and protect the

fashionable shopping and residential sections of the town. In 1905 much of the destructive fury of the distressed was unleashed in the vicinity of the poorer homes and commercial centres. The troops adopted a policy of containment, aware perhaps that many of the warehouses belonged to the unpopular Jews, who handled 90 per cent of Odessa's grain export trade. This policy included holding a line on the Odessa steps that separated the centre of the town from the quayside. That line was threatened on the night of 15/16 June by the mob that was loose in the harbour area. General Kakhanov, Commander of the Military District, reported that

> with the coming of dark the malefactors began to hurl explosive bombs at the troops from the port side as well as from the town side, and began to move upon the troops, with inflamatory shouting and with revolver fire. The crowd dispersed at a run on the opening of gunfire, but then throughout the night it tried in various places to move upon the troops: however, each time it was dispersed with shots. By 4 a.m. the crowd had finally dispersed and the exchange of fire had ceased.[30]

This partisan account tallies with evidence from several other sources of a night-time struggle between troops and civilians, including clashes on the steps, that left hundreds of dead and wounded. The shooting on the steps did take place, but it took place at night and was the frenzied reaction of a military authority trying to prevent a crowd from surging up the steps and not, as portrayed in the film, the cold-blooded daytime murder of a happy crowd innocently waving at the battleship in the harbour.

In his memoirs Eisenstein himself provides supporting evidence for this interpretation. During his visit to the United States he was told by the manager of a cinema in Atlantic City where *Battleship Potemkin* had been shown that the film had reduced one old Russian-American to tears. The manager assumed that he must have been one of the sailors or a survivor of the massacre, but was told instead that he had been one of the soldiers in Odessa.

> Side by side with the others he had fired volley after volley. They had opened fire at something dark, dim, and indiscernable, huddled far below at the foot of the monumental stairway. And now suddenly after twenty years he had actually seen what he had been shooting at on that day. It was only now that he realised that they

had not been firing warning shots, as told, but sending their bullets into living flesh and blood.[31]

Eisenstein's recollection of a cinema operator's story of an old man's remorseful recollections of firing at dark unseen figures does not rank as first-class evidence, but it tallies with several other accounts that speak of rioting and troop action by night but make no mention of a spectacular daytime sweep down the steps.

Eisenstein's invention of the steps' sequence is understandable. It is not easy to understand and accept two aspects of his representation of that event, the composition of the crowd and the conduct of the troops. The crowd on the steps in the film include a high proportion of bourgeois figures, and especially well-dressed bourgeois women. One of the prominent victims, who appeals to the troops for mercy, looks like a middle-aged Jewish schoolmistress. The clash was not portrayed as a class struggle between Tsarist troops and heroic workers, as in his first film *Strike*, or even in the confrontation between officers and men on the battleship itself. Presumably Eisenstein was suggesting that in 1925 and 1905 urban revolution could still be interpreted as a petit bourgeois preliminary to the full-blooded workers' and peasants' victory in 1917.

In the film the soldiers display no hesitation or remorse in their march down the steps, shooting unarmed women and children. At the foot of the steps mounted Cossacks disperse the crowds with enthusiasm. Occasionally Eisenstein gives us a glimpse of an officer giving an order to fire, but does not stress that the soldiers are being driven to act as the unwilling agents of their class enemies. They behave very differently from their comrades on the *Potemkin* where a firing squad, in the presence of the Captain and urged on by Gilyarovsky, refuse to execute their shipmates. This contrast in behaviour lies at the heart of the film and gives a confusing political message. It bears out Trotsky's verdict that the 1905 Revolution was broken on the bayonets of the peasant army, but that is not an interpretation one would expect to find in a film made in 1925.

This sequence is followed by the sailors' only gesture of solidarity with the townspeople, the bombardment of the military headquarters. There was in fact little co-operation between the two groups. The film excuses the failure of the sailors to join forces with the strikers with the sub-titles 'The people of Odessa look to you for their liberation. Disembark now, and the army will join forces with you.' Answered by 'we cannot disembark. The admiralty squadron has begun to move against us.'

On the morning of 16 June the ship did send a party on shore, to seek permission from the military commandant to bury Vakulenchuk in the military cemetery. They asked permission: they did not seek to dictate terms. The June heat that had putrified the meat made it essential to bury the martyr quickly. Approval was given and the ceremony took place at 5.30 p.m. Only twelve sailors and the priest attended from the ship. But the cortège was followed by thousands of townsfolk. Eisenstein surprisingly did not recreate the funeral procession which, in Matyushenko's words,

> marched through the town . . . In the streets new masses of people joined us. On the balconies, in the windows and on the roofs of the houses, there were crowds of people. Shouts could be heard. 'All honour to the dead hero!' 'Down with the tyrants!' 'Long live the *Potemkin!*'[32]

Feldmann thought the only incongruous figure was the priest, Father Parmen.

> This minister of God presented a pitiful appearance. During the mutiny somebody had hit him on the nose with a chair, and the bandage would not keep in place on his thick, fleshy nose. It was coming down every minute and he was entirely absorbed in dealing with it.[33]

The funeral was not molested by the troops, but on the return journey the ship's delegation was attacked. Three men failed to return. They were either killed or wounded, or perhaps took the chance to abandon a losing cause. The attack on the burial party settled the debate on the ship whether or not to bring the *Potemkin*'s guns into action against a meeting of military officers in the town theatre.

Instead of the defiant, accurate bombardment shown in the film as an immediate reaction to the ferocity of the troops, only two live rounds were fired from a six-inch gun after several hours of argument among the crew. The massive twelve-inch guns remained silent. Initially three blank shots were fired. Fifteen minutes later (a delay which presumably enabled all the officers in the theatre to disperse) two live rounds were despatched. One failed to explode and the other damaged residential property hundreds of yards from the theatre and finished up outside the house of the Italian Consul General. Disheartened by their failure to get the range of a target less than two miles away while firing over open sights from an anchored platform, the sailors quickly ended their single act of defiance since the mutiny itself. Eisenstein's picture of an aroused lion flatters this two-shot 'barrage'.

This section of the story ended, not as in the film with a successful counter-attack, but in anxiety, as the ship's crew awaited the arrival of heavy land artillery that would force them out to sea and into the arms of the other units of the fleet.

The film ends with the encounter between the *Potemkin* and the ships sent to recapture her. Eisenstein builds up the fear and tension during the approach of the fleet. Action stations are mounted and the *Potemkin* steams towards the line of ships. Matyushenko emerges at last as the dominant figure and organises the resistance. But she is greeted with cheers not shells, and passes through in triumph. The film closes on this exultant note, leaving unresolved the fate of the revolt in Odessa and even of the mutineers themselves. *Potemkin* is not shown as victorious, nor has she at that moment been subdued.

This section of the film falsifies nothing, but it conveys less than the truth by ignoring the tragic anti-climax of *Potemkin*'s defiance. The ship's mutiny collapsed as abjectly as the 1905 Revolution itself after Tsar Nicholas II had made concessions to the liberals in the October Manifesto, splitting the moderate revolutionaries away from the more radical movement. Once the government had recovered from the shock of defeat in the Russo-Japanese War and the internal conflicts of the autumn and winter of 1905-6, many of the constitutional concessions made in the October Manifesto were revoked or watered down. By 1907 the autocracy was back in power, building up fresh resentment for the final collapse in 1917. In that year whole armies, not single battleships or military detachments, mutinied, and could not be defeated in isolation as the crew of the *Potemkin* was in 1905.

The battleship did sail out of the harbour on 17 June to meet a force of three battleships, a cruiser and four torpedo boats. Although the numerical odds were against her, the *Potemkin*'s range, weight and speed of fire made the disparity less marked than it seems on paper. She had two encounters with the squadron. On the first occasion the Tsarist forces turned away at a distance of four miles and the *Potemkin* returned to harbour. Later that day the force reappeared, strengthened by the addition of two more battleships. *Potemkin*, however, sailed towards them. She was not fired upon, passed through the squadron and returned back through the lines of ships. Some crews acclaimed her, and one ship, the *Georgy Pobyedonosets*, returned with her to

Odessa: the others crept back to their base at Sebastopol. The Commander-in-Chief of the Black Sea Fleet, Admiral Chukhnin, was so alarmed at the possibility of further disaffection that he sent most of the ratings on leave and immobilised ships' engines so that the vessels could not be made operational. *The Times* suggested that 'the Black Sea Fleet has virtually ceased to exist'.[34] Up to this point the encounter was an even greater victory than Eisenstein suggests, but the rest of the story was a humiliating anti-climax.

This brief encounter had solved nothing. The *Potemkin* had not been subdued, but the mutiny had spread to only one other ship. Back in Odessa the sailors were even less willing to join forces with the rebels on land, who were coming under increasing military pressure. Even the crew of the *Georgy Pobyedonosets* were short-lived allies. The ship attempted to slip away to Sebastopol. Discouraged by the menace of *Potemkin*'s guns, she ran aground and the crew abandoned both their ship and the revolutionary cause. The *Potemkin* was desperately short of coal and water. The men were divided about their future course of action. Soon even Matyushenko, the revolutionary leader, agreed that they should sail for a neutral Rumanian port.

On 19 June they reached Constanza. Their welcome was formal and apprehensive. Failing to secure the supplies they needed, but not yet completely cowed, the *Potemkin* sailed away in search of coal. She called at the Russian port of Theodosia, but the townspeople evacuated their homes in terror, and troops opened fire when the crew attempted to take over a coal barge. The ship finally limped back to Constanza. The crew surrendered on 25 June, accepting assurances that they would not be handed over to the Russian authorities.

They did not settle easily in Rumania. Some returned home to face trial and varying lengths of sentence. Others found work on the Rumanian land harder and even less rewarding than in the Ukraine. In 1908 32 of them arrived in London through the good offices of the German Socialist Party and the 'British Friends for Russian Freedom'. This organisation, the committee members of which included Dr G.M. Trevelyan, appealed in *The Times* for £300 to resettle in one of the colonies a party made up of 'strong vigorous men of peasant extraction and all under thirty'.[35] A letter from Mr Trautmann, a British resident in Odessa in 1905, reminded potential subscribers that the refugees had murdered their officers, and had been guilty of theft, insubordination, murder and arson in Rumania. 'Will they be desirable settlers in our colonies'? he concluded.[36] Eventually they departed, not to join the descendants of British convicts in Australia, but to the Argentine.

Matyushenko did not stay long with his ship-mates. By the time they surrendered the crew were bitterly opposed to the man who had driven them so hard for so little purpose. One of the crew, Reshkitin, jumped the ship on its first visit to Constanza, claiming he had fled 'because he could not tolerate Matyushenko's earthy and coarse manner towards the crew. Those who dared to oppose either the committee or Matyushenko were threatened with death'.[37] The Rumanian socialists welcomed Matyushenko and he left Constanza on the first night, according to one report 'because he was afraid of being torn to pieces by the sailors of the battleship *Potemkin* for his inhuman conduct towards them.[38] A year later he was in the United States, working from June 1906 to March 1907 in a Singer factory. On his way through London he was seen by R. Rocker, a German working with Jewish revolutionary groups in the office of Kropotkin's newspaper in Stepney. Rocker found 'it hard to believe that this simple kindly man had been the ringleader of the *Potemkin* mutiny'.[39] In the spring of 1907 he returned to Europe and passed through Paris, en route to further underground agitation in Russia. But he was soon picked up by the police on 3 June in Nikolaev near Odessa in the company of a group of Anarchist-Syndicalists, living under the name of Fedorenko. He was recognised, charged for his part in the mutiny and for a personal responsibility in the murder of the officers, and hanged at dawn on 20 October 1907 in Sebastopol.[40] Feldman was captured in Theodosia, but escaped from prison and resumed his revolutionary career. A police report claimed that he had been seen but not arrested in January 1911. During the preparations for the filming of *Battleship Potemkin* Feldman attended an 'Evening of Reminiscences of Contemporaries of the Year 1905'. Also present were Agadzhanova-Shutko, Alexandrov and Eisenstein, taking notes for the film.[41]

The *Potemkin* herself was punished for her misdemeanours. The ship was collected from Constanza and returned to Sebastopol. Renamed the *St Panteleimon*, she participated in a second, more extensive mutiny in November 1905. The red flag was run up on the cruiser *Ochakov*. The *St Panteleimon* and several other ships joined in the revolt led by Lieutenant Schmidt who sent a telegram to St Petersburg proclaiming the formation of a Black Sea Republic. The rising was subdued after attacks on the rebels by the guns of the *Rostov* and the *Dvenadtsat' Apostolov* (*The Twelve Apostles*), two of the ships which had failed to overawe the *Potemkin* outside Odessa. This mutiny, although more important historically, is less well known. Lieutenant Schmidt was the hero of a poem by Boris Pasternak, and the *Potemkin* affair provided the subject for an opera by Chishko. In the opera the sailors to be shot are covered by a tarpaulin. Neither of these works, however, attracted the attention given to Eisenstein's film.

The *St Panteleimon* continued an undistinguished naval career. In April 1917 she became the *Potemkin* once again but in May was given a third name, *Borets za Svobodu* (*Fighter for Freedom*). She was not in action during the First World War and was finally sunk by order of the Soviet authorities in 1918 to prevent her capture by counter-revolutionary forces. She was later refloated but never brought back into commission.

When Eisenstein made the film in 1925 the *Potemkin* no longer existed. Eisenstein wrote that he used 'her sister ship, the once famed and mighty *Dvenadtsat' Apostolov*'. [42] *The Twelve Apostles* was a contemporary, but not a sister ship, of the *Potemkin*, a cruiser of 8,560 tons, compared with the 12,600 tons of the *Battleship Potemkin*. In 1925 *The Twelve Apostles* was lying rusting at anchor in a creek near Sebastopol. It was one of the few pre-1905 ships still in existence. Very few Russian naval craft of any vintage were still seaworthy. The Black Sea Fleet consisted of two cruisers and three destroyers. It is not surprising that for the shots of the main squadron sailing towards the *Potemkin* Eisenstein had to use pre-World War One stock footage of battleships at sea.

The scenes on board the *Potemkin* were mostly shot on *The Twelve Apostles*, which was given a face-lift by Eisenstein's technicians. The ship had been neglected and was used as a floating mine store. The decks had to be reconstructed. Below decks were thousands of mines. Actors and technicians had to move about carefully for fear of disturbing the dangerous cargo. Later Eisenstein suggested that 'the ship on the screen seemed imbued with their explosive power'. [43] *The Twelve Apostles* could not move through the water, so some of the material was filmed using another vessel, a 1905 cruiser, the *Pamyat' Merkuriya* (renamed by the Bolsheviks *Komintern*), which was still in service as a sea-going training ship.

These ships were used to create a film the splendid artistry of which transformed an unsuccessful revolt into one of the most famous naval mutinies in history, and in the history of the cinema.

Notes

1. D. Mayer, *Sergei M. Eisenstein's Potemkin* (New York, 1972).

2. H. Marshall, *The Battleship Potemkin* (New York, 1978), p.5.

3. Quoted in M. Seton, *Sergei M. Eisenstein* (London, 1978), p.74.

4. Written in 1939 and included in an introductory essay to S. Eisenstein, *The Battleship Potemkin* (London, 1968), p.8.

5. S Eisenstein, *Notes of a Film Director* (London, 1959), p.23. Ironically Eisenstein makes this assertion when discussing his use of the tarpaulin during the execution of the mutineers and, as I suggest later, claims to be distorting the truth when he was in fact following the true course of events.

6. Ibid., p.29.

7. H. Marshall, *Battleship Potemkin,* p.59.

8. Ibid., p.338.

9. Lars Kleberg, in *Scando-Slavica*, vol. XXIII (Copenhagen, 1977).

10. F.T. Jane, *Fighting Ships 1905-6* (London, 1906).

11. F.T. Jane, *The Imperial Russian Navy* (London, 1904).

12. Report by G. Woodhouse, British Consul in Riga, 2 May 1905: Public Record Office, London.

13. Kirill Orlov, memoirs published in V.I. Nevsky, *Vosstanie Na Bronenostse 'Knyaz' Potemkin Tavrichesky', Vospominaniya, Materialy Dokumenty* (Moskva-Leningrad, 1923/4).

14. Matyushenko's letter published in Nevsky, *Vosstanie Na Bronenostse,* p.337.

15. Orlov, in Nevsky, *Vosstanie Na Bronenostse,* p.321.

16. K. Perelygin, in Nevsky, *Vosstanie Na Bronenostse,* p.230.

17. G. Babin, *L'Illustration* (Paris, 22 July 1905), p.55.

18. Matyushenko, in Nevsky, *Vosstanie Na Bronenostse,* p.302.

19. Published in Eisenstein, *Notes of a Film Director,* pp.18-31.

20. Report by H. Dundas, Acting Consul General, Galatz, 12 July 1905: Public Record Office, London.

21. Perelygin, in Nevsky, *Vosstanie Na Bronenostse,* p.233.

22. Yon Barna in his *Eisenstein* (London, 1973) writes on p.98 that Eisenstein received a 'letter from another surviving mutineer, who also maintained that he had been under the tarpaulin; Eisenstein did not disillusion him, but was amused that the power of empathy could outweigh that of memory'. Barna notes that 'it is difficult to determine the truth, but there seems no reason for doubting Eisenstein's word'. Further study of the stories of the tarpaulin and the court case suggests that there is some reason for so doubting.

23. Report by C.S. Smith, British Consul, Odessa, 1 July (Western calendar) 1905: Public Record Office, London.

24. Eisenstein, *Notes of a Film Director,* p.27.

25. Seton, *Eisenstein,* p.75.

26. M. Straukh, quoted in N. Swallow, *Eisenstein a Documentary Portrait* (London, 1976).

27. *L'Illustration* (Paris, 8, 15 and 22 July 1905) contains material on the events in Odessa and in Rumania.

28. *Illustrated London News,* 8 July 1905..

29. This comment is in the version of Matyushenko's memoirs published in London (1931) as A. Matyushenko, *Eleven Days on the Potemkin. The Revolt on the Armoured Cruiser Potemkin,* but does not appear in the account by Matyushenko in Russia in the work of Nevsky, *Vosstanie Na Bronenostse.*

30. Telegram from the Commander of the Armed Forces of the Odessa Military District, Cavalry-General Kakhanov, to the War Ministry, 16 June 1905,

published in Nevsky, *Vosstanie Na Bronenostse*, p.367.
   31. Published in *Soviet Weekly* (London), 7 September 1961.
   32. Matyushenko, *Eleven Days on the Potemkin*, p.15.
   33. C. Feldmann, *The Revolt of the Potemkin* (London, 1908), p.75.
   34. *The Times* (London), 4 July 1905.
   35. *The Times* (London), 16 September 1908.
   36. *The Times* (London), 29 September 1908.
   37. As reported by Melas, Russian police informant in Constanza in Nevsky, *Vosstanie Na Bronenostse*, p.270.
   38. Ibid., pp.276-7.
   39. R. Rocker, *The London Years* (London, 1956), p.173.
   40. Report by the Temporary Deputy Commander-in-Chief of the Black Sea Fleet, Rear-Admiral Viren, 20 October 1907, in Nevsky, *Vosstanie Na Bronenostse*, pp.329-30.
   41. Marshall, *Battleship Potemkin*, p.58.
   42. Eisenstein, *Notes of a Film Director*, p.20.
   43. Ibid., p.22.

References

1. General Works

Baynac, J., Engelstein, L., Girault, R., Keenan, E., and Yassoun, A. *Sur 1905* (Paris, 1974)
Bennett, G. 'The *Potemkin* Mutiny', *Journal of the Royal United Service Institute* (London, November 1959)
Harcave, S. *First Blood. The Russian Revolution of 1905* (London, 1965)
Hough, R. *The Potemkin Mutiny* (London, 1975)
Jane, F.T. *The Imperial Russian Navy* (London, 1904)
———, *Fighting Ships 1905-6* (London, 1906)
Mayer, D. *Sergei M. Eisenstein's Potemkin* (New York, 1972)
Taylor, R. *Film Propaganda, Soviet Russia and Nazi Germany* (London, 1979)
———, *The Politics of the Soviet Cinema 1917-29* (Cambridge, 1979)

2. The Making of the Film

Barna, Y. *Eisenstein* (London, 1973)
Eisenstein, S. *Film Form* (London, 1951)
———, *Notes of a Film Director* (London, 1959)
———, *The Film Sense* (London, 1968)
———, *The Battleship Potemkin* (London, 1968)
Kleberg, L. 'Ejzenstein's *Potemkin*, and Tretjakov's *Ryči, Kiaj, Scando-Slavica*, XXIII (Copenhagen, 1977)
Kleiman, N.I., and Levina, K.B. *Bronenosets Potemkin* (Moscow, 1969)
Leyda, J. *Kino. A History of Russian Film* (London, 1960)
Marshall, H. (ed.) *The Battleship Potemkin* (New York, 1978)
Nizhny, V.B. *Lessons with Eisenstein* (London, 1962)
Seton, M. *Sergei M. Eisenstein – A Biography* (London, 1978)
Shklovskii, V. *Eisenstein* (Moscow, 1973)
Swallow, N. *Eisenstein, A Documentary Portrait* (London, 1976)

3. Accounts of the Mutiny and of Events in Odessa

Reports by the Belgian Consul in Odessa. Archives du Ministère des Affaires Etrangères, Brussels
Reports by the British Consul in Odessa. Public Record Office, London

Reports by the British Acting Consul General in Galatz, Rumania. Public
    Record Office, London
Reports by the British Vice-Consul in Sebastopol. Public Record Office, London
Reports by the French Consul in Odessa. Archives du Ministère des Affaires
    Etrangères, Quai D'Orsay, Paris
Reports by the Italian Consul in Odessa and from the Italian Legation in
    Bucharest. Archives del Ministero degli Affari Esteri, Rome
Reports by the US Ambassador in St Petersburg. Foreign Relations, USA.
    State Department, Washington, 1906

Accounts by:

Lt Colonel Budakov
The Gendarme Administration of the City of Odessa
Melas (Police Informant in Constanza)
A.F. Matyushenko
K. Orlov
K. Perelygin
B. Prokhorov
Colonel Shul'ts
Colonel Zagoskin
(All published in Russian)
V.I. Nevsky. *Vosstanie Na Bronenostse, 'Knyaz' Potemkin Tavrichesky',
    Vospominaniya, Materialy Dokumenty,* Moscow-Leningrad, 1924
C. Feldmann. *The Revolt of the Potemkin* (London, 1908)
A.F. Matyushenko. *Eleven Days on the Potemkin* (London, 1931)
G. Babin. *L 'Illustration* (Paris, 8, 15, 22 July 1905)
St Petersburg *Official Messenger* (5 July 1905)

3 MOVIES AND NATIONAL CONSCIOUSNESS: GERMANY AND FRANCE IN THE 1920s

Paul Monaco

In a recent review essay on books written in English on motion pictures, Ian C. Jarvie explores the interrelated problems of writing history based on feature film documentation and creating a history of the movies that is truly historiographical. The essay is divided into two sections, one entitled 'Movies as a Window', and the other 'A Window on Movies'.[1] Jarvie has long been a constructive critic of attempts to study the social significance and/or the social function of motion pictures. With this essay he asks us: What is the central question of motion picture history? Or, rather, what is the intellectual core of the problem into which we are inquiring? Any response inspires the debate that should ensue whenever scholars of the cinema speak to each other.

Some might protest that Jarvie's metaphor of the window is inept. Movies are more a mirror than a window. Moreover, this 'mirror' is not of a clear silver finish; it has distortions, like the 'funny glass' mirrors at carnivals. Such studies deal with one distorted image (films as a distortion of the time and place in which they are made) reflected through a second distortion (our contemporary perceptions of the meanings of these films). The nature of these distortions is illuminated only by first clarifying our notion of what the cinema is.

The cinema is a popular art! Motion pictures are produced by collectivities, groups or committees – they are collaborative creations.[2] Movies are widely accessible; moreover, on the surface, they are usually readily understandable. Motion pictures are, at once, both a creative and an interpretative art; though one of these elements may outweigh the other in any given instance. The totality of the motion picture is a *Gesamtkunstwerk*, to which neither Richard Wagner, nor anyone of his epoch, could have attained. Its form of presentation is continuous, uninterrupted; its mode of representation is discontinuous. The thinking in motion pictures is 'surface', associative or non-linear thinking.[3] Motion pictures transmit *images* in motion. They are related to, but quite different from, that creation which transmits *data* in motion – the computer.[4]

The elements which define motion pictures as a popular art are aesthetic criteria, not commercial ones. That millions see a movie is, in itself, not definitive of the type of art to which motion pictures belong. Millions see the 'Mona Lisa' annually; millions read Shakespeare. Motion picture companies sometimes make staggering profits, but then so do certain publishers or gallery owners.

To grasp the significance of the motion picture as a popular art it is necessary to acknowledge and accept that all people have 'aesthetic urges' which are satisfied in many different ways. There is some kind of art available for everyone. Motion pictures, television, popular songs and the other popular arts fill the cultural milieu. They are 'democratic' arts, not as regards the content of any specific object of them, but in their inherent nature.[5]

The aesthetic urges can be enumerated:

1. the general receptivity to the expression of fears and wishes;
2. a demand for knowledge and wish fulfilment about society;
3. the desire to spend free time away from work.[6]

In considering how the first two categories of 'aesthetic urge' are satisfied, attention must be given to the nature of the symbolic and the signifying. It may be said that the expression of fear and wishes is symbolic; the demand for knowledge and wish fulfilment is semiotic. Carl Gustav Jung has gone a long way toward clarifying the distinction between sign and symbol. He excludes from the category of 'symbol' the function performed by language. A five-letter word, 'chair' for example, stands for a particular object usually meant for sitting. But to say that the word 'symbolises' the object or is a 'symbol' for it is misleading. Jung argues that what is involved in the use of the word 'chair' is not a matter of symbolism, but a case of signification. 'Chair' is a sign, not a symbol. The word 'chair' serves a 'semiotic' function; this occurs when a word or image is used 'as an analogous or abbreviated expression of a known thing'.[7] When, however, a figure or object is used to refer to 'a relatively unknown thing', its function is not semiotic but symbolic. This excludes language proper from being symbolic. It also calls to our attention an important item. The symbolic function of cinema has nothing to do with the so-called reading of a film. Movies are not read, they are experienced. Motion pictures do not have a 'grammar'.[8] Motion pictures do not create a language, in that their expressions (images) do not lead to standard meanings which are systematised. Furthermore, in the Jungian view the symbolic expresses something unknown toward which the psyche is reaching. Symbols, then, are not a means of 'communication', as that word is normally used. Since symbols reach toward the unknown they are primarily enacted and responded to unconsciously. The symbolic link is fundamental to the relationship of the individual to society. Otherwise put, 'Individual psychic energy develops through the tension between instinctual energy and society, [thus] society functions in terms of and by means of psychic energy . . . the link between [psychic energy and society] is the symbol.'[9]

Both signs and symbols may gratify the aesthetic urges. In movies signs inform us directly about a society. We can observe what certain places looked like in the 1920s, see styles in dress, social manner and gestures; note representations of ethnic types or minorities, handsome men or beautiful women; in sound films we hear inflections, argot and slang. This reveals a society's typologies — its 'surface' values.

Symbolism in a motion picture, or in a group of movies, leads away from the real (the 'semiotic') toward the unknown. This makes sense, however, only if we elaborate on the concept of 'reality' and assert that the unknown is not the same as the 'unreal'. This points to a problem in 'doing' history with or through movies. Our historiography is linear, analytical and rational. Our motion pictures are non-linear, associative and belong to the realm of fantasy. We may study certain aspects surrounding the making of, or consumption of, motion pictures with the methods, conceptions and received ideas offered to us by Western historiography. This might lead, for example, toward an economic history of motion picture production. Studies of film industry structures, the roles of producers, directors and technicians in the movie business, the commercial history of movie distribution and exploitation are all worth while. Or we may pursue the study of movie censorship, describing the political and social forces which lie behind it. These topics, perhaps, have been the ones most successfully treated by 'film historians' so far. The problem is that, while such studies conform well to accepted standards of historiography, they may have little, or nothing, to do with the understanding of motion pictures *qua* motion pictures.

Feature films are fictionalised; they are 'fantasy'. Fiction and fantasy, however, are not the same. Motion pictures create worlds; their styles are their worlds. Motion pictures are realities which relate to other levels of reality.[10] If our purpose is to explore that relationship we must begin with the world the films themselves create. Only from here can we get to there — the connections to other levels of reality.

How we pursue the relationship of movies to 'historical reality' hinges on how we conceive the composition of that reality. It is difficult to argue that feature films, except rarely, reflect relevant, contemporary political issues, the crises of institutions or international diplomacy, economic problems and so forth.[11] Rather we conclude that movies offer insight into the psychic state of the time and place in which they are created. In this conclusion lies the assumption that psyche is a reality, even though its appearance in the world is displaced.

The thought of any motion picture is myth-like. 'Myth' refers to a 'fantastic' story told in an especially powerful way. The purpose behind myth is not to constrict its telling, but to expand upon it, to let the fantasy become unharnessed and to project it into the world as an enactment of power. For its creation a myth requires the release of more energy than could be possessed by any individual psyche. The energy manifested and enacted in myth is collective; this is also true of the motion picture.

In the 1920s Ricardo Canudo claimed that film was 'national folklore'.[12] While he elaborated little on the notion, this conceptualis- ation points in three directions:

1. movies as secular (a displacement from the religious or sacred qualities often present in myth proper);
2. movies as being of the folk (that is, expressing widely shared ideas and attitudes);
3. movies as 'lore' (establishing the cinema as a corpus of works, meaningful beyond the significance of any single film).

In so far as the term 'folklore' was created in the early nineteenth century to distinguish popular tales (of the folk) from myths (which originate with aristocratic or priestly elites) the word descriptively fits the cinema well, but not perfectly. Elites create feature films, but they do so in a symbiotic relationship to the broad public for movies.[13] Folklore is an elaboration on the concept of myth, a broader term which subsumes myth within it. The cinema is then a popular folk art at one remove.

What is the source of this mythic/folkloric creation, the motion picture? It is the major repository of collective psychic energy in modern life — the nation. Movies function as one element in the broader fantasy life of any collectivity to which they appeal. That collectivity is, in the twentieth century, quintessentially, nationally determined.

For it makes remarkably little difference where one finds oneself

in the contemporary world — in Stockholm or Peking, London or
New York. Regardless of location, it is certain that every 'citizen'
has, in the government of his or her 'nation', a fantasy partner who
cannot be excluded from life's largest or most trivial endeavors.[14]

The history of the cinema must be written against this backdrop. In
writing this sort of movie history one is working in an area that might
be called 'history of consciousness'. A body of motion pictures brings
into the world a powerful enactment of collective psychic energy.
It does so through its symbolic functions which mediate between the
source of unconscious energy and the realities of the situation in which
that energy is discovered.

To illustrate the direction of this sort of inquiry, the motion pictures
made in three nations, France, Germany and the Soviet Union, will be
considered. The dates 1919 and 1939 will be parameters for the
illustrations. In doing this, the 'bracketing out' of the creative process
involved in making these movies and the audience receptivity to them
is acknowledged.

In an earlier study my purpose was to reconstruct what stood
behind the 'popular' films of Germany and France in the 1920s.[15] That
was a study in the impulse to creativity. It resulted in a social and
industrial history with implications for the way in which partially
articulated collective concerns, primarily political in nature, were
reflected unconsciously in popular films. Here the interest is in what
stands *beyond* a group of films, that is, what view of the world is
symbolised in them.

A motion picture creates what film aestheticists often call 'off-
screen space'. Our problem is 'off-screen meanings'. In regarding films
as objects it is necessary to recognise that they bear social meaning
only as a group. Movies are stereotyped to a marked degree. They do
not strive toward originality; nor should they. As a symbolic function
of the collective psyche, their purpose is to reiterate and elaborate a
point over and over again. This illustration proceeds at a broad level
of generalisation. 'Worlds' cannot be created in an hour or two;
symbols leading toward the unknown emerge through a body of
repetitious expressions.

The primary symbolism in any motion picture is in its enactment
of temporality (i.e., the 'sense of time' conveyed). From Sergei
Eisenstein to Alain Renais, movie makers interested in the theory of
film have claimed that the elemental characteristic of motion picture
making is a 'playing with time', or a manipulation of temporal

relationships. All motion pictures deal symbolically with temporality. This might be said of many works of art, but there are strong differences. The devices available in cinematography allow that time itself can be recreated (or reconstructed) in motion pictures. Movies are weak at portraying a 'sense of memory'. Flashbacks, for example, even when attempted by talented film makers, usually fail. This is because a motion picture *is* like memory.

The prime filmic function to be looked at, then, is the highly generalised aspect of 'film-time' in its symbolic workings. French movies of the 1920s and 1930s are characterised by the slow pace of their editing and their development. They are, in a word, theatrical in conception and execution. In them entrances into and exits from a scene tend to be from right and left in the frame. There are few instances of a figure coming toward the camera and passing beyond its range in the direction of the viewer. In the inter-war years only the motion pictures directed by René Claire and *La Roue* (A. Gance, 1923) provide consistent exceptions to this pattern. This tendency to a static cinematography is exemplified in the extreme by such commercially successful directors as Roussel, Feyder, Diamant-Berger and Pagnol. It is also present in the movies directed by Delluc, Epstein, L'Herbier, Gremillion, Vigo, Carné and Renior. What is symbolically created in French movies of the 1920s and 1930s is an image of stasis. The popular appeal of historical epics for French audiences is clear. What they portray symbolically as their mode of temporality is a progression that is continuous and rational. These French films are both thematically and cinematographically movies of restoration. They symbolically restore a faith in progress which is incremental, measurable.

The pervasive style of editing in French films between the two wars joins one scene to another, smoothing out the points of transition between them and creating the symbolism of that which flows through time. The introduction of intervening visual material, which would clash with this temporal flow, is avoided. The constrained construction of French movies in this period, the elongation of scenes and the prolongation of a film's action to parallel the passing of 'real time' symbolise an acceptance of that time frame, expressing a desire to live within it. It is noteworthy that, during this epoch, France produced almost no movies which are 'futuristic' in their fantasy. René Clair's *Paris qui dort* (1923) is, perhaps, the most notable of these rarities. The movie, called *The Crazy Ray* in English, wanders along the edges of 'science fiction', portraying a mysterious ray that has frozen Paris.

It does not, as many science-fiction films do, represent the overcoming of time/space or the release from it. Instead, time stands still at the primary level of representation; stasis is total!

The portrayal of spatiality in French movies creates symbolic reinforcements for the mode of temporality. Seascapes and landscapes provide not just a common background for much film action, especially during the 1920s, but encompass the film world of many French productions of the decade. This tendency subsides in the early 1930s, in part, perhaps, because of the initial production constraints that accompanied the coming of sound films for which the French industry was markedly ill-equipped. Yet it re-emerges in the late 1930s, with a vengeance as exemplified in the popular movies directed by Pagnol, such as *Régain* (1937) and *La Femme du Boulanger* (1938), as well as in the films of Renoir, Carné and Feyder. The sea, the pastoral landscape, the earth covered by snow, the atmosphere of mist and fog — these elements combine to reinforce a symbolism of stasis. They are symbols of the immutability of nature, or else they create the sensibility of a muted acceptance of it.

German movies in the same period are markedly obsessed with the question of time, even at the semiotic level. At the surface level, German movies portray repetitious images of clocks, watches, hour glasses and the like. Most importantly, time is treated thematically as a threat, a limitation. This is a reinforcement of symbolism through context. This thematic integration with the symbolism of time passage denotes an especially strong concern with this symbolism. In German movies time is a threat; it is running out. This refers to so-called 'real' time. Lived time offers no hope for salvation or redemption; indeed, not even for success. Hence, it is implied symbolically that the course to overcoming a situation is in the overcoming of time itself. In *Nosferatu* (1922) the vampire perishes only because a young woman of pure heart stays with him until the dawn breaks. In Veit Harlan's *Der Herrscher* (1937), the protagonist is told repeatedly by his children: 'You can't put the clock back.' Another Murnau film, *Der letzte Mann* (1924), explores the theme that time has run out on an elderly hotel doorman. Harlan's *Das unsterbliche Herz* (1939) depicts the story of the inventor of the watch, who is shot and realises it is just a matter of time until the bullet fatally reaches his heart. In the last two instances both protagonists deny what time has brought or is bringing.

The construction of temporality in German motion pictures may be summarised as a mode of parallel editing that results neither in the slow-paced joining together of self-contained scene nor in the visual dynamics of montage. There is, for example, the elongation of time in a sequence such as that found in *Variéte* (1925) as 'Boss' contemplates letting his rival Artinelli fall to his death in their trapeze act. This might be called a 'subjective' elongating of time in the imaginative vision of the protagonist. It is similar to, yet unlike, the elongation of time in the 'Odessa steps' sequence in *Battleship Potemkin*. In that instance there is not only an elongation of imaginative time, but also the prolongation of objective time.

Often in German movies the mode of representation would be best described as portraying the intervention of one time sphere into another. Siegfried Kracauer recognised this tendency, but limited it to the 'stabilised period' in German film making from 1925 to about 1930. He wrote: 'In the grip of the existing paralysis, the German film makers cultivated a species of films presenting a cross-section of some sphere of reality.'[16] Here it is being argued that more generally German movies from 1919 until well into the Nazi period create the appearance of discontinuous time spheres being introduced over-against one another. What is present symbolically is a 'confusion' with regard to temporality. A distinct modification in this confusion is discernible after 1936/37 when movies begin to tend more toward the structures of so-called 'normal' time.

The German cinema produced several 'futuristic films', the most notable of which were *Metropolis* (1927), *Die Frau im Mond* (1929) and *Gold* (1934). It is significant that both *Metropolis* and *Gold* end with visions of destruction — flooding that destroys the worker's underground city in the first case, and the great atomic laboratory in the other. The future is symbolised as clouded, gloomy. The past in German movies is either trivialised as in the films of Lubitsch, romanticised as in *Nibelungen* (1924), or heroicised as in scores of films from *Fridericus Rex* (1922) to *Das unsterbliche Herz* (1939). While the pace of German films slows down in the 1930s, it is still more frenetic than that of French films.

German cinematography tends toward distinct differentiation of whites and blacks. In the interior compositions of the frame there is a clear delineation of line, a failure to create the blending or flow of one image into another. Thematically, German films frequently develop around untimely incidents which turn things sour. There is an accidental quality of causation in German film action; a slip may be fatal. That figure of speech becomes literalised in the popular mountaineering movies which provided German audiences with a

unique and evocative film symbolism from 1919 to 1940. While many
cinemas produce adventure films of one sort or another, they are
rarely this specialised in vision. The mountaineering film was pioneered
in the early 1920s, but remained prominent during the Third Reich
including a remake of *Der Kampf ums Matterhorn* (1936) and ending
with *Der Feuerteufel* (1940).

What we find in German films are symbols of discontinuity; there is
a confusion in the symbolism. The national technique in cinematography
tends toward the introduction of visual materials that are not
discontinuous with a narrative flow encompassed by progression
through real time.

Soviet films tend toward an overcoming of time, especially during
the period of expressive-realism in the late 1920s. The elaboration on
the 'Kuleshov effect', pioneered in 1917, leads toward montage. This
calls for the arranging of various shots of the same subject in quite
different contexts, hence producing contrasting situations. This
clashing of images, which elongates a sequence beyond the
presentation of those images necessary for communication, results in
expanding 'time'. This tendency diminishes, but does not entirely
end, after the eclipse of the first wave of Soviet film making. *We from
Kronstadt* (1936), for example, creates a frantic visual pace; 'everything
is a maximum pitch, with an exhausting effect'.[17] The temporality
created in Soviet film during the 1920s and 1930s leads toward an
evolutionary dialetic of past/present/future through montage or some
modification of it.

There is an almost complete list of the symbolic elements of Soviet
films in this epoch to be found in a letter written by the Soviet author
Vsevolod Vishnevsky. His examples are:

In *Potemkin* — explosion of the mass
In *Arsenal* — fearlessness, denial of death
In *End of St Petersburg* — evolution of individual, and of mass
In *Earth* — pantheism, eternity
In *Ivan* — tragedy of peasantry plus gleam of the new
In *Chapayev* — personal tragedy plus warfare.[18]

In general, symbolism in any group of motion pictures relates to
movements, breadth of scope and power. Although the artistry and
power of the Soviet film seems to have dwindled during the 1930s
as a result of increased governmental intervention in production, attacks
on 'formalism' and the banalities of Shumyatsky's leadership, the basic

tendencies of a cinema of movement, breadth and power are not
eliminated.

Soviet films of the 1920s rarely deal with contemporary society.
They are set, almost exclusively, in the recent past. They portray
Marxist-Leninist heroism, and avoid exploring the efforts to create
proletarian socialism. While in the 1930s the depiction of
protagonists becomes more individualised and the tendency toward
more eclectic film making is promoted, the general thematic
emphasis of Soviet movies changes only slightly. By contrast, Soviet
literature of the 1920s continued an older Russian literary tradition of
exploring 'the unending dialectic between man and his epoch',
frequently portraying contemporary settings rather than those of
the recent past, and exploring such themes as 'sexual freedom' and
'free love'.[19]

The Soviet fashion in the 1920s of not naming individual
characters in a movie marks a tendency toward the allegorical and
away from the signifying. In German or French movies this rarely
occurs. *Der müde Tod* (1921), *Der letzte Mann* (1924), *Verdun,
visions d'histoire* (1927) are the rarities. The shift in Soviet movie
making toward individualisation of characters after 1930 denotes a
partial revoking of the symbolism created in the 1920s.

Words, in general, lead away from symbolism. They limit the
creation of symbolism, especially in movies, where they are present
as dialogue and only rarely, and minimally, used metaphorically.
Words may be put together so as to produce a *feeling* for the unknown.
Images, however, evoke a *sense* of it. Soviet and German silent movies
in the 1920s tend to avoid titles. The French movies, with a few
notable exceptions such as *La Passion et la mort de Jeanne d'arc*
(1927), use titles extensively. Titles in silent movies disrupt the
temporal flow of the film and create a spacing. They act as *caesuras*,
limiting the power of symbol creation. Several German films of the
1920s made in the expressionist style attempt to convey
information through titles, but modify the disruption of the film's
temporal pace by inserting titles which conform visually with the
movie's setting. In the 1930s the transition to sound produced a
cinema that was extensively verbal in France. German movies
resisted this between 1930 and 1933, only then to tend progressively
more markedly in that direction, year by year, from 1933 to 1940.
The Soviet cinema opposed this tendency most strongly. As late as
1934, the Soviet filmic adaptation of Guy de Maupassant's *Boule de
Suif*, directed by Mikhail Romm, was produced as a silent movie on

aesthetic (and, one suspects, symbolic) grounds.[20] The resistance to
language – either written or spoken – represents in Soviet film the
ongoing elaboration and re-elaboration of these motion pictures'
unique temporality.

Suicide is common in German movies up to 1933; after that it
becomes less frequent. French motion pictures avoid the suicide motif
until the late 1930s. In Soviet movies suicide is untreated. But where
suicide is not present or is diminished thematically (French movies in
the 1920s and early 1930s; German films after 1933; Soviet films
throughout the interwar years), sacrificial dying is portrayed. In Soviet
movies sacrificial death is transformed symbolically into a
transcendency. Few Soviet films end in death which do not carry the
articulated hope of that death being for a higher cause. Death is
connected with 'the' future. In French movies sacrificial death is
common, but the mode of representation does not connect such
incidences with the future, but rather with the present. The good done by
dying is meaningful within the present; it absolves the tension or crisis
of the moment immediately preceding. Even in the 'resurrection of the
dead' scene at the end of *J'Accuse* (1919; remake, 1938), the 'rising up'
of fallen soldiers only resolves the tension created by the conduct of
war; it does not point clearly to a future beyond itself. Much the same
is true of heroic, sacrificial death in German movies made between
1933 and 1940. But in the German case there are, as usual, confusions.
The attempts to create the equivalent of the first wave of Soviet film
is found in films produced in the Third Reich such as *Hans Westmar*
(1933) or *Pour le Mérite* (1936), but these films do not succeed, nor
do they seem intended to succeed, in projecting the heroism of
sacrificial death toward the future.

In so far as 'time' is one of the greatest of unknowns that confronts
man, its representation in movies is symbolically of highest significance.
Soviet movies place man in step with the onward thrust of nature; this
imagery is clear in *Mother* (1926), or in *Earth* (1930), or in *Chapeyev*
(1934). Nature represents the onward course of history, and pulsates
toward a future that is not feared. In French movies nature represents
that which is static, unchanging; its symbolism tends toward a sense of
quiescence, and a denial of man's dialectical tension with nature. In
German movies there is a reverse tendency; nature is cruel and
menacing. In a few instances, however, nature is glorified and idealised,
as in *Wege zur Kraft und Schönheit* (1925) or in the numerous
mountaineering films (1919-40).

Symbolism referring to time and nature, life and death, is found in all the arts including the popular arts. We cannot view movies of the 1920s and 1930s and conclude what they *meant* to those who saw them then. Studies in the psychology of perception indicate that motion picture content does not measurably affect viewers in ways which are predictable from knowledge of the film-makers' objectives. This poses a great problem for what amounts to a content analysis of movies in relationship to the audiences. Indeed, a given viewer may see what he or she wants to see, modifying what is objectively presented in the film.

It is through symbols that psychic energy and society are connected; symbolic functions relate to movie *content* only peripherally. Motion pictures may be studied as objects that symbolise the transformation of collective psychic energy within themselves. Modern nationalism is mythic. This does not mean it is unreal. Its reality, while not quantifiable, is of immense power. Nationalism creates, as well as exploits, symbolism. The French 'Marianne', the German 'Swastika', the Soviet 'Stakanhovite Worker' — these are symbolic formations which focus collective energy.

French movies of the 1920s and 1930s reflect a consciousness which is modern, but not contemporary. Their symbolism does not confront discontinuity and disruption. It elaborates on traditional symbols primarily rather than creating symbols of transformation. By contrast symbolism in Soviet films addresses the dialectical and the flow of evolution. It presents an imagery of a transcendence which is not sacral but represents the overcoming by man of a set of pre-established circumstances.

German movies create symbols of transformation, but also rely on traditional symbols. This confusion is paralleled in the lack of resolution found in the thematic materials of many German movies. Soviet movies present a constructive, but limited, symbolism pointing towards transformation. The symbolism of German films is fragmented and points toward nihilism.

What has been pursued here is not concerned with either the source of such symbolism or its 'influence' in society. This symbolism reflects a state of consciousness. Through the myth of nationalism, and in the 'fantasy partner' of the nation state, modern man is confronted with a replacement for the agencies in civilisation through which time, death, nature and the dealing with others were rendered meaningful. Religion is in eclipse, the family shows signs of disintegration. There is scant evidence, however that man's 'religiosity' in disappearing or that a sense of 'kinship' has become unnecessary as the basis for meaningful inter-subjective relationships of all sorts.

The historical 'realities' realised in any epoch hinge on the ways in which the flow of psychic energy is symbolically transformed into images of collective consciousness. Collective psychology, like individual psychology, is not deterministic. Motion pictures are like dreams. They portray the mental landscape at a given moment through symbols. Dreams do not determine what we will do, nor do movies determine what will happen. But what is done and what happens is likely prefigured in the indicative potential of the direction of psychic energy as symbolised in dreams or movies at a given moment.

Does the symbolism of the 1920s and 1930s in French movies point toward Vichy, that in Soviet movies toward Stalingrad, and that in German movies toward Potsdam? This is possible, perhaps even probable. But the exploring of that set of connections is part of another agenda. Inappropriately, I have run out of time and space.

Notes

1. I.C. Jarvie, 'Seeing Through Movies', *Philosophy of the Social Sciences*, vol. 8, no. 4 (December 1978), pp.374-9.

2. Ibid., pp.379 and 390; the argument is not uncommon and has been documented and articulated in a variety of ways.

3. One of the best pieces on linear thinking (writing) and surface thinking (image making) is Vilém Flusser, 'Line and Surface', *Main Currents in Modern Thought*, vol. 29, no. 3 (January-February 1973), pp.100-6.

4. Mark Slade, *The Language of Change* (Toronto, 1977), p.5.

5. A fine, extensive treatment of this notion is found in Garth Jowett, *Film: The Democratic Art* (Boston, 1977).

6. Herbert Gans, *Popular Culture and High Culture* (New York, 1974), pp.73, 74.

7. Ira Progoff, *Jung's Psychology and Its Social Meaning* (Garden City, 1953), pp.160, 161; an excellent refinement on Jung's definition of symbolism, specifically related to movie analysis, is found in Don Fredericksen, 'Jung/Sign/Symbol/Film, Part I' *Quarterly Review of Film Studies*, vol.4, no.2 (Spring 1979), pp.167-92. The second part of Fredericksen's argument is forthcoming.

8. Here I am arguing against the orientation of a semiotic approach to film. The title of James Monaco's *How to Read A Film* (Oxford, 1978) reflects clearly this confusion; so does the title of Raymond Spottiswoode's *A Grammar of Film* (Los Angeles and Berkeley, 1958; original publication in London, 1935).

9. Progoff, *Jung's Psychology*, p.173.

10. Jarvie, 'Seeing Through Movies', p.394.

11. A recent example of this rarity is *The China Syndrome* (USA, 1979, directed by Michael Douglas). There is a parallel between the film's content and an event that occurred shortly after its release (the 'Three-Mile Island' nuclear 'accident'). This, however, is a case of 'life imitating art'. The portrayal of actual events, especially of a political nature, is rare in movies, except when they are treated as 'historic incidents'.

12. Ricardo Canudo, *L'Usine aux Images* (Paris, 1927).

13. This occurs in nearly every movie-making situation. Citations elaborating this in 'free-market' situations are numerous. An excellent source, still, exploring this in a state-controlled cinema is David Rimberg, 'Motion Picture in the Soviet Union, 1918-1952: A Sociological Analysis', unpublished dissertation, Columbia University, 1959.

14. Attributed to Henry Ebel, contributing editor of *The Journal of Psychohistory: History of Childhood Quarterly.*

15. Paul Monaco, *Cinema and Society: France and Germany During the Twenties* (New York, Oxford, Amsterdam, 1976).

16. Siegfried Kracauer, *From Caligari to Hitler* (Princeton, 1947), p.181.

17. Jay Leyda, *Kino* (New York, 1973), p.333.

18. Ibid., pp.336, 337.

19. George Huaco, *The Sociology of Film Art* (New York, 1966), p.72.

20. Michael Gould, 'Maupassant on Film', paper presented at the West Virginia University Colloquium on Modern Literature, 21-23 September, 1978; publication forthcoming.

4 JEAN RENOIR AND THE POPULAR FRONT[1]

Elizabeth Grottle Strebel

By the late thirties, Jean Renoir had established himself as one of, if not the, major French film director. His artistry within the realm of commercial feature-length film was hailed both nationally and internationally. His 1937 film *La Grande Illusion* broke box office records across France and was by far the most commercially successful French film that year.[2] At the same time, Renoir had become highly politicised and actively involved in leftist politics. He was entrusted with the over-all direction of the French Communist Party's first feature film, *La Vie est à Nous* (1936). He also served on the Administrative Council of the CGT organisation Ciné-Liberté, which between 1936 and 1938 produced a number of films by various workers' syndicates, notably those of the railway workers, builders and metalworkers, and sponsored Renoir's own film *La Marseillaise*.[3] Renoir was moreover one of the editors and frequent contributors of the organisation's review by the same name.

Yet, however great his enthusiasm for the leftist cause, Renoir never became bound to party or ideology. Although he worked with the Communist Party and had many friends and collaborators who were committed party members, Renoir himself never became a member. His sympathies lay more broadly with the Popular Front and he was always more of a fellow traveller, a humanist socialist. When he writes for the short-lived review *Ciné-Liberté*, amidst caustic pieces on censorship and rigorous discourses on trade union activities, it is to celebrate the genius of Charlie Chaplin's *Modern Times*.[4] Much of Renoir's commitment to the left derived from the instinctive predilection for the organic bonding of a small group of *copains*, or 'pals', like those that appear in so many of his films and like his own team of cinematographic collaborators, which at the time functioned very much as a sort of extended family. Still, although never ideologically bound, his receptivity to and active involvement with the French left played a critical role in shaping his artistic vision at a time when he was consciously evolving his own cinematic language.

The following study is an in-depth analysis of two of Renoir's feature-length and commercially distributed films of the period, *Le Crime de M. Lange* (1935) and *La Marseillaise* (1937), two major artistic expressions of Popular Front consciousness. Situating each of these films very specifically in terms of its particular socio-historical context, this study aims, on one level, to look at specific images, characters, themes, or the more manifest content, and, on another level, to examine narrative structure and cinematic language (*mise-en scène* and montage), or a more latent content. This in-depth study effectively broadens our understanding of Popular Front iconography, attitudes, mentalities.

In the thirties, the majority of films, French and otherwise, were stylistically patterned along the lines of what has become known as Hollywood 'découpage classique'. Cuts followed the dialogue in shot/reverse shot fashion. It was, as Alfred Hitchcock so aptly put it, 'The photographing of talking heads'. Although all this was done very skilfully to produce 'seamless editing', the over-all effect was still highly fragmented. Jean Renoir's films were different. He de-emphasised montage and exhibited instead a marked preference for long takes, in-depth shooting with foreground and background equally clear, panning, tracking, movement within a fixed frame, all indicative of his respect for the continuity of dramatic space and time, which gives a unique sense of organic wholeness to his films.

The evolution of the cinematic language in Jean Renoir's thirties films has been much commented on. His development of the ontological aesthetic has been particularly heralded by one of his most enthusiastic proponents, film critic and historian André Bazin.[5] Renoir stands out from his contemporaries with a radically different approach to film making, at the same time as he is linked to those lonely giants of the twenties, Murnau, Von Stroheim, Flaherty.

Although the stylistic distinctiveness of Renoir's films is well known, there is no explanation for why this exists, other than attributing it to the genius of the great artist Renoir unquestionably was. It is striking that, whereas film studies have often linked evolution in narrative and thematic content to the socio-political milieu, they are less inclined to associate stylistic evolution with such a context. It is as if stylistic developments occur in a sort of vacuum, guided by some intangible and almost mystical inspiration. I would argue, however, that the cinematic language is also inextricably tied to its social context and that Renoir's work, particularly in this period, provides us with a prime example. Renoir's distinctive approach to filmic writing was very much related to the social and political realities of the day and to Renoir's own intensive politicisation in the period.

Jaques Brunius, with his insightful insider's view of the period in

En Marge du Cinéma Francais, points to *Le Crime de M. Lange*, without much further comment, as 'one of the most important' of Renoir's films.[6] Certainly, in terms of the evolution of his cinematic language, the film is pivotal. We do, of course, have depth of field and highly fluid camera movements before, notably in *La Chienne, Boudu Sauvé des Eaux* and *Toni*, but in *Le Crime de M. Lange* the new style is more fully elaborated in explicit dialectical opposition to the more traditional aesthetic, thus demonstrably linking it to a pronounced ideological framework.

Le Crime de M. Lange was made in October and November of 1935 under a very special set of circumstances which were indicative of significant changes that had occurred both in the French film industry and in French society as a whole. The year 1935 saw the financial collapse of Pathé and Gaumont, the two big conglomerates which had dominated production and distribution of films in France since the introduction of sound. This led to an influx of a plethora of smaller, less tradition-bound, production companies and to a correspondingly freer atmosphere for film making.[7] This comparatively freer climate was extremely important in terms of Renoir's ability to express himself artistically. Renoir's whole career exhibits a tension between his personal artistic vision and the dictates of commercial interest, and in 1935 the balance swung in favour of his own artistry. It is not without significance that the films widely regarded as his greatest masterpieces were made between 1935 and 1939.

For *Le Crime de M. Lange*, Renoir was given greater freedom than ever before in choosing his own artistic collaborators. Usually, working in commercial cinema, a director was assigned a standard technical team at the discretion of the producer. For this film he drew heavily upon members of a radical cultural organisation known as the October Group. The October Group was formed in 1929 on a co-operative basis with the aim of furnishing a radical alternative to the 'bourgeois' theatre of the Grands Boulevards, creating a theatre which would be more truly representative of the working masses. It also took an active interest in the cinema, a number of its members writing criticism for *La Revue du Cinéma*, the *Cahiers du Cinema* of its day. Again, its aim was a radical alternative to commercial cinema. It produced its own film, *L'Affaire est dans le Sac* (1932), which was an early example of co-operative film making and a satirical spoof on bourgeois mores.

The October Group was affiliated with a larger organisation known as the Fédération du Théâtre Ouvrier, which was sponsored by the French Communist Party. At political demonstrations, of which there

were many, particularly after the Concorde riots of 1934, the
Fédération du Théâtre Ouvrier and in particular the October Group
were often called upon for artistic presentations. During the strikes
of June 1936, the October Group provided entertainment for the
striking workers in the form of plays, poetry readings and
improvisations. The chief inspiration of the October Group was
anarcho-Communist poet of the Left Bank, Jacques Prévert, who was
largely responsible for the script of *Lange*. As group member Jean-Paul
Le Chanois put it, 'We are a young team made up of those who
expressed a complete devotion to Jacques Prévert because he was
Jacques Prévert our *raison d'être* and to a certain extent the director
of our consciousness.'[8] *Lange* was the only occasion which marked the
unique instance in which Prévert and Renoir worked together, and
Prévert's participation is critical in understanding the thematic layering
and theoretical underpinnings that lie at the heart of the film.[9]

Other members of the Group who collaborated on the film included
set designer Jacques Castanier, assistant director Pierre Prévert, actors
and actresses Sylvia Bataille, Jacques Brunius, Guy Decomble, Marcel
Duhamel, Florelle, Fabien Loris, Brémiaud, Maurice Baquet, and music
writer Jo Kosma. These names would reappear time and time again
in the period, making up the artistic and technical teams of virtually
all of Renoir's and also Marcel Carné's films from 1935 to 1939. They
would also figure prominently in connection with Communist Party
and CGT film making which began in earnest in 1936. All of this is
indicative of an interesting and unique period of cross-fertilisation
between leftist political film making and a certain segment of French
commercial cinema, that which was largely responsible for the so-called
'poetic realist' movement.[10] Renoir's own acquaintance with the
October Group stemmed from his collaboration with the Spaniard
Jacques Castanier, who had furnished sets for *La Nuit du Carrefour,
Chotard et Cie* and *Boudu Sauvé des Eaux* and who would provide the
central idea for *Le Crime de M. Lange*.

Le Crime de M. Lange reflects Renoir's growing politicisation. Even
if one knew nothing of his involvement with leftist politics, this would
be apparent in comparing it with the film he made just prior to it,
Toni (1934). Filmed under the patronage of independent producer/
director Marcel Pagnol, *Toni* is a remarkable film, a dramatic departure
from standard commercial cinema, with its heightened realism,
authenticity of setting, real social types, use of non-professional players,
true accents, and a narrative which was a direct outgrowth of an actual
police file, albeit tempered by Renoir's plastic and poetic sensibility.

Yet although it was made in 1934 and focuses on the migrant working classes, it is far from the Popular Front film that *Lange* is.

In *Toni* we are dealing exclusively with a rural milieu, characterised by its initial appearance of openness, with an emphasis on exteriors captured in long shots with a wide angle lens. But if nature is often associated with openness, in *Toni* we find a nature that is pressing in, confining, like the massive rock surfaces of the quarry which dwarf the workers and threaten to crush them. The narrative is centred upon the fatalistic ebb and flow of passion, and overt social commentary is oblique, occurring as a sort of parenthesis around the film, with the migrant workers returning year after year to a fated existence. Toni dies in the arms of a comrade; but in 1934 the prospect of a mass movement based on working-class solidarity was still a distant hope and the tone is overridingly pessimistic.

With *Le Crime de M. Lange* Renoir turns from a rural milieu to an urban milieu, from man and nature and forces seemingly beyond human control to man and society, where he is given the possibility of seizing control of his existence. Ostensibly, everything about the film is more closed. First of all, we are dealing mainly with interiors. The narrative centres around an enclosed circular courtyard, and the film keeps returning to the courtyard as a focal point. Moreover, the very structure of the narrative presents itself as a closed circle, with the bistro setting fading out to the extended flashback that comprises the bulk of the film, only to return again to the self-same bistro at the end. And on one striking occasion, the camera itself even forms a tightly closed circle in the celebrated 360-degree pan which precedes Batala's murder. Yet, in spite of all this, within the courtyard setting, as we shall see, there is a greater openness, a sense of overcoming limitations, the potential for breaking with prescribed patterns, leading to an open-endedness at the end of *Lange* which is quite the reversal of *Toni*. Circularity here, then, is used to signify solidarity and organic binding.

Le Crime de M. Lange is the Popular Front film *par excellence*, full of the exuberance, optimism and confidence in the ability to transform social conditions which characterised that movement. The thematic references to the Popular Front and its ideology abound. There is a bankruptcy and predictable collapse of capitalist enterprise, proletarian solidarity and the setting up of co-operative enterprise. Lange, the story writer, dreamer, artist intellectual, with his solidarity with the working class (printers and laundresses), is representative of the artistic/proletarian alliances against Fascism like the Comité de Vigilance des Intellectuels Anti-fascistes and the Association des Ecrivains et Artistes Révolutionnaires, which figured so prominently in the period. Indeed, one of Lange's publications has in it a marked reference to the Cagoulard Movement. However, the whole alliance as initially depicted by the film is somewhat curious and less than natural, even humorous. Valentine laughs when Lange reveals his first name to be Amedée, evocative of Mozart, grace, elegance, aristocracy. But that somewhat surprising alliance is shown to be feasible as the relationship between Lange and Valentine develops.

Raymond Durgnat has pointedout that the name Lange is a clever Prévertian play on words between 'l'ange' meaning angel and thus by cultural inference divinely inspired artistic inspiration, and 'linge', meaning laundry, with its reference within the context of the film.[11] The whole idea of the laundresses and clean linen is itself suggestive of class divisions. In the opening scene, Valentine comments that for once they will have clean sheets to sleep on whereas the laundresses are always running into Batala's office to assure him of a fresh change of clothing. In the iconography of the period the ruling class had the luxury of clean sheets whereas the working class simply did not. The same imagery is found in other feature films of the period. There is, for example, a reference in Carné's *Quai des Brumes* (1938) where one of the down and outs who frequent Panama's bar has the exquisite pleasure of sleeping on clean sheets for the first time in his life.

The image of the working class in *Lange* is certainly romanticised and poeticised, particularly as the dialogue flows from the pen of Prévert. But then was not perhaps the Popular Front's view of the working class also highly romanticised? In *Lange* there is no question of dealing with an industrialised proletariat. Indeed, there is a conspicuous absence of an industrialised proletariat in French feature films even at a time when organised labour and its social struggle had come to the forefront as in the mid-thirties. On the other hand, a number of economic historians, notably David Landes and Jesse Pitts,[12] have pointed to the dominance of French industry by the small family concern, of which the Batala publishing company has to be a prototype.

The portrait of Batala, sleek, slippery, urbane womaniser and financial wheeler dealer, and even his violent death, are reminiscent of Stavisky and the Stavisky scandal. The name Batala evokes the town in Portugal, Batalha, celebrated for its fifteenth-century Dominican abbey; and Batala's return in the guise of a priest interjects a note of traditional, leftist anti-clericalism that is pure Prévert.

A somewhat more obscure reference to the Popular Front is the tearing down of the billboard advertisement which covers up the only window in Charles's room. Fresh air, health, housing, leisure time, the general quality of the working man's living and working milieu, were to become a central preoccupation of the Popular Front. Léo Lagrange would head the newly created Office of Sport and Leisure Time under the Popular Front Government; the *auberges de jeunesse* would expand dramatically; the Socialist Party's Faucons Rouges youth movement would celebrate fresh air and fitness. Indeed, the most enduring contribution of the Popular Front was probably the paid holiday to the sea. Charles's graphic liberation from the dark, claustrophobic confines of his room admirably anticipates all this.

Another way in which Renoir reflected Popular Front attitudes was in his approach to women. His focus here is on working-class women, but with subtle psycho-sociological distinctions. There is the classic tart that has appeared before in Renoir's films, Batala's secretary, who uses her favours to attain upward social mobility and is willing to prostitute herself to Batala and elsewhere on his behalf. But there is also the working-class woman Valentine, resourceful, independent, mature, an active seductress, clearly a woman with a 'past', yet refusing to be exploited, who has no illusions about everlasting love with Lange. Here is chronicled a rather progressive attitude towards love, sex and marriage, certainly for French cinema of the period. One cannot help but be reminded of Léon Blum's book *Du Marriage* (1905) with its celebration of premarital sex which so shocked French society. Indeed, in Renoir's earlier film *Boudu Sauvé des Eaux*, he has the free-wheeling Boudu spit on Balzac's *Physiologie du Marriage*, a cultural reference coupled with his portrait of Valentine which has Renoir anticipatory of Simone de Beauvoir's chapter 'Marriage' in her book *The Second Sex*. Perhaps one of the most remarkable insights gained from Renoir's treatment of women in the film comes with Estelle's loss of Batala's bastard baby. This is greeted by Estelle and her comrades with gales of laughter, a reaction which can only be seen as an allusive appeal for the right to abortion.

The film's epilogue gives us still another insight into Popular Front attitudes. Here, Lange is given a trial by the people. The bistro *copains* have to decide whether or not to turn him in, and their decision to exonerate Lange and abet him in crossing the border confirms his crime as just and implicitly conveys a rather radical message. But perhaps even more revealing than this is the whole underlying concept of popular justice being somewhat superior to institutionalised justice which was so dear to the French left. It was an attitude similar to that which, for example, called for the abolition of all official film censorship. As Léon Moussinac, film critic for *L'Humanité*, advised, the public should exert its own censorship by hissing or applauding films. It was an attitude that had millions of French workers sitting in and taking over the factories after the Popular Front had won its electoral victory and gained legitimate control of the governmental institutional framework.

We have been looking at the film in terms of theme and character, but the real power of *Le Crime de M. Lange* as an expression of Popular Front consciousness derives not so much from what is said but from how it is said, in other words from Renoir's special use of the cinematic language. In this film we are dealing with two completely different models of structural organisation, in terms both of the *mise en scène* and of the montage.

The first model defines the world of Batala. Here the *mise en scène* is generally closed. We most often see him inside, in his office, forever shutting doors and windows, especially when he is involved with his deals and exploitation of women. Corners are used to emphasise the idea of 'huis clos'. Estelle is trapped in a corner by Batala before he seduces her. And he himself is trapped at the end of the film in a corner of the courtyard. Even on a staircase, which is generally assumed by the codes of graphic arts to imply some sort of dynamic, continuous motion, either upward or downward, Batala is shown to represent an arrestation of movement. While arguing with creditor Buisson, who is trying to collect on a loan, he starts up the stairs only to come down, up again only to come down, an action which is repeated seven or eight times.

In terms of the editing, there is a similar arrestation of fluid movement. In many scenes and sequences that involve Batala, Renoir resorts to the distinctive cutting back and forth between characters, the old Hollywood 'découpage classique'. This is most notably true when Batala confronts a character like Baigneur over whom he exerts exploitative control. Moreover, in this same scene with Baigneur, there is further fragmentation and distortion through traditional dominant/submissive angle shots. However, in scenes with characters like Lange and Valentine who, although temporarily exploited by Batala, ultimately emerge as stronger than he, there is a marked absence of fragmentive editing or angle shots. As far as the camera and framing goes, for the Batala model it tends to be traditional and static. The camera rarely explores physical space. It more often than not frames a theatrical proscenium view and there is virtually no feeling of off-camera space. All of this is supposedly uncharacteristic of Renoir, but is in fact an approach he uses to define the world of the capitalist.

The structural model of the world of Lange and the workers is markedly different. We are first introduced to it by a rambling, exploring camera, which investigates the room where he does his writing late at night. In a very long take, a roving camera eye takes in all the marvellous artefacts which adorn his walls, the gun holsters, cowboy hat, the map of the United States, all sources of his inspiration for Arizona Jim. The room is small, yet how spacious and open it seems with this roving camera. How much more geometrically confining is Batala's office where he is visually hemmed in by desk and filing cabinet and a rigidly held fixed frame.

In terms of kinetics or body language, there is a parallel opposition between Batala and Lange. Batala is the grand old actor of the established French theatre, full of the elaborate theatrical gesture which appropriately matches his eloquence and verbosity. Lange is much more cinematic. With the exception of our first view of him, as he simulates a horse rider in a fit of inspiration, he is generally highly reserved in his gesture, as in his speech, communicating meaning through more subtle movements or no movement at all. Nowhere is this more graphically illustrated than in the scene towards the end of the film when Batala returns in the guise of a priest and confronts Lange with his intention of taking over the co-operative. Batala faces the camera. He mugs, he gesticulates, he carries on the stentorian fashion. We see nothing but Lange's back. He is immobile, silent, but how communicative is the emotional appeal. Throughout the film, Lange is associated with openness and space. Whereas Batala closes doors and windows, Lange leaves them open. In fact, we often see him framed by an open window or doorway. Similarly, his interactions with women tend to be out in the open. When he tries to charm Estelle, it is on a park bench, and when this fails, he merely lets her run off.

With the world of Lange, in contrast to that of Batala, there is a marked avoidance of fragmentation on all levels, through longer takes shooting in depth and extensive use of panning shots as well as the rhythms of the actors within the frame. Fluid camera pans serve to bind characters together. At one point in the film, as Lange's relationship with Valentine develops, they are bonded by a smooth camera sweep from Valentine in the courtyard to Lange framed by an

open window. But camera movement and shooting in depth serves not
only to produce male/female bonding but also to evoke the fraternal
solidarity of the workers and of the co-operative. When we are dealing
with the printers and laundresses, it is through panning and tracking
and shooting in depth. Crucial to this shooting style is the very
architecture of the set.

The initial idea of using an entire courtyard came from the set
designer Castanier.[13] Here again the stress upon the importance of one
of Renoir's collaborators avoids too much of an exclusively auteurish
approach. Castanier's realisation represented a major departure from
the standard commercial film of the day, which employed the
three-sided theatre set for all interiors and even for many exteriors.
The dramatic contribution in *Lange*, a true innovation, is to use a very
real courtyard setting, a four-sided physical space. (Among the numerous
allusions in the film to Renoir's own cinematographic profession, Lange,
while filming the Arizona Jim series, refers to his abhorence of
phoney sets.) It is the courtyard setting which sparks the fraternal
solidarity that leads to the setting up of the co-operative upon the
presumed death of Batala, and perhaps nowhere is that solidarity
better captured than in the scene where the poster is torn from
Charles's window and the camera pans slowly back and forth to
various members of the co-operative framed in windows. Given the
ideological significance of the panning and tracking in the context of
this particular film, the celebrated counter-clockwise 360-degree pan
takes on added meaning. Not only does this pan, as André Bazin
suggests, constitute 'the pure spatial expression of the entire *mise
en scène*'[13] but it also implies the solidarity of the entire co-operative
behind Lange's violent act of murder. And since the spectator is forced
to follow the self-same path as the camera tracks Lange from his
office and down the steps, and then to experience the 360-degree turn,
there is a certain degree of complicity required.

Throughout our analysis of *Le Crime de M. Lange*, we have been
witnessing a sort of reflection of Renoir's own unique approach to
film making, his own new aesthetic. Like Lange, Renoir was in
rebellion. Like Lange, who rebels against Batala who would have him
plug Ranimax Pills in the Arizona Jim Series, so too did Renoir
struggle against having to subject his artistry to commercial restraint.
He rejected the idea that he should have to film the farce *On Purge
Bébé* in four days (which he did in 1931) to prove to producers that he
could make money. He fought against a situation which had the
producers of *La Chienne* deny him editing access to his own work

because they were dissatisfied with his approach. In opposition to arbitrarily assigned technical teams and hierarchically determined film making decisions, Renoir offered his own conception of co-operative film making. In opposition to scripts based on commercially successful plays or books, Renoir offered the script based on original ideas and improvisation. In opposition to a cinematography of classical Hollywood *mise en scène* and montage, Renoir offered his own free-wheeling camerawork, as well as his organic conception of sets which explored real social entities.

Renoir was also extraordinarily sensitive to the current multifaceted larger societal struggle. This awareness stemmed directly from the fact that his own profession, being both capital and labour intensive, was a microcosm of that larger societal struggle between capital and labour which came to a head in France in the thirties. In 1936 cinema 'workers', technicians as well as artists, fought for and won their own collective contract on the lines of the Matignon Agreements. Along with the regulation of salaries, wages and working conditions, one of the important provisions of this collective contract was to give autonomy to the film director *vis-à-vis* the producer. Here was a very real 'politique des auteurs', long before Francois Truffaut put forth the concept to become a popular battle-cry of the fifties. Jean Renoir anticipated all of this with *Le Crime de M. Lange* and thus, in a sense, the film can be seen as an expression of the social and artistic redressment of an entire professional cadre.

But in the final analysis, the most striking aspect of *Le Crime de M. Lange* is the concordance between the film's manifest (thematic) content and latent (cinematographic) content, which makes the film's message particularly powerful. Indeed, it is the dramatic contrast of the two structural models that gives the thematic conflict its poignancy. On the one hand there is the world of the capitalist exploiter, Batala, closed, windowless and claustrophobic, captured by a cinematography that is traditional, static, fragmentive. To this is opposed the world of Lange and the workers' co-operative, open, airy, fluid, where the bonds of organic solidarity prevail, all translated through Renoir's radical new aesthetic of extensive use of long takes, panning, tracking, in-depth shooting and concentration on movement within the fixed frame. Such was this cinematographic vision of the deep cleavage in French society on the eve of the electoral victory of the Popular Front.[15]

In comparing *Lange* with *La Marseillaise*, filmed in the summer and autumn of 1937, there are many points of similarity, thematically, structurally, cinematically. However, the whole tone and over-all conception of the film is more markedly defensive. The financing of this Ciné-Liberté-backed film through popular subscription has by now become well known.[16] Promoted by a broad spectrum of Popular Front organisations, the public, presumably the working-class public, was also encouraged to purchase its tickets for the viewing of the film in advance, thus contributing to its financial backing.

The choice of the French Revolution as subject-matter for the film was clearly grounded in the social and political realities of the day. The Popular Front was the closest France had come to a revolutionary situation since the Paris Commune of 1871, and revolutionary élan, however romanticised, was high in 1936. By 1937, however, enthusiasm for the Popular Front had already begun to wane. Although wages had been increased through the Matignon Agreements of June 1936, prices had spiralled and the net gain to the average working man was wiped out. Moreover, there was deep resentment created by the Popular Front Government's decision not to intervene in the Spanish Civil War on behalf of the Spanish Popular Front. A film on the French Revolution of 1789-92 could perpetuate and wherever necessary rekindle the élan of May and June 1936. As Communist film critic George Sadoul wrote in 1937:

> The points of resemblance between this period and our own, the similarity of popular sentiment which saved France and liberty in '92, and the sentiments which today animate the people of France, have not failed to strike us on the strictly historical level.[17]

In preparation for the film, as Renoir revealed in a highly illuminating article published in *Regards*, he carefully undertook to research in the Archives of Marseille the social backgrounds of the 500 members of the Marseille Battalion.[18] Besides trying to establish historical veracity, Renoir had another motive for engaging in such research, a very contemporary motive. This was to explode the popular myth of the revolutionary, especially as promoted by anti-Communist propaganda, as a wild-eyed, irrational, criminal type on the fringes of society. As Renoir wrote:

> This slogan has helped fix in the mind of the bourgeois public this prefabricated image of the revolutionary as a sort of ravenous, dirty, ragged bandit who spends his days inflicting immoral, indecent

and bloody injuries. Naturally, venality is another characteristic that one can tie to this image. Everyone knows that revolutionaries are always bought, as it has been said in a play on Marie-Antoinette that is presently having a run in a theatre on the left bank.[19]

In the *Regards* article, Renoir went on to refer to a number of slanderous descriptions of the Fédérés by royalist and other conservative writers and historians, portraying them as undesirable alien elements which had permeated French society and were the cause of its undoing. The relevancy to the situation in the thirties was striking, for the right-wing press had engaged in a virulent anti-Semitic campaign against Popular Front leader Léon Blum. He was considered to be an outsider, a subversive alien, because he was Jewish and therefore somehow un-French.

Documents in the archives enabled Renoir to disprove the charges against the Fédérés that they were foreigners, particularly Italians. Renoir examined the list of names and ranks of the Marseille Battalion and found that their nationality was unquestionably French. To establish them as honourable citizens instead of bandits, he cited the conditions under which they were admitted to the Battalion: apparently one had to prove that one had financial resources to support one's family while serving as a volunteer, show that one was free from debts, have never been indicted before a court of justice, and have had some sort of military background. All of these qualifications are faithfully recorded in the film to press home the point. Finally, by examining the professional backgrounds of the volunteers, Renoir showed that, far from being social outcasts or misfits, the Fédérés were made up of former officers from the royal army, city magistrates, stonemasons, carpenters and agricultural workers. He concluded:

> Thus, we are quite far from the troop of bandits so magnificently described by anti-revolutionary writers . . . Let us hope that by frequenting this friendly troop, our revolutionary comrades of today will be consoled in the face of calumnies which a certain press inflicts upon them.[20]

Apparently, there was some controversy over the choice of the film's title. This was a time when the tricolor vied with the red flag and 'La Marseillaise' with the 'Internationale' Popular Front mass meetings and demonstrations. For Renoir, it was 'unbelievable' that such a petty

controversy should come to the forefront at this particular moment.[21]
It is often asked of films sponsored by political groups: are they
preaching to their own supporters or are they trying to win new
converts? Renoir's insistence on the title *La Marseillaise* points to an
attempt to reach the broadest cross-section of the population. Yet
another consideration was censorship, since the Communist Party
film *La Vie est à Nous* (the over-all direction of which had been
entrusted to Renoir) still was not granted a censorship visa for
commercial distribution even after the Popular Front Government
had taken office. As was expressed in the *Ciné-Liberté* article
'Comment Naguit le Scénario?',

> Thinking that the film could be projected without risk of censorship
> and without being attacked by our enemies because it traces an
> acknowledged glorious period of our history, so that it could serve
> as French propaganda at Exposition 1937 and in various countries
> that would be inclined to purchase it, we adopted the project with
> unanimity.[22]

There was an additional dimension to focusing on the actual song
'La Marseillaise'. There is a pointed dialogue reference in the film to
the fact that the tune was originally a Jewish pedlar's song, which was
then taken up by the Army of the Rhine. Here again Renoir confronts
France's currently virulent anti-Semitism, as he also does in *La Grande
Illusion* and *La Règle du Jeu*.

As the original script outline shows, Renoir was particularly
conscious of distinguishing his approach to the French Revolution
from the numerous Hollywood renditions of the same subject. In
explaining why he did not commence with the classic fall of the
Bastille, he wrote:

> The taking of the Bastille seemed to us cinematographically
> dangerous. The Americans have already filmed several sumptuous
> films in which this event figures prominently, and they have
> offered admirable period set reconstructions of which we musn't
> think. This is the material reason that has pushed us to begin our
> film in a village.[23]

Hollywood films on the French Revolution had, according to Renoir,
put forth all kinds of myths and clichés that had become embedded in
public consciousness. *La Marseillaise* was to be an act of demythification,

and the first myth Renoir was trying to explode was the idea that the Revolution consisted of a few glorious and spectacular events like the storming of the Bastille. It is significant that the film starts with the day after the fall of the Bastille and traces the Revolution up to the victory of Valmy, conceiving of it as a day-to-day struggle.

Renoir was also trying to get away from viewing the Revolution as the work of a few heroic figures like Mirabeau, Danton or Robespierre. Instead, he focused on the common men who made the Revolution possible, the band of 500 volunteers from Marseille who travelled to Paris to defend the Revolution against the attack of counter-revolutionary forces and who also participated in the overthrow of the monarchy on 10 August 1792. Renoir pointed out the persistence of the 'hero myth' of the French Revolution in an anecdote published in a brochure put out by the Société d'Exploitations et de Productions Cinématographiques. While making plans for the film, a woman came to Renoir's office, having prepared the role of Charlotte Corday, Marat's assassin. She was convinced that any film on the French Revolution would have to have a Charlotte Corday, and was utterly taken aback to discover that they had no use for her. 'There was also a reincarnation of Mirabeau who visited us frequently. When we swore to this man that the great tribunal had no place in our film, he stared at us blankly suspecting some sort of conspiracy.'[24] It may be argued, of course, that, at the same time as Renoir was exploding various myths, he was setting up his own set of myths, especially as the film was consciously intended as Popular Front propaganda. As Pascal Ory has pointed out, Renoir's Revolution was one of the most bloodless of all times, and in a very calculated fashion, when blood is finally spilt, it is foreign, Swiss blood rather than French.[25]

Renoir was opposed to certain Hollywood clichés, myths and card-board sets. He was also, once again as with *Lange*, opposed to the classical Hollywood aesthetic, which by the grace of American cultural imperialism had so thoroughly permeated French cinema. Therefore, just as he had done in *Lange*, Renoir set up in *La Marseillaise* a structural stylistic opposition between two worlds, that of the king and aristocrats versus that of the people, a static model of the past versus a dynamic model of the future. With the world of the king and the court, we are drawn into interiors, drawing-room settings, framed by a relatively static camera, capturing a theatrical proscenium view. When the king and his courtiers finally emerge into nature it is only to enter a Le Nôtre-inspired classical garden which mirrors their own rigidly symmetrical positioning. In this poignant scene, it is only the young

Dauphin who is able momentarily to break out of the rigid pattern by cavorting in a pile of leaves.

The world of the people, on the other hand, belongs largely to exteriors, settings in nature. There is a great deal of movement, disorder, confusion, both visually and with a highly complex soundtrack of superimposed sounds, dialogue and music. We have a repetition of the lengthy takes, in-depth shooting, heightened camera mobility and movement of actors within the frame that were previously associated with the world of *Lange*.

One of the key scenes which are revealing of this sort of aesthetic is the one in which the Marseille 500 assemble and prepare to march off to Paris leaving loved ones behind. For this scene, Renoir had constructed a special crane which enabled him to make an extraordinary crabbing shot of the Fédérés in one of the most distinctive long takes in the film. The whole way in which Renoir handles the crowd is illuminating. It is very rare that one sees the Fédérés and townspeople *en masse*, and this at a time when mass demonstrations both of the right and of the left dominated the newsreels. Renoir preferred to focus on isolated groups within the larger crowd. Avoiding fragmentive editing, he tracked back and forth with his camera to stress the organic bonds of solidarity between these groups. Indeed, he never strayed far from that small, intimate bistro cameraderie of *Lange* even within the massive scale of the French Revolution. Although it was Renoir's predilection to film in this manner, it also made effective propaganda for would-be converts, who might have been deterred by high, wide angle shots of huge crowds.

This study of two of Renoir's Popular Front period feature films has dealt with how various external socio-economic and political factors shaped the films' form and content. In the case of *Le Crime de M. Lange*, the emphasis was on the state of the French film industry and Renoir's relationship to that industry as well as on his growing political consciousness and association with left-wing collaborators. In the case of *La Marseillaise*, the stress was on the health, or rather lack of health, of the Popular Front.

La Marseillaise was an unusual film, in that a good deal was written about it at the time it was being made, particularly by Renoir himself. On the whole, during the first fifty years of film history, directors, producers, artists and technicians were too busy making films to write for posterity. With *La Marseillaise*, however, Renoir and Ciné-Liberté were highly conscious of their historical mission and propagandist role, and they have provided the historian with abundant documentation as to their conscious intentions as well as with details on some of the controversy surrounding the inception of the film.

Nevertheless, the historian must still look to the films themselves as the central documents, and a major aspect of this study has been to examine cinematic form and content as an expression of the times. Borrowing from structuralist and semiotic analytical concepts, the latent content of the filmic discourse has been uncovered, illustrating the complexity of the cinematic text, the 'galaxy of signifiers', in the words of Roland Barthes, revealing some of the tensions and dilemmas of France in the crisis years of the Popular Front.

Notes

1. A version of this article first appeared in *Sight and Sound* under the title 'Renoir and the Popular Front' in the Winter 1979/80 issue. This article appears by courtesy of the British Film Institute.

2. *La Cinématographie Française,* 25 March 1938.

3. In recent years, there has been increased attention focused on leftist and workers' cinema in France during the thirties. Among the studies there are: Geoffredo Fofi, 'The Cinema of the Popular Front in France (1934-38)', *Screen,* vol.13, no.4 (Winter 1972-3), pp.5-57; Pascal Ory, 'De Ciné-Liberté à la Marseillaise, Espoirs et Limites d'un Cinéma Libéré (1936-1938)', *Le Mouvement Social,* no.91 (April-June 1975), pp.153-75; Elizabeth Grottle Strebel, 'French Social Cinema and the Popular Front', *Journal of Contemporary History,* 12 (1977), pp.499-519.

4. Jean Renoir, 'A Propos de Temps Modernes', *Ciné-Liberté,* no.1 (20 May 1936), p.1.

5. See André Bazin, *Jean Renoir* (Editions Champ Libre, Paris, 1971).

6. Jacques Brunius, *En Marge du Cinéma Français* (Arcanes, Paris, 1954), p.172.

7. For a detailed examination of this evolution see E.G. Strebel, 'French Social Cinema of the Nineteen Thirties; A Cinematographic Expression of Popular Front Consciousness' PhD dissertation, Princeton University, 1973.

8. Jean-Paul Le Chanois, 'De la Rue Dauphine au Studio', *Ciné-Club,* no.4 (January 1949).

9. *Premier Plan* devoted an entire issue to Jacques Prévert that is very useful in this regard.

10. This cross-fertilisation comprises a whole fascinating topic in and of itself. I have, for example, noticed thematic and visual borrowings by Duvivier in his film *Fin du Jour* (1939) from Jean-Paul Le Chanois' Communist Party film *Le Temps des Cerises* (1937). Both have to do with the dignity of the aged and old-age pensions, and there is an arresting montage sequence, of old people dramatically lifting bowed heads with pride, that figures in both films.

11. Raymond Durgnat, *Jean Renoir* (University of California Press, Berkeley, 1975). See the chapter on *Le Crime de M. Lange.*

12. See particularly David Landes, *Unbound Prometheus* (Cambridge University Press, Cambridge, 1972).

13. Bazin, *Jean Renoir,* pp.37-8.

14. Ibid., p.42.

15. In the collective contract it was also specified that the director could have the free choice of his technical team.

16. Pierre Leprohon has described this in *Jean Renoir* (Seghers, Paris, 1967), pp.92-3.

17. Georges Sadoul, 'Un Film sur la Révolution Française', *Regards*, 15 February, 1937.

18. Actually it was Mme Jean-Paul Le Chanois (Dreyfus) who poured over and sifted through the archival material.

19. Jean Renoir, 'Honneur aux Marseillaise', *Regards* (10 February, 1938), p.3.

20. Ibid., p.5. In the last few months, missing issues of the review *Ciné-Liberté*, including a special issue of 12 March, 1937 devoted to *La Marseillaise*, have been rediscovered by the Dutch historian Bert Hogenkamp. This issue provides further insight into the genesis of the film and includes a copy of the original script outline for the film submitted to the Société des Auteurs et Compositeurs.

21. Jean Renoir, 'Notre Film', *Ciné-Liberté*, Edition Spéciale, (12 March, 1937), p.1.

22. 'Comment Naguit le Scénario', *Ciné-Liberté*, Edition Spéciale, (12 March, 1937), p.1.

23. 'La Révolution Française' ('Note pour le découpage'), *Ciné-Liberté*, Edition Spéciale (12 March, 1937), p.2.

24. Georges Sadoul, private collection: 'La Marseillaise de Jean Renoir', *Brochure de la Société d'Exploitations et de Productions Cinématographiques.*

25. See Ory, 'De Ciné-Liberté à la Marseillaise'.

FEATUREFILMS AS HISTORY

ED. K.R.M. SHORT.

1981

CROOM HELM
LTD.

5 IDEOLOGICAL CONSENSUS IN BRITISH FEATURE FILMS, 1935-1947

Tony Aldgate

The popular image which has often been drawn of Britain in the 1930s and 1940s is one which suggests that Britain went through three distinct phases. The first phase lasted throughout the thirties, until 1939, and saw Britain beset by innumerable crises both at home and abroad, and divided as a result of them. The crises on the domestic front ranged from depression, unemployment, disarmament, to rearmament, and more; on the international front, the problems were how to deal with emergent Nazism in Germany, Fascism in Italy, aggression in Abyssinia and Civil War in Spain. All conspired, so the argument went, to produce a 'Divided Britain' both socially and politically. Indeed one historian, Kenneth Watkins, used that very phrase as the title and gist of a book which attempted to assess the impact on one of those crises, the Spanish Civil War, upon British opinion.[1] (My own recently published book reaches a somewhat different conclusion based upon a reading of the evidence offered by the British cinema newsreels and their coverage of the Spanish Civil War.[2])

The second phase, from 1939 to 1945, found Britain beset by perhaps the biggest crisis of all, the onset of war and the threat to survival. The direct sense of menace posed by Hitler, the German conquest of Western Europe in 1940, the prospect of invasion, and the aerial blitz which followed, all served to unite the country and the British people once again, under the charismatic leadership of Churchill. Hence the surprise, in some quarters at least, when the 1945 General Election ousted Churchill and replaced him with the Labour leader, Clement Attlee. The immediate postwar years, constituting the third phase which lasted from 1946 to 1951, saw the country confronting the problems of austerity and reconstruction, but with new-found policies of nationalisation and socialisation. Imperial greatness was on the way out, but the Welfare State was definitely in, and with it benefits like national insurance, a free National Health Service and reforms in education. Such positive and determined moves on the part of the Labour Government culminated in the sort of national identity expressed by the grandly symbolic 1951 Festival of Britain. That heralded the end of the immediate postwar period (and,

ironically, Labour's term of office) and, in the words of Herbert
Morrison, the government minister responsible for it, amounted to a
'great demonstration of the British way of life'.

Thus, the argument went: from a divided kingdom to a United
Kindom in three distinct stages. Of late, however, many of the basic
suppositions which lay at the heart of that thesis have come under
further review and greater scrutiny. Historians in recent years have
been tempted to ask such questions as: how divided was Britain really
during the thirties; how united was the country in the Second World
War; were the policies of the postwar Labour Government so very
new; and how much of a sense of national identity and integration
had been truly fostered by 1951? The answers put forward to
these questions have resulted in much more emphasis being placed
upon the idea of an inherently stable Britain and the notion
of a progressively evolving 'consensus' within British society. It has
been suggested that this 'consensus' existed throughout the 1930s
(though some would argue it was an 'imposed consensus' in the
thirties), was somewhat interrupted and changed as a result of the
stresses and effects of World War II, but came to fruition in a
modified form in the postwar years. This notion of consensus has,
in turn, prompted some historians interested in the realms of film
and history to explore the mass media generally, and the cinema in
particular, to see what part they might have played in engendering
consensus, of whatever variety.

However, before turning to the films themselves, I would just
like to look briefly at the historical works to which I have alluded, in
order that I might elaborate upon the arguments being developed
there.

John Stevenson and Chris Cook, in their book entitled *The Slump*[3],
addressed themselves to the question of 'the hungry thirties', and came
up with the over-all conclusion that for Britain the thirties were not,
after all, a period of total depression and unmitigated misery. In
some areas, in fact, there was slight growth and economic expansion.
Certainly there was undue hardship in the depressed areas but, while
wages, for instance, did not increase, the cost of living actually fell
by one-third between 1919 and 1939. Stevenson and Cook agree that
some of their arguments are by no means new arguments, and
they point out that both A.J.P. Taylor and C.L. Mowat have
suggested in the past that the hardships of the thirties were unevenly
spread.

Interestingly, however, C.L. Mowat would also appear to have subscribed to the 'Britain Divided' argument. He considered, for example, that the crisis of the Spanish Civil War increased 'the disunity of the country for a time' and 'widened existing divisions', though he also believed that it was a 'united country' which went 'into the war for its own survival in 1939'.[4] One is left wondering how it was that a divided nation could so suddenly and readily become reunited in time to face the threat of war. On the other hand, the implication to be drawn from the findings of Stevenson and Cook is more logical and credible, for their suggestion is that Britain had not in fact been deeply divided by the various threats to its social and political fabric during the thirties. Indeed, their investigations into the police records of the time and the results of local and general elections show, first, how little social conflict there was in British society and, second, how much political stability there was. The evidence suggests, they would argue, that the National Government would have won yet again had a general election been held in 1939 or 1940.

A note of dissent enters into the proceedings here for, as I have hinted, the argument has also been advanced that, while Britain may well appear after all to have been a united and stable nation by 1939, nevertheless this was only a superficial appearance. The sociologist Tom Burns, for example, talks of 'the imposed consensus of the thirties'. From his study of the media of press and broadcasting at the time, he concludes that they served to promote only 'an appearance of national, social and cultural integration'. His belief is that the country was still 'deeply divided' and 'fearful of the destructive forces present and gaining strength in Britain and abroad'.[5]

On the one hand, then, Stevenson and Cook martial their evidence to suggest that the country was comparatively stable and integrated. And on the other hand Burns surveys his evidence and decides that, while consensus appeared to exist, it was only a 'projection of Britain' which glossed over the realities of the situation. Who is to judge whether Britain was truly a divided nation or not by 1939, what the image and what the reality? Perhaps it is worth while adding, though, that, whether genuine or fabricated by the media of the day, consensus is believed to have existed in Britain at the time. That in itself may have been enough to account for social and political stability. The newsreels, for instance, were consistently putting forward a picture of 'Wonderful Britain', to cite the title of but one Gaumont British News story[6], and that projection repeated often enough could have been as potent a force as the 'reality' itself, whether it accurately reflected that 'reality' or not.

the
witchway

ADULT

Lancashire 1

£4.00

Valid

Wed, 30 Oct 19

Service X43 Bus
Drv9787 Ticket104444
Journey3021 Stage 43

Great having you on
board with us!

Tweet us @burnleybuses
Lancashirebus.co.uk

What is of less dispute, at least, is that, as Michael Howard puts it, 'a national consensus did exist to be focused' in Britain by 1940. Of course, he goes on to add that in fact the national consensus in 1940 owed a lot of the new-found circumstances of a country at war; but he also notes how much it owed to the prewar years, when pointing out that 'Britain was probably still the most socially cohesive major nation in Europe between the wars'. As he explains, that cohesion may indeed have been 'increasingly eroded by political and industrial conflict' during those years, but it ultimately survived strong enough to withstand the onset of war and the initial military setbacks. France, by contrast, it is suggested, was not 'reasonably coherent'. It had become socially polarised during the thirties and was torn by political strife. It did not take much of a shock to bring the nation down. To make his point further, Howard quotes Hitler's boast that he would never strike until he believed his adversaries politically ready to fall. The enemies' social cohesion as well as military capacity had to be taken into account before a move should be made. Hitler was proved right in May 1940 over France and also justified, indirectly, by his reluctance to launch an invasion of Britain: 'whatever the military problems involved, Britain was not politically ripe for the plucking'.[7]

It would be foolish, though, to pretend that Britain remained the same throughout the thirties and the war years, that social and political cohesion were underpinned by a consensus which varied little between 1935 and 1945. Arthur Marwick, especially, has demonstrated often enough that war did effect social change in Britain.[8] His four dimensions of the relationship between war and social change show that to be the case: 'destruction-disruption', involving damage and upheaval but leading to a desire to rebuild better than before; the 'test' dimension, challenging society, imposing new stresses and strains, inducing the collapse of some institutions and the transformation of others; 'participation' of underprivileged groups in the national effort and cause, bringing consequent social gains; and the 'psychological' dimension, by which war provides a great emotional experience, again with concomitant results.

Similarly Paul Addison charts the significance of the war in effecting political change. After the fall of France and the ignominy of Dunkirk, there was a distinct swing to what might loosely be called 'the left' in Britain. The removal of Chamberlain and his replacement by Churchill did not go far enough to stem this new tide of popular feeling, despite the latter's obvious popularity as a war leader. Paul Addison makes effective use of Home Intelligence Reports to show that this current of feeling among the population was not necessarily of a political character, nor indeed was it necessarily always chanelled along Labour Party or socialist lines. But it was 'directed against the Conservative Party' in so far as this represented 'the so-called "Men of Munich", the "old gang", "Colonel Blimp", and similar diehard types'. It was, first of all, a feeling of revulsion against 'vested interests' and 'privilege' and, secondly, a general agreement that 'things are going to be different after the war'.[9]

The war did effect social and political change, but Britain remained an integrated and cohesive society, with a new consensus. As Addison notes, the species of consensus which had existed before the war was 'a consensus to prevent anything unusual from happening' and one of 'safety first', whereas 'the new consensus of the war years was positive and purposeful'. It was this which brought Labour to power in 1945, since it was thought that the Labour Party would be the party most likely to manifest such a shift in the form of new legislation (though it should be remembered that new laws on family allowances and education were actually introduced during the war).

It was also this new consensus which provided the inspiration for Labour's attempts to lead Britain towards improved economic welfare and social equality. Several of its great reforms had been prepared and virtually laid out for it during the war by men outside of the party system, such as William Beveridge and John Maynard Keynes. So, far from being a party of radical change and innovation, it might be said that the Labour Party simply capitalised upon the wartime consensus. It did not help its cause that the country, for its part, came out of the war with its coffers well-nigh empty and pretty-near flat broke.

The country did emerge, however, as a far more homogeneous society in 1945 than it had been in 1939. That is a point noted briefly by Michael Howard in his article, already cited; and it is a point particularly well exemplified by Arthur Marwick's latest research into class in Britain. During the course of a lecture which he delivered on the topic, for instance, he commented that 'the working class in 1945 assumed a position in British society analogous to that assumed by the middle class after the passing of the Great Reform Act of 1832'. Furthermore, when surveying the immediate postwar years in Britain he came to the conclusion that 'From the implicitly dichotomous models of class held in the 1930s' there developed in the late forties a movement 'away from contempt and conflict, towards consensus and integration'.[10]

Consensus — the word occurs over and over again in recent historical writings and accounts of Britain in the 1930s and 1940s. But what of the film evidence from the period: does that justify the continued use of the term?

To judge from Sir Michael Balcon's comments, the historian of the thirties, at least, would expect to find very little of value in British feature films of the time. Balcon has suggested, in retrospect, that 'Hardly a film of the period reflects the urgency of these times.' Balcon did well to qualify his generalised overview, for there were one or two lesser-known films, though perhaps moderately significant, which did to some extent address social and political issues: films like John Baxter's *Doss House* (1933) which tried to tell 'an unpretentious story of life in the lower depths' and was set in the sleazy doss houses of London, or Michael Powell's 1934 film of *Red Ensign* with its plot of rivalry between Clyde shipbuilders during the depression, which, incidentally, gained the new title of *Strike* on the film's release in America.[11]

Yet even if Balcon's description of British feature films were essentially correct, at the obvious level of depictive reality, then the British cinema would still be significant to the historian for what it chose not to say, or to deal with. For Balcon misses one very important dimension of all films, regardless of their overt content or subject-matter, and that is their ideological dimension.

The ideological role of the media, and the cinema by implication, has been well summarised by Stuart Hall.[12] He argues that the ideological role and function of the modern media is of a threefold variety. First, there is the provision and selective construction of social knowledge, of social imagery, so that the 'worlds' of others, and our own, can be imaginarily reconstructed, made intelligible and coherently grasped as a 'whole'. The second function is *to reflect* and *reflect upon* the apparent plurality and varieties of life patterns, to classify, rank and order the different types of social knowledge. The social knowledge which the media selectively circulate is ranked and arranged within preferred meanings and interpretations, in order that we can not only know more about 'the world' but also make sense of it. 'Here the line', as Hall puts it, 'between preferred and excluded explanations and rationales, between permitted and deviant behaviours, between the "meaningless" and the "meaningful"... is ceaselessly drawn and redrawn, defended and negotiated.' The third function of the media is to bring together what they have selectively classified, so that what has been made visible and classified shapes up into an acknowledged order. However fragmentarily and plurally represented, some degree of integration and cohesion, some coherence and unity, begins to be constructed. Hall adds that it is

> from this difficult and delicate negotiatory work the problematic areas of consensus and consent begin to emerge . . . This forms the great unifying and consolidating level of the media's ideological work: the generative structure beneath the media's massive investment in the surface immediacy, the phenomenal multiplicity, of the social worlds in which it traffics.

The production of consensus, the production of legitimacy, this is the third key aspect of the media's ideological role.

Selective representation, selective classification of social knowledge, the production of coherence, cohesion, consent and consensus: what evidence is there of the British cinema fulfilling its ideological role and function?

Clearly, there is a lot, even if we take Michael Balcon's description of feature films in the thirties at its face value. For he is surely saying there is selective representation. The fact is that at that level, he is for the most part proved right.

There was little of divisive issues or social problems in British films of the thirties. Unemployment and depression, for instance, barely merited a mention. The successful northern comedian, George Formby, sang about such matters in *Boots, Boots* (1934, Bert Tracey) and joked about them fleetingly at the beginning of *Off the Dole* (1935, Arthur Mertz). Significantly, both films were made for John E. Blakeley's small film company which was based in Manchester, before Formby was snapped up by Basil Dean for Associated Talking Pictures. Gracie Fields displayed great pride and dignity when leading the workers into unemployment and out again during the course of *Sing as we Go* (1934, Basil Dean), for all that the film itself is ultimately compromised when the mills are saved from permanent closure by a last-minute 'technological miracle'.[13] From the rest, there was an almost complete silence on these issues.

Victor Saville's film of *South Riding* (1938) was based upon the Winifred Holtby best-selling novel, which had a background plot of social problems and business corruption. The opening credits and titles of the film must have looked forbidding when one of them recounted:

Winifred Holtby realised that Local Government is not a dry affair of meetings and memoranda: but 'the front-line defence thrown up by humanity against its common enemies of sickness, poverty and ignorance'. She built her story round six people working for a typical County Council.

Another title which followed a short time later, however, would have put that first one into perspective, when adding: 'Beneath the lives of the public servants runs the thread of their personal drama.' Despite all that high-principled rhetoric, it was a love story after all. In an interview about the film several years later, the director Victor Saville pronounced quite correctly: 'I never attacked the establishment in any way.'

Interestingly, one of the most sympathetic novels of these years, Walter Greenwood's *Love on the Dole* (1933), was not filmed until some time later and released in 1941 when the changed circumstances of the war made it favourable to do so.[14] Then it was John Baxter, once again, who faithfully transposed it to the screen. During the intervening years, Greenwood for his part had turned up as scriptwriter on the George Formby comedy *No Limit* (1935, Monty Banks). It was a hilarious film and incredibly successful at the box office, but it contained a typically caricatured vision of the British working class. Still, that was where the money lay, and in a similar fashion J.B. Priestley was brought in to script two of the Gracie Fields pieces.

It is not at all surprising that Balcon looked back over those years and could see little in the way of 'a genuine reflection of reality'. One looks in vain, if that is what one looks for. As both Roy Armes and Charles Barr have argued in their respective surveys of the period,[15] the British film makers turned their backs on the everyday reality of British life. British cinema consisted of an amalgam of Alexander Korda spectaculars. Jessie Matthews musicals, Conrad Veidt spy melodramas, Hitchcock thrillers, light-hearted farces from Tom Walls, vehicles for the talents of George Arliss, or Jack Hulbert and Cicely Courtneidge, and comedies from Formby, Fields and Will Hay. If there were any over-all trends discernible, then Roy Armes suggests they were between, on the one hand, prestige productions with literary pretensions and international casts which were made with an eye on the American market but which, with the exception of the Korda epics, generally failed to make money, and, on the other, the commercially successful but critically despised comedies aimed at the domestic market from the northern comedians such as Formby, Fields and Hay. And their representation and classification of social knowledge and imagery were highly selective indeed.

The projection of Britain which the two must successful and distinct British cinemas depended upon was a glorious vision of Empire abroad, as shown in Korda's efforts, and domestic harmony at home, as in the stereotyped comedies. Few film makers consciously sought to upset those images or to break such a consensus. One should not forget the contribution made during the thirties by the documentary movement in Britain; but their films were rarely shown in the commercial cinema and hence attracted comparatively small and committed audiences. Furthermore, their occasionally critical tone was decidedly muted in view of the fact that many were sponsored by financial backing from the government and other establishment sources.

Korda's films were particularly important for expressing what Jeffrey Richards has called 'the national ideology in its purest form on film'.[16] Korda, born Sandor Kellner in a town near Budapest, arrived in London in 1931. *The Private Life of Henry VIII* (1933) was probably his greatest success but it was his trilogy of films with imperial themes, *Sanders of the River* (1935), *The Drum* (1938) and *The Four Feathers* (1939), which perhaps best expressed the Korda vision. Each was produced by Alexander Korda, directed by his brother Zoltan and had set designs by yet another brother, Vincent. Together with films from Herbert Wilcox such as *Victoria the Great* (1938) and *Sixty Glorious Years* (1939), they painted a picture of a vast and glorious British Empire ruled over by a benign and benevolent monarchy. Like the domestic comedies, they offered little to trouble the conscience.

British feature films went their own insular way throughout the 1930s. The imperial films propagated the imperialist ethic, the domestic comedies fostered social integration, and occasional war films, generally set during the First World War, preached nationalism and patriotism. Anthony Asquith set the tone there with his film at the beginning of the decade, *Tell England* (1931), which dealt with the Gallipoli landings and ended with the words over a grave reading: 'Tell England, ye who pass this monument, we died for her and here we rest content.' Walter Forde's *Forever England* (1935) continued in the same vein, being a naval drama 'which finds its lofty, unforgettable theme', said one trade paper review, 'in the true maxim "Breed will Tell" '.

Only in the second half of the decade were any incursions made into the insularity of British films. But the vogue for spy thrillers and melodramas, particularly the films of Alfred Hitchcock, did hint unwittingly at events taking place abroad. The stress on secret agents and political assassinations appeared with the escalation of the Nazi threat to Europe and Raymond Durgnat argues that, in the case of Hitchcock, this was deliberate.[17] Hitchcock's film of *The Thirty-Nine Steps* (1935) was bedecked with spies in Gestapo-looking leather coats and upper-class Mosleyite collaborationists. His fears for the democratic process were actually shown in the scene where the escaping Hannay inadvertently stumbles into a political meeting and is immediately mistaken for the guest speaker. Hannay improvises a speech on the spot, includes a stream of bland but stirring generalisations, and yet is roundly applauded by the audience. Such fears were rarely disturbing, however. In *Cheer Boys Cheer* (1939), director Walter Forde includes a shot of an avaricious British businessman at his desk, with a copy of *Mein Kampf* by his side, but the film remains a whimsical comedy and boy gets girl in the end.

The role of British feature films in the thirties and the part they played in engendering consensus has been most effectively summarised by Roy Armes when he concludes:

> The characteristic works of 1930s cinema do not therefore lay bare social contradictions or express directly the feelings and aspirations of the underprivileged majority. They are rather films which organise the audience's experiences in the sense of fostering social integration and the acceptance of social constraints. Emotional problems are shown to find an easy solution in matrimony, and potentially explosive political or legal issues are defused by being personalised and turned into mere clashes of character. It is simplistic to treat such a form of cinema as merely harmless — or even harmful — escapist entertainment. The Odeons of the 1930s did not offer oblivion on the lines of the gin palaces of Victorian times. Instead they consistently gave their audiences a deeper reassurance through a facsimile world where existing values were invariably validated by events in the film and where all discord could be turned to harmony by an acceptance of the *status quo*.[18]

The war which began in 1939 was to change many of the features inherent in that *status quo*, though not overnight. Alexander Korda, for instance, thought that patriotic jingoism, of the sort which had accompanied the opening of the Great War, would be called for once again in 1939. He rushed into production and released within a matter of weeks a film called *The Lion Has Wings* (1939). It was propaganda of an obvious and hollow kind. The film attracted large audiences. But Mass Observation surveys of audience responses to the film found that people went to see it out of a sense of duty more than anything else, and said they liked it 'because they thought it the right thing to say'. Even then, though, the staged scenes in which German pilots 'screamed with fright when they came in over London and discovered the anti-aircraft balloons' were judged to be particularly laughable and puerile.[19]

The fact is, quite simply, that a film like *The Lion Has Wings* misjudged the mood of the people. Both the British government and the people were aware that the distinction between the front line and the home front, between 'over there' and 'back home', which has been so marked during World War I, would not be so obvious with the onset of hostilities in 1939. The point had been graphically reinforced during the 1930s with copious British newsreel coverage of the aerial bombardment of cities such as Guernica and Barcelona in the Spanish Civil War. The entry made in his diary by one London bus driver during the early stages of the blitz perhaps best summed up the new mood: 'We are all in the "Front Line" and we realise it.'

Many of the film makers also came to realise what effects such events as the blitz, evacuation and participation of the population in total war were having upon British society, and to recognise what new-found feelings were being engendered therein. The war brought changes which were reflected and manifested in the films of the period, and the selective lines of representation and classification of social knowledge in the cinema were redrawn to accommodate those changes. In part, the film makers were greatly helped by the almost total lack of interest in propaganda shown by the wartime leaders of the day, Chamberlain and Churchill (unlike the Nazi leaders). Chamberlain contemplated closing down the BBC and the Ministry of Information. Churchill, despite his own prolific use of radio, was reported to have said that he was not interested in propaganda 'because he knew it would not win the war'. He was right, of course. Propaganda did not win him the war, though it might be said to have contributed to his losing the peace when the 1945 election came round. This lack of interest at the highest level, coupled with some woefully inept propaganda from the MOI in the first year or two of the war, created a space which the likes of the BBC and the film makers were quick to fill and to capitalise upon. As a result, the British cinema, for one, reached a maturity which had never been evident before.

Working-class life, mining communities and the depression were the subjects of films such as *The Stars Look Down* (1939, Carol Reed), *The Proud Valley* (1940, Penrose Tennyson) and *Love on the Dole* (1941, John Baxter). They were by no means radical or uncompromising films. Carol Reed admitted in an interview in 1971, for example, that he had no polemical intention in making *The Stars Look Down:* 'I simply took the novel by A.J. Cronin. I didn't feel particularly about his subject (nationalisation of mines). One could just as easily make a picture on the opposite side.' Tennyson's film presented a largely idealised picture of working-class life; and, for all its apparent fidelity, Baxter's film has one or two melodramatic moments. But at least they were dealing with subjects which would not have been produced in the years before the war. Furthermore, the treatments afforded to such subjects got better as the war progressed. Baxter, in particular, went on to make a series of films with such suitably evocative titles as *The Common Touch* (1941), *Let the People Sing* (1942) and *We'll Smile Again* (1942).

The question of class in British society was another taboo subject which came to the fore in feature films. At first it was brought forth only as a peripheral matter. Walter Forde's re-make of the Edgar Wallace novel *The Four Just Men* was actually released in June 1939. Even then its message of ruling-class decadence and its inference that appeasement had come from that quarter and had amounted to treachery were clear. Just to make those points further, in the context of war, however, the film was re-released in July 1944 with the addition of a newly made newsreel-style epilogue, which showed that the Four Just Men had been right all along. Thereafter, films as diverse in intent as the George Formby comedy *Spare a Copper* (1940, John Paddy Carstairs) and Alberto Cavalcanti's *Went the Day Well?* (1942) played either unwittingly or wittingly upon the idea of traitors in higher-class places. The former film saw George in the police force, winning the day against 'a pillar of the community' determined to sabotage the efforts of a local shipyard. Cavalcanti's film, based upon an idea and story by Graham Greene, fantasised about German paratroopers, disguised as British soldiers, taking over an English village as a prelude to an invasion of the country. They win the village easily enough with the help of a treacherous village squire, and they are only finally betrayed to the military authorities, and the village relieved, by the heroic endeavours of the local poacher (who loses his life) and the working-class, Cockney evacuee lad (who gets through).

With a more positive, less dichotomous, vision of class, *Millions Like*

Us (1943, Frank Launder and Sidney Gilliat) viewed war as the great leveller of class divisions in British society and told a story of girls from all social groups coming to live together in happy harmony, for the most part, by working together on the factory front. By way of contrast, Anthony Asquith's film from that same year of 1943, *The Demi-Paradise*, played ironically upon the belief that class divisions were as strong as ever in Britain. Nevertheless it still forcefully acknowledged that advances had been made, that changes had come about since the advent of war, and that Britain was one great integrated community. The plot utilised to make those points was simple enough: the young Soviet marine engineer (played by Laurence Olivier) arrives in England early in 1939. He stays the weekend with an eccentric, millionaire shipbuilder and returns home convinced that Britain is hidebound with tradition and imbued with little else. When he comes back in 1941 he finds a country at war and a different land. The smugness, laziness and indifference are gone, and the class tensions relaxed. His conversion complete, he falls for the shipbuilder's daughter, of course, and promises to return yet again, when the war is over.

These were the sort of images, then, the visions of Britain undergoing change and transformation as a result of war, to be found in the feature films of the time. It would be easy to exaggerate their existence or influence. There were still many films, particularly set against a military background of one variety or another, which purveyed the patriotic clarion calls of old. Sergei Nolbandov's *Ships with Wings* (1941) and the Noel Coward-David Lean *In Which We Serve* (1942) provide two such examples. The former, something of an aberration for the Ealing Studios which on the whole produced excellent works in the war, was an archetypal story of wartime heroism and daring: dashing young Fleet Air Arm officer is dismissed from the service in disgrace before the war starts; with the advent of war he tries to re-enlist, but in vain; however, pilots are in short supply for a vital but dangerous mission; so, fearing nothing and daring all, he succeeds though at the expense of his own life. 'I knew he wouldn't come back', says one officer at the end of the film. 'I think he'd have preferred it that way', concludes another. Stock responses abounded in the film, as they did ultimately in the Coward-Lean production with its condescending and patronising flashbacks in the lives of the captain, an officer and a rating on their warship's ill-fated maiden voyage.

But for every *Ships with Wings* and *In Which We Serve*, there were films of the quality of *The Way Ahead* (1944, Carol Reed) and *The*

Way to the Stars (1945, Anthony Asquith). Reed's film observed a band of conscripts from every rank and station in life going through the process of being turned into a fighting unit. Most of all, as Roy Armes notes, 'The class consciousness of Lean and Coward's work is replaced by a more detached and uncondescending view of ordinary soldiers.' Asquith's film put aside mock heroics and the like, and dealt more convincingly with the intrusion of war into people's private lives. The young RAF pilot, played by John Mills, sees his comrades regularly fail to return from missions over Germany and deliberates whether he should marry after all, as planned, when such sacrifices are called for. John Pudney's 1942 poem 'For Johnny' provides a *leitmotif* in the film, and its final verse highlights an answer to the pilot's dilemmas:

> Do not despair
> For Johnny-head-in-air;
> He sleeps as sound
> As Johnny underground.
>
> Fetch out no shroud
> For Johnny-in-the-cloud;
> And keep your tears
> For him in after years.
>
> Better by far
> For Johnny-the-bright-star,
> To keep your head,
> And see his children fed.

But what of the new wartime consensus of which we have talked; where was the best exemplified? Perhaps it is seen nowhere better than in the films of Michael Powell and Emeric Pressburger, and in particular their film of *The Life and Death of Colonel Blimp* (1943). Furthermore, the furore which greeted this film demonstrated better than anything could the nature of the official response (Churchill's especially) to film makers who chose to manifest too obviously the new-found consensus of wartime.

The original screenplay for *Colonel Blimp* was written by Emeric Pressburger early in 1942, and it was then called 'The Life and Death of Sugar Candy', 'Sugar Candy' being the nickname of Clive Candy, the leading character in the story. Director Michael Powell planned to shoot the film between July and September of 1942 with Laurence Olivier in the role of Candy. It was at that stage that Powell and Pressburger hit upon the idea of approaching the cartoonist David Low to see if they could use the name of Blimp in the title for their film, the purpose being to show cinematically, in Powell's words, that 'Colonel Blimp was a symbol of British procrastination and British regard for tradition and all the things which we knew and which were losing the war'. David Low stipulated only that Powell and Pressburger take full responsibility for the production and, most of all, that Blimp be proved a fool in the end. Since this was also what Powell and Pressburger wished to show, agreement was reached. In one respect, therefore, it was not as though the film were trying to say anything that was new. After all, the Blimp cartoon had been in existence for many years and the figure of Blimp had been shown to be a fool on many occasions in print. But, as Churchill likely knew, the MOI's Home Intelligence Department had pointed out that between 1940 and 1942 British public opinion in general was itself highly critical of what were called the 'men of Munich', the 'guilty men' and the 'Colonel Blimps'. Chamberlain had gone, of course, in 1940, but many of the politicians associated with him and his policies were still in the House and the Conservative Party. Home Intelligence reported that there was a widespread feeling of revulsion against 'vested interests', 'privilege' and what was referred to as 'the old gang', coupled with a belief that it was these vested interests which were hampering the war effort and were to blame for 'ills of production' and the like. As a result, it is easy to see why, at that particular point in time, a proposed film with the name of Colonel Blimp in the title took on added significance in Churchill's eyes.

Furthermore, there were elements in Powell's earlier films which might not have constituted the best of recommendations in certain governmental quarters. In 1939, for example, he had directed *The Spy in Black*, a First World War story about a daring German spy ring which almost succeeds in scuttling the British fleet. Then in 1941 he had come up with *49th Parallel*, partly financed by MOI money, about a German submarine crew on the run across Canada and showing great initiative during the course of a fruitless attempt at escape. Some critics praised the depiction of the German crew for avoiding a one-sided and partisan characterisation, but many wondered whether the film was not perhaps better propaganda 'for the enemy than ourselves'.

In any event, when once the film on Blimp was brought to Churchill's attention, he became determined to stop it if he could. The

War Office then stepped in and refused Laurence Olivier release from
the services to take part in the film, and refused to give any support
in the way of uniforms, guns and other props. Churchill's thoughts on
the matter, his persistent attempts to stop the film, and the arguments
which took place over the film at Cabinet level, can be accurately
gauged from the memoranda on the subject of Blimp in the Public
Record Office.[20] In the final analysis, Churchill could not stop the film
being made or released, though it was later cut down, making it 'much
less abrasive'. Churchill then tried to stop the film from being
exported. However, the film enjoyed great success at the box office.
David Low, for his part, decided that what Blimp represented was
still very much in existence and revived his cartoon figure after a year's
absence. *Time* magazine was also prompted to wonder whether 'Blimp
was dead after all'.

The Blimp incident showed just what happened when somebody
chose to depart from Churchill's line regarding acceptable wartime
propaganda. Yet it also revealed that there were other channels of
opinion which perhaps better expressed the currents of popular
feeling in wartime Britain than did anything emanating from the
official propaganda machine. The British cinema was one channel
which highlights, in retrospect, 'The Road to 1945'.

The postwar cinema began, as no doubt did much of the country,
in a mood of idealism and enthusiasm. Michael Balcon declared,
in the pages of the trade paper *Kinematograph Weekly*, during 1945,
that he wanted to see films project 'the true Briton to himself and to
the whole world'. They must see 'Britain as a leader in social reform in
the defeat of social injustices and a champion of civil liberties'. They
were grandiose ambitions which were to disappear when economic
problems beset the British film industry as readily as they did the rest
of the country. Thereafter the British cinema was to continue along
its path of old, and it became, once again, a matter of financial
survival. Ironically, within just a few years of Balcon's statement
his studios, more so than any others, were well on the way to
generating the sort of stereotypes and caricatures to be found in the
Ealing comedies. Films such as Robert Hamer's *It Always Rains on
Sunday* (1947), praised at the time for depicting 'the audible and
visible surfaces of life east of the Aldgate pump', soon gave way to
the same director's *Kind Hearts and Coronets* in 1949.[21] The postwar
consensus, in large part a left-over from the war itself, ossified and
atrophied.

Before it did so, however, it was well served once again by the team of Powell and Pressburger, especially in their film entitled *A Matter of Life and Death* (1946). This is the film which Raymond Durgnat comments upon in detail during the course of his book *A Mirror for England* (1970).[22] Durgnat's book is exciting, thoughtful and stimulating, but he has surely miscalculated in his analysis of *A Matter of Life and Death.*

Durgnat talks of 'explicit ideological positions like the High Tory moral of *A Matter of Life and Death*' and states that 'the film's preoccupation is not with Britain's survival in war, but with her survival in peace'. On two counts, Durgnat is certainly correct — the film does adopt 'explicit ideological positions' and, despite the wartime setting, it is assuredly a film with a message for Britain at peace. But it is definitely not a film with a 'High Tory moral'.

Durgnat's arguments read thus:

> *A Matter of Life and Death* is generally taken as an extravaganza, a vague, eccentric, enjoyable contraption advocating closer ties with the U.S.A. But the politics of this 'Halfway Heaven' are far more precise. They express perennial Tory criticisms of the Socialist Utopia — that is, the Welfare State . . . This Heaven is a futurist Utopia. It's a planned society. It's machine like . . . As Tories claim planning drains colour from life, so, here the Technicolour of earth pales to celestial monochrome. Heaven's values are those of the collectivity (as opposed to the selfless individualism of romantic love). Planned, bureaucratic, idealistic, totalitarian, colourless, theoretic — these are all the words Tories like to use of Socialism.

Durgnat assesses the film, then, and decides that it is for the most part an anti-socialist tract, a Tory critique of socialist plans and ideals for postwar Britain.

John Russell Taylor comes nearer than Durgnat to capturing the essence of *A Matter of Life and Death,* when he says of Powell's films generally: 'much of Powell's work is concerned with the rapprochement, if not the total reconciliation, of opposite ideals.'[23] That is, essentially, what *A Matter of Life and Death* is all about: the rapprochement and reconciliation of opposite ideals. It is, finally, a film about compromise and consensus. That consensus is put at its most explicit in an opening scene where David Niven describes himself and adds: 'Politics . . . Conservative by nature, Labour by experience'.

The words put into the character's mouth at that point are surely Powell and Pressburger's comment upon Britain by the end of the Second World War, a Britain 'whose life and imagination have been violently shaped by war', to use a phrase from the introduction to their film. 'Conservative by nature, Labour by experience' accurately describes the nature of the wartime and immediate postwar consensus in Britain.

Consensus and integration, not confrontation and conflict, were the order of the day once again in 1946 as they were so often in the British cinema. But the consensus as expressed in *A Matter of Life and Death*, at least, was infused with optimism and hope for the future, as was shown during the long trial scenes in the film. Such hopes soon gave way to disillusion. A year later, the Boulting brothers were to convey disappointment and discontent with the way the postwar consensus was going in their film of *Fame is the Spur* (1947), a story of compromise and the loss of ideals. By the end of the 1940s, the Ealing comedies were to show how far this consensus had atrophied, and by 1951 the stage was set for Anthony Kimmins, who had written and directed most of George Formby's less interesting films in the late 1930s, to come up with *Mr Denning Drives North*, as supreme a celebration of hidebound and conservative virtues as one could possibly expect to find anywhere in the British cinema.

For a while, then, the bounds of consensus had been enlarged to embrace the changes brought about by the Second World War. However, the ideological role of the British cinema in fostering harmony and social integration had changed in few other respects.

Notes

1. See K.W. Watkins, *Britain Divided* (London, 1963). Watkins states that 'It is, in fact, arguable that nothing since the French Revolution had so tragically divided the British people as the Spanish Civil War' (p.11).

2. Anthony Aldgate, *Cinema and History: British Newsreels and the Spanish Civil War* (London, 1979).

3. John Stevenson and Chris Cook, *The Slump. Society and Politics during the Depression* (London, 1977).

4. C.L. Mowat, *Britain Between the Wars, 1918-1940* (London, 1968), pp.577-8.

5. Tom Burns, 'The Organization of Public Opinion', in James Curran, Michael Gurevitch and Janet Woollacott (eds), Mass Communication and Society (London, 1977), p.63.

6. Gaumont British Issue No.278, 27 August 1936.

7. Michael Howard, 'Total War in the Twentieth Century: Participation and Consensus in the Second World War', in Brian Bond and Ian Roy (eds), *War and Society: A Yearbook of Military History* (London, 1975), p.220.

8. See Arthur Marwick, *Britain in the Century of Total War* (London, 1968) and *War and Social Change in the Twentieth Century* (London, 1974).

9. Paul Addison, *The Road to 1945* (London, 1975).

10. Arthur Marwick, 'World War II and Social Class in Great Britain', paper delivered to the Sixth Anglo-Dutch Historical Conference.

11. John Baxter's work is discussed in John Montgomery, *Comedy Films 1894-1954* (London, 1954), and a review article by Jeffrey Richards of *Say it with Flowers* and *Music Hall*, in *Focus on Film*, no.30 (1978), pp.48-50. *Doss House* is held by the National Film Archive. Michael Powell's work has been the subject of much discussion of late, including Ian Christie (ed.), *Powell, Pressburger and Others* (London, 1978). *Red Ensign* is held by the NFA.

12. Stuart Hall, 'Culture, the Media and the "Ideological Effect" ', in Curran Gurevitch and Woollacott (eds.), *Mass Communication and Society*.

13. The comedies depended for their success upon caricature, stereotype and hackneyed situations, but they can be a rich source none the less. Formby's 1935 film of *Off the Dole* is for the most part what producer Blakely describes it as being in an opening credit, 'A Merry Musical Burlesque'. Yet the opening scenes in an employment exchange contain some clever banter, equating capitalist American ideas on 'market economy' with those of the Communists ('You buy something you don't get, with money you haven't got, from someone you never see'), and claiming that neither the Americans, nor the Russians, nor the British government for that matter, have much idea how to solve unemployment. Similarly, Gracie Fields in *Sally in our Alley* (1931) displays some acute differences of reaction to the workers and 'the toffs', during the course of a film which highlights, perhaps inadvertently, the immense gap between the social classes in Britain.

14. I am grateful to Jeffrey Richards for providing me with information regarding the attempts to film *Love on the Dole* in 1936. On two occasions in that year the censor rejected scripts submitted to him, claiming that 'I think this subject, as it stands, would be very undesirable as a film.'

15. See Roy Armes, *A Critical History of British Cinema* (London, 1978), and Charles Barr, *Ealing Studios* (London, 1977), though more particularly for the 1930s, see Barr's two articles in *Screen* (1974).

16. Jeffrey Richards, *Visions of Yesterday* (London, 1973), p.114.

17. See Raymond Durgnat, *The Strange Case of Alfred Hitchcock* (London, 1974).

18. Armes, *British Cinema*, pp.113-14.

19. 'Public Reaction: *The Lion Has Wings*. A Mass Observation Report on Audience Reaction', *Documentary News Letter* (February, 1940), p.5.

20. File PREM 4 14/15, cited in Addison, *The Road to 1945*, and reprinted verbatim in Christie (ed.), *Powell, Pressburger and Others*.

21. *It Always Rains on Sunday* has been the subject of two interesting articles in *Framework*, no.9. Barr's *Ealing Studios* pursues the notion of consensus in greater depth with regard to the Ealing films of the time.

22. See Raymond Durgnat *A Mirror for England* (London, 1970), pp.29ff.

23. John Russell Taylor, 'Myths and Superman', *Sight and Sound* (Autumn 1978).

6 THE FIRST REALITY: FILM CENSORSHIP IN LIBERAL ENGLAND

Nicholas Pronay

The fact that censorship of films existed in all European countries as well
as overseas is known to all. By the outbreak of the First World War, in all
countries in which the cinema had already become a medium of popular,
not necessarily yet a mass, entertainment, some form of censorship of
films had also come into being. In terms of organisation it ranged from
fully established state censorship organisations, such as in Russia,
Germany or Denmark, to censorship organisations run locally, by a
collusion between the local authorities, whether they be the government
of the state or city or county, and some powerful vigilante-type
organisation, usually based on a religious body. The Roman Catholic
Church had already taken a serious view of the importance of the
cinema both in the positive and in the negative sense. In most
countries where the Catholic Church was powerful it contributed to
the budding film censorship system of that locality that long
experience which the Roman Church had accumulated in all matters
of censorship, in terms both of organisation and of intellectual
framework. In the United States of America all these types of film
censorship could be found side by side within a constitution which
relegated such matters in the first instance to state and local
legislatures.[1]

The censorship organisations before the First World War were
primarily concerned with moral censorship, but this word 'moral'
should not be constructed, even in this early period, too narrowly.
It did not mean only the suppression of photographic pornography
or of blasphemy, in the form, for example, of religious images being
portrayed on the screen in an unacceptable manner, or the
suppression of the presentation of criminal actions which could be
copied by youngsters from the screen. It also extended to what was
described as 'public morality'. Public morality meant a defence of
the ethical bases of the society concerned: the institution of
monogamous marriage, parental authority and so forth, and to
some extent at least the protection of the idea that the existing
institutions for law and order were just and fair and necessary.
The degree to which 'public morality' would shade into a more

113

directly politically motivated censorship depended largely on the
interplay between the degree of sophistication of the particular political
system and the extent to which it had as yet taken note of the cinema.

In the course of the First World War the potentials of propaganda
came to be generally recognised as a weapon of particular significance
in a war which was fought by conscript armies and in which the morale
of the population at home was subjected to unprecedented privations
and demands for industrial production. The collapse of the Central
Powers was in the last resort an internal collapse, a failure of morale,
albeit in the face of growing military superiority on the part of the
enemy. In this collapse of morale the propaganda work of the
Allies was widely seen as playing an important, perhaps even crucial,
role.[2] Whether or not the work of the Allied propaganda
organisations did or did not help much to 'Win the War' is immaterial
for our purpose here: the important point is that it was believed at the
time both by those who had been in charge of the armies of the
Central Powers and by those who were in charge of the propaganda
offensive mounted against them. Wide official currency was given to
the statements of General Ludendorff, for example.

> We found ourselves, bit by bit, attacked by enemy propaganda,
> in speech and writing through the neutral countries, especially
> across our land frontiers, from Holland and Switzerland, through
> Austria-Hungary, and even our own country, and finally from the
> air, with such cleverness and on such a scale, that many people
> could no longer distinguish between enemy propaganda and
> their own sentiments . . . The collapse of our morale at home,
> with its effect on our fighting capacity, the campaign against
> the home front and the spirit of the Army were, undoubtedly,
> the chief weapons whereby England hoped to conquer us, after
> they had given up hope of a military victory.[3] . . . We were
> hypnotised by the enemy propaganda as a rabbit is by a snake.[4]

After the publication of *Mein Kampf*, equally well publicised was
Hitler's assessment:

> In the year 1915, the enemy started his propaganda among our
> soldiers. From 1916 it steadily became more intensive, and at the
> beginning of 1918, it had swollen into a storm-flood. One could
> now see the effects of this gradual seduction. Our soldiers learned
> to think the way the enemy wanted them to think.[5]

Equally well known in British official circles were the pronouncements of General Hindenburg and of various German Army commanders all claiming that the German Army and people came indeed to be 'hypnotised like a rabbit is by a snake' by the propaganda work of the Allies, and that it was the failure of the German government to carry out effective and far-reaching counter-propaganda at home and amongst the troops which resulted in a collapse of the will to fight. The reports of the psychological subsection of the US Army were also influential, claiming 'scientific' evidence for the collapse of the Central Powers as a result of successful subversion of the spirit and political will of both German and Austro-Hungarian soldiers during the summer of 1918.[6]

The victors were also aware of the shaky morale of some of their own troops, as manifested in the well-known mutinies in the French Army in 1917, but also in the mutinies in British and Commonwealth units in 1918-19. While news of these were successfully kept from the public, they deeply disturbed the government, as did the disaffection in several British police forces in 1919. These demonstrations that good morale could not be taken for granted even amongst victorious troops added to the general awareness of the importance of propaganda amongst the broad masses of the people. Finally, the impact of the Soviet Revolution and of the industrial unrest and agitation which coincided with it in many European countries, including the victors, from 1917 to the early 1920s, greatly reinforced the belief that governments must keep a close eye on those media through which the industrial working classes, in particular, could be reached.[7]

The development therefore of a political approach to the censorship of the cinema, which from the First World War onwards was the mass medium *par excellence*, has to be seen against the background of what were then taken to be the lessons of the First World War and of the widespread feeling that, while the war against the Central Powers had indeed come to an end, the war against industrial subversion, and even potential revolutionary tendencies amongst the industrial working classes, certainly had not. We must also bear in mind that there was not only one potential source of ideological subversion. The seductive notions of populist democracy, powerfully projected by the United States, also constituted a danger. As late as 1945, it was thought that, while general statements to the effect that government should be for or even ultimately by the people were fine, it was most un-Ally like for the *Why We Fight* films to go on spelling it out: 'Government by the people; *not* by the *best* people . . . but by all the people'. The series was thought undesirable, at least widely, to be shown in England, and *War Comes to America* was effectively kept off British screens. The United States' popular culture represented on one level an even more fundamental political/ethical challenge: social, moral and ethical standards and aspirations should not be imposed by an educated elite but, on the contrary, people should be entitled to do their own thing, to pursue happiness, in their own way. These ideas, this ideology, were in many ways as fundamental a challenge to British and also European systems of government as the socialist and Communist ideas put about amongst the industrial working classes. So were the Wilsonian notions of 'self-determination', 'open diplomacy' and the rest on the ideas of how international relations ought to be conducted, and by whom, since they went manifestly against the idea of foreign policy as the special preserve of the experts and mandarins of the various European Foreign Offices. The projection of individualist populism in place of an ordered, hierarchical, elitist concept of politics and society, ultimately, but only ultimately, devoted to a liberal aim, was also thought to be part of the agencies of dissolution after 1918. Above all, this less obvious invasion by an ideological challenger was of paramount importance because it came as an integral part of the invasion of Europe by American popular culture. Jazz (containing, as *Pravda* once explained, 'the exceptionally subversive idea that instead of educated musical artists performing works of Art from properly written scores, ignorant persons should vent their emotions through musical instruments, and thus reduce the sacred Art of Music to chaos'), Tin Pan Alley ballads and 'Western' songs with highly suggestive messages almost wiped out indigenous popular music. American films which implicitly, and quite often explicitly, projected American social, moral and political values practically wiped out mass-appeal film making in England, and in much of Europe, which had flourished before the war, as did British and European popular music.

It is against this background — the supposed lessons of First World War propaganda about the practicability and potential of mass persuasion, the belief that the war against a revolutionary threat from the working classes had not ended in October 1918, and the flood of American popular culture bearing the challenge of American populist ideas — that the development of political censorship in Europe in general and in Britain in particular has to be seen.

Censorship of the cinema in Britain, in institutional terms, was a characteristic compromise between censorship exercised by local authorities thus responding to local opinion and censorship by a central national body of professional censors with a broader and more intellectually thought-out set of criteria for judging the suitability of films. The so-called British Board of Film Censors was a central body residing in London, staffed by dedicated and professional men, but its judgement on films was, at any rate in law, only advisory for the actual power to allow or not to allow the showing of a film in a cinema rested with the local authorities. The local authorities were not left entirely to their own devices, of course; the Home Office took a very close interest indeed in seeing the local authorities did follow the rulings of the British Board of Film Censors, and the President and through him the Secretary of the British Board of Film Censors were in practice appointees of the Home Secretary. On the other hand, the British Board of Film Censors was a body actually financed by the fees charged for examining films, and not by 'public money'. Consequently, it did not come within the definition of a state organisation run by the Home Office. The Home Secretary, while he was indeed regarded as a person to whom enquiries in Parliament and elsewhere about the working of censorship in general could be addressed, could claim therefore, with much convenience, that he was not personally responsible, nor was his office, for the banning or permitting of any particular film. In order to maintain this sensible and convenient arrangement, the Home Office handled any recalcitrant local authority with tact and leniency.[8] One Home Secretary actually explained that a state censorship board would mean that Parliament could scrutinise and debate each individual decision which would make the work of censorship 'impossible'.[9] The system was further buttressed by agreements with organisations such as the Cinematography Renters Association, which distributed films. They made it a precondition of membership (which in turn meant in practice the opportunity to operate in the business at all) that members should only handle films which had been approved by the British Board of Film Censors. Only very occasionally were the wider powers of the Home Office brought into play, such as the power to forbid the importation of any article which was likely to be injurious to the country,[10] or the powers of the police in countering subversion in general. The ultimate powers under the law, such as seditious libel or sedition itself, were never explicitly invoked, at least in peacetime, although it has been made clear on occasions that the Home Secretary would not hesitate to use all his powers, if absolutely necessary, in the last resort.

The question which needs to be examined in the first place is whether the censorship of films in Britain was conceived and operated for protecting political stability or whether it was concerned with straightforward moral protection against pornography and blasphemy. In order to approach that question we must first define by what criteria we can talk about a 'political' as opposed to a 'moral' censorship system.

A political system of censorship must first of all be based on a coherent set of political principles to determine what kind of arguments and even facts the censorship should prevent from being brought to the attention of the people. These must be laid down in a detailed and co-ordinated list of banned topics. The existence of a coherent set of principles and the existence of a detailed and co-ordinated list constitute the first criterion of ideological, or political, censorship, as is shown by that archetype of this approach in Western Europe, the Roman Church's Holy Office with its Index Prohibitorum.

Second, political censorship must actually be conducted by officials who possess specialised political expertise and have contact with the highest level of the political structure. In other words, it must be run by men who are themselves politically highly placed, just as the officials at the Head of the Holy Office of the Roman Curia were always close to the very centre of decision making.

The third criterion is that it must be effective. Intent is not good enough. Censorship or, to give it its technical name, counter-propaganda, the suppression of ideas other than those approved, can only work if it can indeed prevent publication. Positive propaganda, provided that it is dominant, need not be monolithic or comprehensive. It can operate in a market place of ideas. Censorship, that is propaganda through the suppression of alternative ideas and information, must, however, be comprehensive and monolithic in order to operate at all. Of course, nothing in real life can ever be suppressed 100 per cent, but it must come near enough to that, at least as far as its target groups in society are concerned.

The British Board of Film Censors operated on the basis of a detailed list of 'exceptions' — a term usually preferred by the Board although it also used the word 'rules' interchangeably with it — which were appended to its Annual Reports from 1919 until 1932. A copy of these 'exceptions', referred to this time as 'rules', was also sent to any film studio or importer who asked to know what the Board's rules were. Until 1928, the Board also issued from time to time a set of general principles in the form of a booklet. After 1928

these principles were regarded as 'set' and enquirers were sent a copy
of the 1928 booklet *Censorship in Britain*.[11] The 'exceptions' were
phrased in the form in which the 'general principles' had been applied
in practice, in dealing with new manifestations of the 'themes' which
the Board disallowed, in the course of the last year covered by the
Report. The list was subdivided into a number of categories which
remained largely unchanged, both in name and order, from the first
Report of the Board in 1919 until the Second World War. Taking the
year 1930 as typical, there were the following nine categories:

1. Religious
2. Political
3. Military
4. Administration of justice
5. Social
6. Questions of sex
7. Crime
8. Cruelty
9. Titling and sound ('Titling only before 1929).[12]

There was a certain degree of mobility in terms of which particular rule
was entered under which particular heading, particularly between
Political, Military, Administration of Justice and Social. For example,
'Inciting workers to armed conflict' had appeared at various times under
'Political', 'Social' and 'Military'.

There was no question, however, of the Board not being perfectly
open about exercising censorship over political as well as other matters
which might be communicated through the medium of the cinema
screens. The Board also made it clear that its rules were in principle
fixed, in practical application cumulative. Producers were invited to
acquaint themselves with *all* the particular 'exceptions' taken by the
Board over the years in order to be sure of understanding what the
principles of the Board meant in practice.[13] If a particular 'exception'
did not appear in a particular year's list, that only meant that no film
was submitted in that particular year which breached that particular
rule.

By 1931, the list of political subjects, or 'themes', which the Board
would not permit to be *either* the principal subject of the story of a film,
or shown in any incidental form within a film, consisted of the following:

1. *British officers* and *forces* shown in *disgraceful, reprehensible* or

equivocal light.

2. The presentation of *inaccurate* or *objectionably misleading themes purporting to illustrate parts of the British Empire*, or representing *British possessions* as *lawless* or *iniquitous.*

3. The presentation of *British officials overseas* or the *wives of responsible British officials* in *reprehensible light* or *unfavourable reflection*; The presentation of *white men* in general in *a state of degradation amidst Eastern or native surroundings*; or the showing of *liaisons between coloured men and white women*; or the showing of *equivocal situations between white men and coloured people* and of *equivocal situations between white girls and men of other races*, not necessarily 'coloured'.[14]

4. The presentations of *lampoons on the institution of monarchy, libellous reflections on royal personages* or *families*, whether British or not.

5. All subjects were banned which dealt with *relations between capital and labour*, or included the showing of *inciting of workers to armed conflict*, whether in a British or foreign setting; all subjects dealing with *industrial violence and unrest*; *conflicts between the armed forces of a state and the populace*, whether in British or foreign setting; any *films or scenes showing soldiers or police firing on defenceless population* and *mobs attacking unarmed police.*[15]

6. Subjects or incidents which *conveyed a false impression of the police forces in Britain* or involved *reflections upon the administration of British justice* or upon *judges* and other *responsible officials of the law or public institutions*, or upon *public characters.*

7. Subjects, themes or incidents *likely to wound the just susceptibilities of friendly nations.*[16]

There can therefore be little doubt that, as far as the first criterion of political censorship is concerned, the existence of a set of clearly political rules organised in a coherent form and systematically restated and applied, did in fact exist in Britain. Let us now turn to the second criterion, the question whether the censorship organisation was actually conducted by person(s) possessing high political standing close enough to the political decision-making process and endowed with high-level political and propaganda expertise.

The British Board of Film Censors evolved gradually. From its beginnings in 1912 until 1917 it was in the charge of Mr G.A. Redford, who had served from 1875 to 1912 in the office of the Lord

Chamberlain, first as Licenser and then as Examiner (Censor) of Plays.
Redford was certainly no novice to the idea of political censorship in a
liberal setting, for the censorship of the theatre in Britain had its origins
in the threat which the theatre was supposed to have represented to
political stability in the eighteenth century. Redford himself rather
distinguished his tenure of the office during the first decade of the
century by an uncommonly extensive list of heavily 'political' bans.
In addition to banning *The Mikado* when the Anglo-Japanese Alliance
was about to be cemented involving the visit of the Japanese Crown
Prince, and *Secrets of the Harem* when Turkey was being wooed, and
similar acts belonging to the old, silly, traditions of political stage
censorship, Redford inaugurated a new and much more controversial
approach. Under the rule of 'no controversial politics' he banned plays
which argued *against* there being a 'German menace', while licensing
those which set out to 'warn the country'. For example, a play entitled
An Englishman's Home, written by an author called 'A. Patriot' — in
fact by Guy du Maurier who actually called it a 'propaganda play' —
and arguing that war with Germany was inevitable and that Britain
was already under attack from German spies and saboteurs, was one which
Redford failed to spot as 'controversial political propaganda'. A skit upon
it — actually called *Another Englishman's Home*, put on while the
original was still running and arguing that, on the contrary, there were
certain circles in Britain and France who were whipping up anti-German
moods, the expressions of which appeared to be menacing to the
Germans — did, however, stike him as 'controversial' and he
absolutely and irrevocably banned it. G.B. Shaw's *John Bull's Other
Island* (1903), which ridiculed the Liberals when they were in
opposition and which included such characters as "Ballsquith',
did not impress him with having relevance to the rules against either
'controversy' or the 'representation of living persons'. *Press Cuttings*
(1908), which ridiculed the Conservatives, however, as well as being
an ironic treatment of dreadnoughts, German invasion scares,
conscription and kindred issues, which the author (also G.B. Shaw)
regarded as issues got up by a combination of the press and other
warmongerers, Redford did ban.[17] Nevertheless, there can be
no doubt that Redford was a small man without access to confidential
information or high-level contacts, who was acting under intermittent
and unco-ordinated political instructions from a variety of masters,
usually the Foreign Office, who should have known better — had
they *seriously* considered regular political censorship in the first
instance.

In 1917 Redford was succeeded by T.P. O'Connor who had been, and remained after his appointment as President of the Board of Film Censors, a Member of Parliament and, from 1924, a Privy Councillor — thus being entitled to receive confidential information and being bound to official secrecy. He was a man on terms of intimacy and political trust, indeed friendship with all the leading politicians of that period, including Churchill, the Chamberlains, Lloyd George and Ramsay MacDonald. In 1929, he was succeeded by Sir Edward Shortt, a former Chief Secretary for Ireland, member of the Cabinet and Home Secretary whose particular field of political expertise lay in counter-subversion, having been specially appointed by Lloyd George to deal with the Bolshevik threat, the police strikes and the threatened General Strike in 1919, and who continued to be involved in the contingency planning against subversion during the 1920s. In 1935 Shortt was followed by Lord Tyrrell, whose career apexed as the Permanent Head of the Foreign Office. Tyrrell specialised from before the First World War in the new developments of political intelligence, news propaganda and cultural diplomacy. He was successively in charge of the FO's Political Intelligence and News Department, and was Chairman of the British Council. The last position he retained in conjunction with the Presidency of the British Board of Film Censors, thus for the first time linking up positive and negative 'cultural' propaganda. Of course, both Tyrrell and Shortt were also Privy Councillors and thus properly approachable by ministers and others with confidential matters. Lord Tyrrell remained in office until after the Second World War.[18]

From the emergence of the cinema as the prime medium of the industrial and urban working-class masses and the recognition of its potentially major political danger at the end of the First World War, the Presidents of the British Board of Film Censors were men of increasingly high political position, background and connections — not men of a moralist or educationist complexion — and they had the necessary high level of political contacts, standing, access to information and also broad expertise in the field of propaganda/counter-propaganda, which political censorship requires.

Turning to the third criterion for the political censorship of films, as a measure of counter-propaganda, namely the question of effectiveness, the story falls into two halves. From the outbreak of the First World War until 1930 (essentially the period of the silent film) the Home Office concentrated on gradually bringing all of the 144 local authorities to accept and abide by the decisions of the

British Board of Film Censors without legislation having to be introduced specifically for the purpose. This was very largely successful but not wholly so. The problem was that, in the absence of legislation, the aggrieved film makers whose films got heavily cut or banned altogether by the British Board of Film Censors, involving them in heavy financial loss, could only have redress against the decision by appealing, not to the British Board of Film Censors, but to a particular local authority, since it was its power as vested in the law which produced the actual ban. Time and time again local authorities petitioned the Home Secretary to introduce a state censorship board. This was not because, on the whole, they believed the British Board of Censors was too severe, for in many ways local authorities regarded its standards as far as *moral* matters were concerned as far too liberal — which was hardly surprising in view of the personalities of the Presidents of the British Board of Film Censors — but because they felt that in the case of the political suppression of films they were neither qualified to judge nor should carry the onus for it. As the Birmingham Justices put it: 'It is desirable that whenever . . . questions of public policy or of national character are involved . . . the censorship of films should be controlled by the Government.'[19]

Matters came to a head in 1928 and the then Home Secretary, Sir William Joynson-Hicks, actually wrote that he thought that the establishment of a state censorship board would be an inevitable necessity, however preferable the existing system might in fact be.[20] Extensive parliamentary debating took place over this issue and eventually resulted in a compromise in 1931 whereby a Cinema Advisory Council, made up of Chief-Constables, Justices and representatives of the local authorities, was set up under Home Office auspices to liaise with and advise the British Board of Film Censors.[21] The actual effectiveness of the system before 1930 in terms of actually keeping 'unsuitable' films, on political grounds, from reaching mass audiences had been considerable. Constant debates and complaints about censorship, thus advertising its existence, are inhibiting factors on the effectiveness of such a system: political censorship must operate as far as possible without public debate if it is to be effective — particularly if its purpose is to protect a liberal political system.

After 1931, in response to these problems and partly as a result of the appointment of Sir Edward Shortt, there came a change of policy. Instead of cutting or banning films already made, production

companies came to be encouraged to submit scenarios to the British
Board of Film Censors before they actually embarked on the making
of the film. This obviously made good sense as far as the production
companies were concerned: if the Board told them that the film they
proposed to make would not be passed they would save themselves
the cost of making it. By 1932 this system was operating with fair
efficiency. In that year the Secretary of the Board, Mr Brooke
Wilkinson, who served in that office from 1913 to 1948, except for the
war years during which he was in charge of the production and
distribution of films for propaganda in neutral countries, and an
ex-Northcliffe journalist by training reported:

> it is the general practice with producers in this country before
> they commence operations at Elstree or wherever the studios may
> be to submit to us either the story they propose taking or if they
> have no doubts about the story, the complete scenario. As a
> matter of fact at the present moment there are five film plots
> lying on my table to be dealt with this week.[22]

Five years later, on the occasion of the closure of the old Gaumont
Studios, the then President of the BBFC, in recording his sorrow
at the closure of 'an organisation with which the Board has had a
close relationship for years' could say: 'the scenario or synopsis of
every film produced by that vast organisation was submitted to the
Board for its observations before operations would commence in the
studio, and many were the letters of thanks and appreciation received
from them.'[23] In the same year Lord Tyrrell could also report on an
aspect of the work of the Board 'which I find of immense importance
. . . the weekly and monthly correspondence we have with the Empire
Censors. They certainly look upon the Board as the Mother of Censors.'[24]

The moving over from post-censorship, of films already made, to
the censorship of ideas for films solved the problem of quiet
effectiveness most satisfactorily. In 1937 the President of the Board
of Film Censors reported that, while they certainly would not ban
all films which some silly people regarded as subversive, there was
not 'a single film shown today in the public cinemas of this country
which dealt with any of the burning questions of the day'.[25]

The cinema audience was composed by the late 1930s of some
20 million people each week. They were predominantly from the
working classes, amongst whom nearly 80 per cent of the men and
women under the age of 35 went to the cinema at least once a week

or more often, and who in a period of massive unemployment and ideological challenge could so easily have been inflamed. But they were effectively and successfully kept from being subjected to the powerful impact of images and stereotypes designed to undermine their faith in the good intentions of their rulers and in the beneficial effectiveness of the political system under which they lived. Instead of powerful, emotionally backed calls for taking matters into their own hands, for viewing their government as their enemy 'class' or otherwise, and their plight as the result of the system of government, they were encouraged to regard their economic and social condition as a personal and not a political problem, to take a joy and pride in the institutions, historic and 'fair', of their country. In short, harmony and hope of better days, arising from the innate strength and justice of the system in which they lived, which was suffering only the temporary impact of a world-wide depression, were most successfully and effectively fostered. This was not done through counter-productive sermonising on 'propaganda', but through the exclusion of any alternative viewpoint from the medium which they regarded as their chief escape into a world of dreams. Dreams are powerful stuff and so are visions: visions of our country, of other lands and of the future. Censorship ensured that dreams were not turned into nightmares of doubt and distrust and that there were no alluring visions of alternative new orders.

How did such a wide-ranging, well-run and effective ideological censorship come to be accepted? Was there a consensus of opinion amongst the educated, politically influential groups in British society that, in order to defend the essentially liberal political institutions of Britain, it was necessary and acceptable that a comprehensive system of political censorship should operate in the cinema? Was this matter discussed and debated at all or was it something which had simply been quietly carried out by some group of faceless officials?

Awareness of the importance of propaganda in general, and of films in particular, was indeed widespread both at the Cabinet and at the parliamentary and civil service levels of government as a result of the experience of the First World War. As early as August 1918, for example, Stanley Baldwin spoke at length about propaganda in the House of Commons. He began by saying 'propaganda is not a word that has a pleasant sound in English ears' and, after outlining the wartime need for propaganda, he went on to say:

there is another aspect of this question which I wish to put before the House. Public opinion today has a far greater weight in the moulding of governments and of policy in various countries than it has ever had before and unless people have faith in their allies and have faith in their cause it is impossible for them to hold together.

Nor had he any illusions about the nature of propaganda work as being quite different from merely distributing literature or posters. He also, significantly, believed that it was something which could be properly carried out and assessed:

Propaganda work is very like anti-submarine work. It is work which is necessary, it is work as to which you cannot disclose to your adversaries how you are doing it and it is work that can be and must be judged by results.

Almost exactly 20 years later at the end of his political career, in the course of which, although an old man, he learned to use the cinema very effectively and as Prime Minister and Leader of the Conservative Party placed a great emphasis on propaganda in general and films in particular, Baldwin explained his understanding of the needs of the period over which he so largely presided:

Science has brought the nations of the world jostling together and ideas laugh at boundaries. And there are ideas so loaded with dynamite that they may blow systems which appear founded on rock into fragments. I need not tell you that such ideas are those of bolshevism and those propagated by the Nazis and the fascists . . . of one thing be clear, they cannot exist within the same boundaries of what you and I understand as democracy.[26]

Ramsey MacDonald, perhaps the second most important political figure who, together with Baldwin, dominated the interwar period, was also under no doubt whatsoever about the importance of propaganda in general and the cinema in particular. It was Ramsey MacDonald, in fact, who handled the negotiations with some of the newsreel companies and it is amongst his papers that the formal agreement between the Ostrer Brothers and the National Government is found, undertaking 'to place at your disposal the whole machinery of Gaumont British News, the Gaumont Studios and of the newspapers under our control'.[27] And, of course, it was MacDonald's administration which appointed

Sir Edward Shortt to the highly sensitive post of the President of the
British Board of Film Censors.

Neville Chamberlain, as Head of the Research Department and
Chairman of the Conservative Party, was directly instrumental in
developing the remarkably efficient and far-reaching cinema
propaganda organisation of Central Office.[28] It included such modern
devices as comparative field trials to assess the effectiveness of the use
of the cinema as compared with all the other means of party political
propaganda. Chamberlain worked in close association with Sir Joseph
Ball, head of the propaganda section of Central Office and later in
charge of the National Publicity Bureau. Central Office developed the
sound cinema-van (in fact the '1922 Committee' purchased in 1927
one of the earliest sound-film patents in Britain) and believed that
film propaganda was substantially responsible for the very much
larger majority gained in 1935 than had been expected. Albert
Clavering, who, as Organising Director of the Conservative and
Unionist Film Association, was in charge of Conservative film
propaganda, was knighted for his work after the election.

As far as the Liberal leadership was concerned, Sir Herbert Samuel
had been involved with the cinema and with censorship ever since he
introduced the 1908 Act which empowered local authorities to supervise
cinemas. He was Chairman of the Joint Committee of Both Houses on
Stage Censorship in 1909 and, as Home Secretary in 1916, he wished to
establish a state censorship board. When he returned as Home Secretary
in 1931, it was he who actually established the Cinema Consultative
Committee at the Home Office. At its first meeting he gave his views,
confidentially, on the tasks of film censorship:

Gentlemen, there are two issues before you upon which you should
concentrate. The first is the old question of the protection of
children and the question of the A or adult certificate. I am sure
I need not say to you much on that subject.

The second problem facing you is the very vexous question of
censorship, not on the grounds of morals but on the grounds of
politics where questions of propaganda arise. We do not want this
country to close its eyes to things that are going on in the world
and that intelligent people should be refused the right of seeing
films which are good in themselves merely because they have some
contentious element in them, of which most of us would disapprove.
We do not want them to be limited to private societies like the
Film Society for seeing these films, on the other hand we do not

want to have films exhibited which may give rise to great controversy
and perhaps lead eventually to breaches of the peace which would be
distasteful to a great many people: so we have to steer a very careful
line. The British Board of Film Censors is well aware of that.[29]

It is perhaps of some significance that only the first part of Sir Herbert's
speech was included in the official communique, but in an expanded
form.

There was an equally wide understanding amongst the vitally
important second level of the political world, the leaders of
parliamentary opinion. Here is, for example, Mr MacNeill, a good,
sound, long-serving Tory MP, speaking in August 1918 on the
effectiveness of propaganda:

> I entirely agree with what was said by an Honourable Member
> earlier in this debate that it was propaganda probably more than
> any other single fact, or factor, which brought about the disaster
> in Russia. However that may be, I do not know anyone who has
> examined the fact of the disaster on the Isonzo earlier in the year
> but can doubt that the overthrow of the Italian Army was almost
> entirely due to an extraordinarily successful propaganda which
> had been at that time pursued by the Germans and the Austrians.
> I go further — and I point to my own knowledge though I have
> some facts which I should not like to disclose — but I can
> certainly say this, that the opposite is also true that the great
> failure which the Austrians have more recently experienced when
> they had to recross the Piave was almost or very largely due to
> propaganda on our part.

And then about the cinema:

> I was surprised to hear objection from the Right Honourable
> Gentleman that the cinema was used to propaganda purposes. It
> seems to him entirely beneath the dignity of this country. . . . I
> think it is extraordinary that this modern up-to-date educational
> engine, the cinema, should be so scornfully spoken of. The cinema
> should be used by us as far as we possibly can use it. My Noble
> Friend, Lord Beaverbrook, is endeavouring to use the cinema as
> much as he can in, I believe, all parts of the world and I have not
> the slightest doubt that it is perhaps the most valuable means of
> propaganda. I believe that the money expended is the most

valuable expenditure that has been undertaken.[30]

In November 1918, in the course of the next debate about propaganda, it was argued by J.H. Thomas, the Labour front bencher, that 'There is I believe general agreement among all who are in touch with the industrial classes that whenever peace comes the problems immediately following it will not only be difficult but will require very delicate handling.' He appealed for restraint in any direct government propaganda during the forthcoming elections in case it made the authority of the new post-election Parliament weaker in the eyes of the industrial classes amongst whom there was much talk about 'what is called industrial action'.[31] Alfred Booth MP argued that, while he too 'would not like the Minister of Information to be doing much in this country during elections', yet 'I do say it is highly necessary that the department should continue its splendid work in foreign countries'. He enumerated the new countries in Eastern Europe and envisaged a cultural propaganda campaign. Also, 'Belgium has got to be re-peopled and re-established in industries and in universities and in schools'; they should be told what Britain 'has done for them and explaining our learning, our schools of philosophy as well as politics and even our business. . . . I would urge the Government', he concluded 'to spend more money. They spend too little on secret service and propaganda.'[32]

Here is Lt Com. Kenworthy, another long-serving MP who has been active all through the postwar decade, addressing the House in 1925:

Suppose that 95 per cent of the schoolbooks used in our schools were edited and published abroad. The position could not be more serious. I believe that a child learns more today from the cinema screen than from schoolbooks and that 95 per cent of the films shown in British theatres are American, German or in a very few cases French origin. I believe in internationalism. I want this to be universal. I want Art not to be one sided. I want Art to have a chance because the production of cinema pictures is a new Art. Do not let us make a mistake about that. Suppose 95 per cent of the newspapers of this country were edited, printed and published abroad. The position would not be very much more serious than is the position shown by the figures in regard to the use of foreign films in this country . . . nearly 20 million of our people go to the cinemas which is far more than read newspapers.[33]

In fact, the parliamentary debates show a high level of understanding of the nature of the cinema as a medium of communications of values and ideas and of the nature of the cinema as a medium of communications of values and ideas and of the nature of the audience upon whom it has a particular impact.

The third level on which the government of Britain functioned was that of the local authorities. The London County Council was by far the largest, most powerful and influential body which in matters of censorship, as in many others, carried very great weight indeed. It took film censorship so seriously that its committee dealing with the matter was headed by Sir Cecil Levita, the leader of the Council, and its members included all the leading figures of the political structure of the government of London. Perhaps the shortest route to explore its ideas concerning the censorship of films, within very extensive documentation over many years, is by looking at the case of the Cinema Societies. These consisted of groups of people who possessed an eminently responsible and adult interest in films, who, as such, acted as a particularly severe test-case for the justifications of film censorship in a liberal society. The Council decided to allow Cinema Societies to exhibit films not passed by the British Board of Film Censors — a course of action approved by the BBFC — but it insisted on itself censoring the films, by the following criteria:

> No . . . film shall be exhibited which is likely to be injurious to morality, or to encourage or incite to crime, lead to disorder, or to be in any way offensive in the circumstances to public feeling or which contains any offensive representation of living persons . . . or which contains subversive propaganda liable in any way whatsoever to endanger the tranquillity of any part of the territory of the British Empire.

In 1930 an attack by Labour members, led by George Strauss MP and Charles Latham, was launched in order to remove the last clause. In the course of a wide-ranging debate the opponents of the clause made the point that 'what may be subversive propaganda today may be the accepted philosophy of tomorrow', to be answered by the point that 'films which are subversive today ought not to be shown today, but tomorrow'. They also suggested that 'what is subversive propaganda will presumably change according to the political complexion of the majority of this council', which was answered by pointing out that the offending clause was a verbatim copy of

Clause 16 inserted by the *Labour* Foreign Secretary, Arthur Henderson, in the 1924 Treaty with Soviet Russia. That treaty itself, of course, is a highly significant indicator of the very serious views held about the importance of propaganda. But the most interesting aspect of the debate was the acceptance of the need for political censorship by both sides. Mr Latham, the Labour spokesman, for example, explained that he was perfectly content that provision in the licences should be made to secure entry for policemen to all shows of Cinema Societies because 'the showing on the films of propaganda (sic) of a subversive character, or indeed of other subversive matter, is surely a question for the Police'.[34] George Strauss, later Labour minister and the person who regarded it as a particular privilege to be able to introduce, in 1967, the Act which abolished the Lord Chamberlain's censorship of the stage, argued not that censorship of films should be abolished but that it should be more flexible and variegated. His views on film censorship in general deserve full quotation:

> In my view, the power of censorship of films is an extraordinarily important one. The number of picture houses has grown by leaps and bounds during the last few years, and the cinema has become a vital part in the life of all citizens, and the question of what films should be shown and what films should not be shown is a very important one and the power of the censorship is one which must be recognised in the effect it has upon the opinion and views which the general public of London are allowed to assimilate through the pictures.

He went on to argue for a system of graduated appeal against decisions and the strengthening of the machinery for wider discussion, in the case of difficult films, within a democratically elected Council. He also wished to draw distinctions between what was or was not effective propaganda, only the former of which needed banning. He quoted with approval the view of a critic concerning the (banned) film by Pudovkin, *Storm Over Asia*: 'The truth is that Pudovkin's film fails as propaganda because of its high quality as a work of Art.'[35]

Other members took a more down-to-earth attitude, summed up in the view of Mr Clyde Wilson:

> Surely it is not seriously contended in this Council that the Film Societies here in the heart of the Empire should have the right to show subversive propaganda. . . . If that is what Honourable

Members opposite are contending for, I shall be very pleased to do all I can against it.[36]

Finally, if we look at the views of those who were particularly concerned with moral censorship, such as representatives of social workers, teachers or churches, it is evident how often even these people also recognised the essentially political nature of film communications.

One such person was Sir Charles Grant Robertson, Vice Chancellor of the University of Birmingham and the leader of the so-called Cinema Equity Movement, which was specifically concerned with the impact of the cinema on children, apparently not in the least a political matter. The Cinema Enquiry Movement demanded that, apart from a tightening up of moral censorship, the government should itself produce films projecting desirable values and all films of which the 'general tendencies were undesirable.' Sir Charles said in 1931:

It is the general attitude of the individual that his or her subsequent values of life will be based [sic] and it is the values of life that ultimately determine conduct; the conduct of the nation as a whole. Any time you want to test what the voters of the nation can do, and practically they are now coincident with adults, they will be judging the issues — I am not thinking of political issues such as what should be the quota of wheat etc. — I am thinking of the great divergencies of opinion that are going to be decided upon these values . . . The extraordinary potency of this instrument of the cinema lies in the kind of sediment it leaves on the mind. We may be undermined slowly by degrees but very completely. The very basis of British civilisation, and I do not put it too strongly, is built on some fundamental ideas and certain fundamental standards upon which we build the British way of life and it is those fundamentals that the cinema is eroding.[37]

The Reverend H. Carter, of the Methodist Church, whose full-time job in the hierarchy was to be the 'cinema expert' and 'liaison officer' with American moralist organisations, extended the point made by Sir Charles Grant Robertson.

The men who have power of control over what is produced are not hundred per cent American, to use the American phrase — they are men who have themselves come from Central and Southern European countries, or whose parents did so and they have brought with them a very different standard of outlook from that of the Anglosaxon race. A little group of men of Southern European birth with no Anglosaxon standards of culture or morality have seized hold of the motion picture industry of the USA and it is their type of thinking which is going out to the nations and into our local cinemas.

He went on to paint a picture:

Somewhere in America, probably in Hollywood, the Paramount fingers are busy. First someone's actual fingers get down on paper the scenario of the play then Paramount fingers are busy drawing the necessary workers from all over the United States . . . and finally Paramount fingers are busy buying up our local cinemas . . . Impressing their outlook on life upon scores of millions of inhabitants of this planet and above all this country.[38]

The Chairman of the British Social Hygiene Council added a further dimension to the pressure of censorship: 'If you attend a number of trade shows in this country you will see to what extent the distribution business is also in the hands of representatives of Southern Europe in this country (sic)' and demanded that 'local authorities should be made to recognise the need for supervising the type of individual who may be the renter of a cinema house'.[39] Nor was this proposal utterly far-fetched in the context of the legal safeguards of British society. In 1916 the London County Council was taken to court for withdrawing the licence of a cinema chain on the grounds that the majority of its shareholders were of German origin. The judgement of the Lord Chief Justice, Lord Reading, upholding the right of the LCC to withdraw the licence, went to appeal, and the Court of Appeal unanimously approved Lord Reading's judgement. It was based on the very sophisticated grounds that, while each film exhibited by that company would be subject to censorship and thus would be blameless, the long-term impact of the mere selection and juxtaposition of *approved* films themselves could have a deleterious import on the minds of the audience.[40] Therefore enemy aliens, on those grounds alone, were properly prevented by the London County Council from owning cinemas.

The evidence is very strong indeed for indicating that the inter-war years in Britain were characterised by a sophisticated and intelligent

understanding of the potential of film as a means of political
communication. At the centre of power in Britain there was no need
to wait until some trendy filmologist or sociologist of the 1960s
would pronounce film to be the 'Subversive Art'. On the contrary,
the potential of film for subverting, or for reinforcing, the loyalty
of little-educated people was fully realised: and no chances were
taken in countering the damage it could have caused. An intelligent,
comprehensive and effective counter-propaganda operation was
established to deal with it, and did so.

Thus the first element of reality in feature film in Britain during
the interwar period is the reality of censorship: it controlled absolutely,
at least where it actually mattered, the relationship between external
reality and filmic reality. It defined what aspects of contemporary
reality could form the subject of a film at all. It defined what stereotypes
about the political system might or might not be put on the screen in
great detail. It determined the degree of verisimilitude the film makers
could employ about contemporary reality in finely calculated
measures. It ensured that the power of the screen could never be
utilised for shocking the public and that its great power for sowing
doubts and for alienating should not be released: nothing was allowed
which could subvert, nothing which could 'demoralise the audience'.

There is, moreover, no need for the historian, who wants to know
why the British cinema did nothing to question, to shake or to
subvert the political system, why there was 'hardly a film of the
period which reflected urgency', why films did not 'lay bare social
contradictions' and so forth, to wander into the territories of
sociologists, psychoanalysts, gestalt-experts. He needs only to
apply his own training and discipline: to find out from the
documentary evidence what happened in practice.

Film production and film distribution, which includes censorship,
the control of what can be shown to the public, are practical,
administrative matters — whatever degree of mystery may be involved
in the 'creative process'. We may not, as historians, be able to explain
why a poet sitting in his garret wrote what he did, when he did:
there are no records to study— which is *our* particular craft. But the
processes of film production and distribution do generate records and
therefore we can establish an historic reality within which the artistic
element of film making operated. That historic reality was, quite
simply, that anyone was free to make a film about anything he wished —
but only films which, in the opinion of a full-time, professional
body of long experience, did not carry political messages conflicting

with those of the government in any fundamental way could be shown to the 'great audience'.

Acknowledgement

I am grateful to Dr D.W. Spring of Nottingham University for reading, criticising and suggesting improvements to this paper, many of which I have incorporated.

Notes

1. For a thoroughgoing legal account of the development of film censorship in England, USA, India, Canada, Australia, Denmark, France and Soviet Russia, see Neville March Hunning, *Film Censors and the Law* (London, 1967). See also Richard Randall, *Censorship of the Movies* (Madison, Wisconsin, 1968), Olga Martin, *Hollywood's Movie Commandments* (New York, 1937), Dorothy Knowles, *The Censor, The Drama and the Film* (London, 1934), Jack Vizzard, *See No Evil* (New York, 1970) and J. Bancal, *La Censure Cinematographique* (Paris, 1934).

2. See Sir Campbell Stuart, *Secrets of Crewe House, The Story of a Famous Campaign* (London, 1920), which was a well-documented and only slightly popularised version of the official history of British Enemy Propaganda Department, and something of a best seller with wide influence. See also D. Brownrigg, *Indiscretions of the Naval Censor* (London, 1920). G.C. Bruntz, *Allied Propaganda and the Collapse of the German Empire in 1918* (New York, 1938) reinforced this view in a scholarly form. Wickham-Stead's memoirs published in 1924 emphasised the same view in a wider context: H. Wickham-Stead, *Through Thirty Years* (London, 1924).

3. Erich Ludendorff, *My War Memories 1914-1918* (English translation, Hutchinson, London, 1920), p.368.

4. Ibid., p.362.

5. Adolf Hitler, *Mein Kampf* (unexpurgated English ed. and translation by James Murphy, London, 1939), p.163.

6. See Bruntz, *Allied Propaganda*, for a discussion of those reports.

7. For a discussion of the views held in Parliament concerning propaganda in general and film propaganda in particular, see below.

8. The best account, as far as the legal and administrative development of Censorship in Britain is concerned, is Hunning's *Film Censors and the Law*. For a good discussion of other aspects, although not historically oriented, see Guy Phelps, *Film Censorship* (London, 1975). For wider aspects, and some parallels to this kind of arrangement in the case of the 'security' censorship of the press, see Paul O'Higgins, *Censorship in Britain* (London, 1972).

9. 'Just imagine the Home Secretary's position if every single film, as might be the case (if a state censorship board replaced the British Board of Film Censors), were to be the subject of a question to this House. It would be an impossible position.' *House of Commons Debates*, vol.214, col.579 (1 March 1928), Sir William Joynson-Hicks.

10. 'I have the power to prevent the importation of any film as of other matter which is injurious to the public interest or security. Such a power is very rarely exercised . . . the powers which I exercise against the importation of

foreign films are only in cases where the film is injurious to the public weal.'
H.C. Debates, vol.214, cols 1209-10 (8 March 1928), Sir William Joynson-Hicks.

11. British Board of Film Censors, *Censorship in Britain* (London, 1928).

12. British Board of Film Censors, *Annual Report* (London, 1930), pp.6-9.

13. O'Higgins, *Censorship in Britain*, pp.3-4.

14. By comparison, the morality-oriented Hays' Office Rules, 1930 considered this issue as one of 'Miscegenation (Sex relationships between the white and the black races'; as item 6 in subsection *Seduction* or *Rape* in Section II, *Sex*.

15. In those states in America where state censorship was practised in the 1920s there were some vaguely similar attitudes; for example, *Battleship Potemkin*, which was banned repeatedly in Britain (for there was no reason why a film should not be tried-on several times, in several versions, for different venues and localities) under all of these rules, was also banned in Pennsylvania on the ground that 'it gave American sailors a blue-print of how to conduct a mutiny'. Knowles, *The Censor, The Drama and The Film*, p.200.

16. The comparison with the Hays' Code is again instructive: 'The history, institutions, prominent people and citizenry of all nations shall be fairly represented.'

17. For an account of the political censorship of plays in the pre-First War period, see Knowles, *The Censor, The Drama and The Film*, pp.50-65, and for the anti-German and spy agitation and kindred phenomena see David Trench, 'Spy Fever in Britain, 1900-1915', *Historical Journal* (1972), p.359.

18. There are no biographies of O'Connor, Shortt or Tyrrell. For O'Connor and Shortt see the articles in the *Dictionary of National Biography*, for Tyrrell see P.M. Taylor, 'The Projection of Britain', unpublished PhD thesis, University of Leeds, 1978, and his forthcoming book of the same title (Cambridge University Press, 1981). O'Connor is the same T.P. O'Connor who is greatly regarded as the inventor of 'new journalism'; perhaps the most successful political, popular journalist since Paine.

19. Resolution of the Birmingham Justices, 4 January 1929, quoted Hunning, *Film Censors and the Law*, p.104.

20. Lord Brentford (Sir William Joynson-Hicks), *Do We Need a Censor?* (London, 1929), p.11. He also said the same with even greater emphasis after the death of O'Connor in speaking to the trade: *Bioscope*, (20 November 1929), quoted Hunning, *Film Censors and the Law*, p.128.

21. This body proved, despite the expectations to the contrary, not a liberal-ising public body at all but rather a confidential committee within the Home Office, conducting its business in secrecy: its papers are one of the clearest indicators of the actual concerns and operation of the censorship. PRO, HO 45/21109/695383.

22. London Public Morality Council, Private Cinema Conference, 12 January 1931. British Board of Film Censors, *Verbatim Reports* (1930-31), British Film Institute Library, p.35.

23. BBFC, *Annual Report* (1937), p.4.

24. Ibid., p.12. In 1932 The Imperial Conference on Film and Radio called for co-ordinating the censorships of the Commonwealth and Empire. Cmd 4175. The Chairman of the Subcommittee was Mr Cunliffe-Lister.

25. Ibid., p.16.

26. *H.C. Debates*, vol.109, cols.1000-1001; Speech on 'Democracy', 17 August 1937 in America and carried by all the newsreels: see John Ramsden, *Baldwin*, Inter-University History Film Consortium (London, 1979).

27. For the relations with newsreel companies and National Government film propaganda in general see the forthcoming article by Timothy Hollins, 'The Conservative and Unionist Film Association', *English Historical Review* (1981).

28. For Chamberlain's involvement and some of his views on film propaganda

see Alan Beattie, David Dilks and N. Pronay, *Neville Chamberlain*, Inter-
University History Film Consortium, Archive Series, no. 1 (1973).

29. BBFC, *Verbatim Reports*. Film Consultative Committee (26 November
1931), pp.2-3.

30. *H.C. Debates*, vol.109, col.1009 (5 August 1918).

31. *H.C. Debates*, vol.110, cols 2399-2400.

32. Ibid., col.2402 (5 August 1918).

33 *H.C. Debates*, vol.186, col.153 (6 July 1925).

34. Meeting of the Council of the County of London, 4 November 1930:
BBFC, *Verbatim Reports* (1929-30), pp.14-15 *et seq.*

35. Meeting of the Council of the County of London, 27 May 1930: BBFC,
Verbatim Reports (1929-30), p.18.

36. Meeting of the Council of the County of London, 4 November 1930:
BBFC, *Verbatim Reports* (1929-30), p.24.

37. Speech at the Birmingham Cinema Enquiry Committee Conference,
'The Cinema and Its Influence Today', 7 November 1930: BBFC, *Verbatim
Reports* (1930-31), pp.9-10.

38. London Public Morality Council Private Cinema Conference,
12 January 1931: BBFC, *Verbatim Reports* (1930-31), pp.19-21. The whole
of this speech, which includes evidence of many trips to the USA and elsewhere
(and much understanding of the way film works), is most illuminating for the
kind of interest and level of activity which lay behind the support of film
censorship on the part of many powerful pressure groups outside the immediate
political arena.

39. Ibid., p.50.

40. Cited in Hunning, *Film Censors and the Law.*, pp.87-9.

CASABLANCA, TENNESSEE JOHNSON AND *THE NEGRO SOLDIER* — HOLLYWOOD LIBERALS AND WORLD WAR II

Thomas Cripps

Times of crises in American history have often released social forces, weakened old structures and revived, in Herbert Croly's phrase, 'the promise of America'. During these epochs, the forebears of 'conscience-liberals' sometimes acquired unaccustomed power and influence that enabled them to press the federal government into service as an advocate of the oppressed. Among their ranks were the Abolitionist opponents of slavery, Radical Republicans of post-Civil War Reconstruction, the spiritual children of the Abolitionists who in 1909 formed the National Association for the Advancement of Colored People (NAACP), and the New Dealers during the Great Depression. During World War II the probability of a similar liberal mood increased and promised to extend into peacetime because liberal beliefs were seen as opposed to the political systems of foreign enemies, and therefore regarded as legitimate fruits of victory.[1]

'Conscience-liberalism' was a loosely defined political faith of the 1940s and 1950s that eventually became part of American public policy as a result of the inclusion of many of its beliefs in the propaganda slogans that expressed Allied war aims to American civilians. 'Conscience-liberalism' as it applied to racial matters began with a generalised support for 'the underdog', a wish for 'fair play' and a vague belief in an open society that provided equal opportunity for all its citizens. During World War II these tenets were broadened to include still less well-defined catchwords that called for unity of all Americans across lines of group and class, tolerance of group differences expressed as 'contributions' to American culture, and brotherhood.

The war provided additional scaffolding for liberalism in the form of advances in the technique and technology of propaganda and a buoyant faith in their ability to convert the faithless. Politically, the war brought liberals and Marxists closer than ever as a result of the 'Popular Front' that allowed the Soviet Union and the Western democracies temporarily to put aside ideological differences. Afro-Americans approached the seats of power coincident with these

political and technical changes because the war marked the first time
that they were conscripted and the government was therefore obliged
to give them a reason to fight.

Racial politics, then, moved from the perimeters of American
attention toward the centres of power. To some degree, motion
pictures reflected and reinforced this trend. In Hollywood movies,
blacks appeared almost as factors in a newly derived equation.
Elsewhere, liberals armed with a newly developed respect for the power
of 16 mm projectors and documentary films looked to a postwar era in
which the wartime catchwords — unity, tolerance, brotherhood — would
spread to classrooms, film societies, churches and trade union halls.[2]

The growth of the liberal spirit from privately held conviction to
government propaganda, supported by advances in the technology of
film usage, may be seen in the circumstances surrounding the three films,
Casablanca, Tennessee Johnson and *The Negro Soldier*, each one of
which must be taken as an exemplar of a stage of the trend. Any
number of films might have been chosen to reveal in a sampling the
drift of liberal strategy from personal faith, to activist intervention in
film making, to government action in the name of an admittedly
oppressed minority. In microcosm, the movies may be seen as
precursors of a line of political action that grew from belief to loosely
organised groups of political activists to an increasingly responsible
government that itself moved from courtroom advocate to protector
of civil rights to source of economic welfare. In this sense, the three
films and the other films for which they speak demonstrate the
usefulness of Richard Dalfiume's account of World War II as 'a
hidden revolution' that provided a scaffolding for the more famous
postwar civil rights revolution.[3]

This line of argument should not be taken as a naive assertion that
liberal reform proceeded headlong. Before 1942, most Hollywood
movies relied heavily on black images derived from ancient Southern
lore created to justify slavery and inferior status. Even well-intentioned
movies often branded blacks with the worst stigmata of Southern history.
D.W. Griffith himself imagined his infamous *The Birth of a Nation*
(1915) to be friendly to blacks. Later, when sound-film provided an
opportunity to present aspects of Afro-American life in a favourable
light to a national white audience, the three most ambitious projects
lapsed into Southern idiom. Although King Vidor's *Hallelujah!* (1929),
Paul Sloane's *Hearts in Dixie* (1929) and Marc Connelly's *The Green
Pastures* (1936) all enjoyed generous, if not unanimous, praise from
the black press, many black critics found them politically empty and

called for indigenous works created by blacks. Indeed, in the generation between the wars a lively 'race movie' industry provided an under-financed and poorly distributed alternative to Hollywood's outdated racial images. Thus, on the eve of war Hollywood movies spoke only through softly sentimental images from a rose-coloured 'plantation legend'.[4]

World War II signalled a revival of black political activity, an alliance with white Quakers and radicals in such groups as the Congress of Racial Equality that added up to 'a comprehensive pressure for Negro rights'. The air was filled with calls for unity, tolerance and brotherhood. As the historian Thomas C. Cochran characterised the era: '"Democracy" became the major slogan of the period' which provided, in John M. Blum's words, 'a prerequisite for wartime and postwar progress toward desegregation' and a motive for the government to act against 'at least some black grievances'. Roosevelt himself, never an enthusiast for racial reform, granted the connection between war and liberalism by asking Americans to refute 'at home the very theories which we are fighting abroad'.[5]

These two trends — white liberalism and black activism — surfaced in almost every medium of show business, including revivals of depression-era social dramas like *The Petrified Forest*, black versions of white music such as Mike Todd's *The Hot Mikado*, black works like Abram Hill's *Walk Hard* at the American Negro Theatre, racial radio programming that included talk-shows such as Roi Ottley's *New World A 'Comin',* and wider distribution of radical films such as Frontier Films' warning of eroding civil rights, *Native Land.*[6] In Hollywood, the trend began in small ways even before the war in films like Warner Brothers' pro-Allied *Confessions of a Nazi Spy* (1939). Conscience-liberalism peered through the cracks of David O. Selznick's *Gone with the Wind* (1939) which he fully intended to depart from the plantation legend. As he wrote in a memorandum: 'In our picture I think we have to be awfully careful that the Negroes come out decidedly on the right side of the ledger.' Moreover, he felt 'quite strongly that we should cut out the [Ku Klux] Klan entirely' rather than risk creating 'an advertisement for intolerant societies in these fascist ridden times'.[7] Despite displeasure at some portrayals, an astonishingly large number of black critics were 'not offended or annoyed'. Indeed, the NAACP organ, *Crisis*, found 'that there is little material, directly affecting Negroes as a race, to which objection can be entered'. The Left was less happy; the Communist Party, despite outward signs of internal debate, blasted the film as a 'rabid incitement against the Negro people'.[8]

Off the screen, Hollywood 'moguls' faced pressure for more direct messages. Symbolised by the NAACP's decision to hold its annual convention in Los Angeles, Walter White, executive secretary of the group, forged a strong link with Hollywood through the defeated Republican Presidential candidate, Wendell Willkie. By the opening of the convention Willkie served both as legal counsel to the NAACP and as Chairman of the Board of Directors of 20th Century Fox. The alliance resulted in a broadly phrased agreement by several studios to depict Negroes on the screen with greater variety and sensitivity. Of all the studios, 20th came to reflect the liberal temper through its production chief, Darryl F. Zanuck, who in the 1940s helped make the studio's logo synonymous with liberal 'message movies'. Throughout the war, Hollywood movies reflected the agreement or derived inspiration from writers who shared its principles. As Bette Davis recalled of her starring vehicle, *In This Our Life* (1941), a script written by Howard Koch, one of the authors of *Casablanca*: 'There was a first in this film. The Negro boy played by Ernest Anderson was written and performed as an educated person. This caused a great deal of joy among Negroes.' Every studio seemed to have its resident conscience-liberal who inserted political bits into otherwise prosaic material. Dore Schary, who recalled no influence from White's direction, asked his scriptwriter Robert Hardy Andrews to bury a Negro role in *Bataan* that would accent its call for patriotic unity while concealing it from Louis B. Mayer and the sales department.[9]

It is this personal intrusion of politics into the studio that *Casablanca* exemplified; like Schary's *Bataan* it spoke for its authors rather than its studio. The lines that American college students now know by heart gave compelling support to the American decision to join the Western alliance. The movie opens with Ferrari, proud 'leader of all illegal activities in Casablanca', lecturing the owner of the Café Americain. 'My dear Rick', he asks, 'when will you realize that in this world today isolationism is no longer a practical policy? – to which Rick replies, 'I stick my neck out for nobody.' The film is the story of the resolution of these two polar opposites in the last reel when Rick shoots the senior German military attaché in *Casablanca* in full view of a Vichy prefect who ignores Rick and merely calls for a perfunctory rounding up of 'the usual suspects'. In the last shot they embrace, with Rick predicting: 'Louis, I think this is the beginning of a beautiful friendship.' The American government's Office of War Information (OWI) wished for an even more pointed argument in favour of war, although Bosley Crowther in the *New York Times*, for one, guessed that 'It certainly won't make Vichy happy.'

It is not possible to allocate credit for the conscience-liberalism that made its way through the various drafts by Howard Koch and Julius J. and Philip G. Epstein; we can only say that Michael Curtiz, the director, took responsibility more for romance than for politics. Perhaps because of this division of labour, the racial thrust of *Casablanca* surfaced with less clarity and force than either its politics or its wistful romantic story.

None the less, running through the story is Sam, a black piano player, friend of Rick, a factor in the politics, and far more than mere furniture, atmosphere or musical accompaniment that he might have been in an earlier movie. In *Casablanca*, Sam sharpens the political issues. To Ferrari and the Germans he is no more than a pawn; to Rick he is a person — indeed, the script insists that 'as far as Rick is concerned, the Negro is a privileged person', a status supported by the fact that Sam owns a piece of the saloon. His solidarity with the plight of the multinational victims of the war is seen when the Vichy gendarmerie raid the place. As he plays his piano to soothe their panic the camera sweeps the room, taking in 'all types of people' tapping out the beat and singing along. Admittedly, Sam's demeanour is a little too old-fashioned to be taken for that of a revolutionary leader; nevertheless, he undercuts older forms of racial liberalism to America's new role in international politics. In one version the connection between American liberalism and war aims is made even more explicit. As the German officer, Strasser, expounds his 'theories about non-Germanic peoples', Rick interrupts, claiming that 'all the best theories are going down the drain these days'.[10]

Of course, *Casablanca* can hardly be taken for a ringing Magna Carta that quickened liberal hearts and converted the conservatives. But along with *In This Our Life, Sahara* and other examples of the studios' wartime tolerance of liberal messages, *Casablanca* helped make the 'movie colony' a centre of liberal advocacy. Indeed, sharp-eyed conservatives seemed to count every 'comrade' in movie dialogue as a sign of encroaching Communism, and engaged in cocktail party debates with the liberals. The director, Sam Wood, a founder of the conservative Hollywood Committee for the Preservation of American Ideals, once refused to work with Dore Schary because of his alleged 'Communist' affiliations.[11]

During the spring and summer of 1942 the NAACP accelerated the liberal trend by mounting a campaign to intrude directly into the film making process, a strategy launched by holding its annual

convention in Los Angeles despite pressure from the Office of Defense
Transportation to curtail needless civilian travel as a means of
conserving gasoline. Together Wendell Willkie, Walter White and the
production chief at 20th Century Fox, Darryl F. Zanuck, reckoned
that they might use the war as the occasion for a full-scale assault on
Hollywood's traditional Negro characterisations. 'I ought to have a tiny
bit of influence right now', Willkie told White. 'Let's go out to
Hollywood and talk with the more intelligent people in the industry
to see what can be done to change the situation.'[12] Their plan coincided
with other favourable circumstances: the abrogation of the Hitler-
Stalin pact brought Marxists and liberals into common cause;
Roosevelt began to express Allied war aims in social terms, even to
the point of taking action such as Executive Order 8802, creating a
federal Fair Employment Practices Committee which guaranteed
Negroes equal opportunities in war industries; OWI established a
Hollywood office; and the Pentagon ordered *The Negro Soldier* into
production.

White gave added momentum to the trend in public statements
such as his essay, 'Race — A Basic Issue in This War' in which he
argued that the need for unity gave 'our traditions of fair play and
equality . . . a new necessity'. Thus the war inspired blacks to seek an
alliance with movie makers. 'In the name of those ideas for which
all of us are now fighting, we ask that the Negro be given full
citizenship in the world of the movie', said White to the 'moguls'. In
his view, conscience-liberalism required constant prodding and the
penetration of the sources of mass communication.

By the summer of 1942, White had arranged several luncheons
and conferences at the end of which Zanuck confessed: 'I make one-sixth
of the pictures made in Hollywood and I never thought of this until you
presented the facts.' White seized the moment and called for films that
showed 'the Negro as normal human being and an integral part of human
life and activity'. In a few days OWI opened its Hollywood office and
joined the blacks as 'one of the opening guns' in a campaign pointed
'in the direction of consideration of the status of the Negro in the war
program.'[13]

Before the war only a handful of leftist documentary film makers
made such political linkages in such scattered films as *Native Land*
(1940), an alarm against the threat of restraints on civil rights,
produced by Leo Hurwitz and Paul Strand, the founders of Frontier
Films. Even then, Marxist class theory softened the racial aspects of
the film. As Hurwitz recalled: 'It is important not to indite the whole

white race and remove the class character of oppression.'[14]

By the middle of the war, left and centre put aside differences of ideology, if not their mutual suspicions. White himself not only spoke at the leftist-sponsored Hollywood Writers' Congress at the University of California at Los Angeles, a conference the trade magazine *Variety* counted as one of 'the attempts of many screenwriters to infiltrate "pink" and "red" propaganda into screenplays, but published in the NAACP's *Crisis* one of the speeches by Dalton Trumbo, one of the soon to be blacklisted "Hollywood Ten"'.[15]

The alliance between left and centre was an indicator of the general rising tide of political and social activity brought on by the war. Another example of the mood, *Tales of Manhattan*, revealed the sharpening political sensitivity of both actors and critics. Laden with sentimental Negro images, yet touched by conscience-liberalism, the film drew not praise but calumny from leftist critics such as Manny Farber of the *New Republic* who blasted its 'white lies', and from its star, Paul Robeson, who offered to picket his own movie. One imagines that before the war it might have received some sort of 'brotherhood' award.[16]

In keeping with the new spirit, between 1941 and 1944 movies grew from individual expressions of conscience-liberalism such as *Casablanca* toward those more consciously shaped by the alliance of left, centre, OWI, Hollywood and the NAACP, or at least Walter White. Blacks increasingly appeared as symbols of Allied war aims as expressed in the slogans of the Atlantic Charter, the 'four freedoms' speech and the catchwords unity, tolerance and brotherhood. In *Sahara, Crash Dive* and *Lifeboat* they fought German forces as a symbolic *quid pro quo* for which they expected a better lot in American life. *Stormy Weather* and *Cabin in the Sky* brought all-black musicals to appreciative white audiences and enthusiastic black ones. As bit actors and extras they appeared in a broadened spectrum of social roles. So rapid was the change, many Hollywood Negroes resented the NAACP and feared for their traditional 'bread and butter' roles.

The first film that felt the united front of OWI, NAACP, Marxists and Hollywood was *The Man On America's Conscience*, a 'biopic' of Reconstruction President Andrew Johnson and his *bête noir*, the pro-black Republican congressman, Thaddeus Stevens. More than any other film it cemented the political alliance — while also demonstrating that heartfelt politics rarely inspired great art. The issue at hand was not a black character but the treatment of Stevens.

Appearing only days after the NAACP meetings in Los Angeles,

The Man On America's Conscience outflanked the blacks' campaign.
David Platt, a veteran film aesthete and reviewer for the Communist
Daily Worker, warned White that two black papers had characterized
[it as a potential *Birth of a Nation'*, perhaps at first merely to needle
him for trusting the promises of Hollywood capitalists.

The *Worker's* critic, perhaps because of his long-term political focus,
correctly discerned the conservative angle of MGM's biography of
Johnson. As early as 1936 Marxist intellectuals James E. Allen's and
W.E.B. DuBois's revisionist view of Reconstruction had challenged
academic historians by taking into account economic and class factors
in Southern life. In their view Stevens was a populist hero in the
vanguard of a movement to provide economic underpinning to
freedmen in the form of 'forty acres and a mule' to be allocated by
the federal Bureau of Refugees, Freedmen and Abandoned Lands.
Conversely, they saw Johnson as a truckling catspaw of the former
Southern landed elite that subverted newly recognised freedmen's civil
rights.[17] Thus, in the midst of a world war purportedly against racism,
MGM rehabilitated a mediocrity at the expense of the hero of the blacks,
Thaddeus Stevens, an event hardly in keeping with the popular mood
that linked liberalism to war aims.

The Man On America's Conscience started out in 1939 as a brief
treatment of a 'sympathetic dramatization of the life . . . of one of
America's noblest, most under-rated and foully used great men'.
Andrew Johnson's humble roots were seen as the source of a stubborn
populism and personal ambition that was to be spoiled by the
'vindictive' Stevens. One early reader warned of its potential
conflict with wartime liberalism, calling it a 'tough subject to handle'
because of its casting Johnson and Stevens as symbols of good and
evil in a historical period 'which some of the Marxist (sic) crowds have
lately been trying to distort'. He warned the studio that 'one doubts it
would be politic to produce'.[18]

By May 1942 a conservative screenwriter, 'an Englishman and a
scholar', John L. Balderston, shaped Stevens into an authoritarian
usurper whose villainy offered a warning against the rise of Fascism.
Although a studio writer sought the advice of an informed Negro
writer, Balderston's was the version that director William Dieterle shot,
thereby setting off the summer-long squabble that drew the
Communist Party, the NAACP and OWI together in a pragmatic alliance
against the movie and conservative Louis B. Mayer.[19]

Mayer was more a Hoover Republican than a Fascist; he simply failed
to see the new meanings given the movie by the wartime political mood,

a naiveté probably shared by his writer and director. Balderston, a Briton who had settled into mere competence after three early gems, *Frankenstein* (1931), *The Mummy* (1932) and *The Bride of Frankenstein* (1935), had never written a political film. Dieterle had plodded through a career in Germany and Hollywood until he hit a streak of well-written biographical scripts to which he gave sensitive direction. His Warner Brothers' movies about Pasteur, Zola, Juarez, Reuters and Paul Ehrlich, discoverer of a syphilis remedy, were models of simplistic Horatio Alger-like aspiration.

Thus, in the hands of Mayer, Balderston and Dieterle *The Man On America's Conscience* blundered into a thoughtless confrontation with black activists. In keeping with the broad outlines of liberal strategy, Walter White in a statement released in August spoke of the film's impact on wartime morale. He demanded a copy of the script from Mayer, asked Mayer's daughter (Mrs David O. Selznick) and OWI to intercede, called upon liberal scholars to rebut the image of a villainous Stevens, and demanded a preview.[20]

In a protest to OWI, he painted Johnson as indifferent to liberal Reconstruction laws and tolerant to the 'black codes' used by Southern States to control Negroes after emancipation. He also called for a softer Stevens, less malevolent toward Lincoln, innocent of contributing to Johnson's reputed drunkenness, and neither card playing partner of Lincoln's assassin John Wilkes Booth, nor an *eminence grise* behind Booth's plot. As White phrased the argument to OWI: 'I strongly believe that the making of this picture at this time would do enormous injury to morale. It would, in my opinion, accent sectionalism which already is at a dangerously high point in Georgia and Alabama.'[21]

In the other camp, Mayer became 'completely upset' and blasted the affair as 'directly a result of the Communists'. What right had a minority to dictate to a studio; how many Negroes had actually seen the script, much less been offended by the Stevens characterisation, he asked. But he relented and granted White a preview.[22]

By autumn, under pressure from OWI and White the studio allowed Balderston a rewrite which Dieterle reshot, with the result that Stevens came closer to his image among blacks as 'the great commoner'. 'There was much reshooting and cutting', reported OWI to White in November. Andrew Johnson became the less politically charged *Tennesee Johnson* — the film's new title. Howard Dietz, an MGM vice president and one of its liberals, arranged for White to have a preview and even sought to hire a black publicist.[23]

The tenuous coalition risked winning the battle at the expense of

the war, for the incoherent movie that went into release promised to
make Mayer a bitter enemy of Negro interests in Hollywood. Indeed,
Nelson Poynter of OWI warned White to avoid the 'mistake' of
winning so easily that all of Hollywood might balk at further dealing
with black activists.

Tennessee Johnson went out and took a beating at the box office,
from carping reviewers and on the picket lines set up by more than
twenty Negro organisations. 'Perhaps white America needs this form
of hypocrisy to survive', explained a Howard University sociologist to
a Washington film distributor. John T. McManus of the newspaper
PM spoke for the left finding it a device 'to bring disorder into
the ranks' and a posturing, lacklustre period piece which will probably
never get to first base with movie audiences'. The more centrist *Time*
magazine probably agreed with the review but attributed it to a victory
for 'Negrophiles'.[24]

Walter White effectively co-operated with the coalition of left and
centre, OWI and black groups, thereby appearing to marshal forces that
demanded a broadening of black roles as a fulfilment of the pledges
of 1942. Thus the campaign against *Tennessee Johnson* was made to
seem a part of a movement of pervasive proportions against which
conservative forces could not possibly prevail. White's brand of
conscience-liberalism had thus taken a giant step toward a stage of
combining liberal sentiments with direct action in turn supported by
liberal elements of government agencies. *Tennessee Johnson* therefore
became far more important as a *cause célèbre* than as a film, largely
as a result of a pioneer testing of the eventual coalition of interests
that formed the centre of the modern civil rights movement:
conscience-liberals, organised blacks and government agencies.

By the end of 1943 the liberal mood had become so self-propelled
and commonplace that many liberal films owed no direct debt to
the political activism. William Wellman's tight little film of Walter
Van Tilburg Clarke's anti-lynching novel, *The Ox-Bow Incident*, for
example, owed its existence at least in part to its star, Henry Fonda,
who recalled that he 'browbeat' Zanuck into making it. *Mission to
Moscow* (1943), a film which featured Leigh Whipper as Haile Selassie,
the Lion of Ethopia, spoke not to conscience-liberalism but to the
strategic need to present 'our awkward ally', the Soviet Union, to the
American public. *Sahara* came from the typewriter of the Marxist,
John Howard Lawson, by way of a 1937 Soviet film by Mikhail Romm.
Sometimes the NAACP, fearing to loose its grip of the situation,
reasserted its presence through press releases that depicted each liberal

project as an 'outstanding contribution toward the objective stated by Mr White'.[25]

Thereafter the coalition began to crumble in a train of fortuitous events that revealed the continuing need to involve government agencies as dependable political allies. In the studios the vast collaborative system of film making impeded the flow of liberal messages downward from the executive offices. In the summer of 1944, for example, the Negro composer William Grant Still resigned from 20th Century Fox's all-black musical, *Stormy Weather*, in a bitter fight over the authenticity of the musical score. As he told White: 'It may happen that the big people to whom you talk are perfectly willing and eager to do something constructive, but their efforts are nullified by the little people at the heads of the departments.'[26]

Outside of the Hollywood studios the situation also deteriorated. Race riots in Harlem, Detroit and Los Angeles mocked the calls for unity, tolerance and brotherhood, and threatened to stall the release of *Stormy Weather* and other films. Zanuck, the most zealous ally in Hollywood, left to serve with the army in North Africa. Congress eviscerated OWI's budget, thereby reducing its influence in Hollywood. Finally, Wendell Willkie died shortly after the Republican Convention of 1944, leaving a void that White could never fill. 'With the tragedy of Willkie's death in 1944 most of those responsible in Hollywood for changing the pattern appeared to feel that the pressure upon them had been removed', he recalled in his memoirs.[27]

Momentum for social change shifted to other media. In publishing alone in 1943 and 1944 three books appeared that set an agenda for the future without recourse to movies: Roi Ottley's *New World A'Comin'* (New York, 1943), a black journalist's essay that became a pioneering black radio programme; Gunnar Myrdal's *An American Dilemma* (New York, 1944), a monumental anatomy of American racial life financed by the Carnegie Foundation; and Rayford W. Logan's colloquy of famous Negroes' demands, *What the Negro Wants* (Chapel Hill, 1944).

With the decline of Hollywood's attention to racial themes, many organised Negroes forged the last link in the chain of conscience-liberal politics by returning to the federal government as the advocate of last resort. Early in the war, the first in which blacks had been conscripted, Judge William Hastie, a black civilian adviser to the War Department, had complained of racial discrimination and violence in and around military posts. The army reluctantly commissioned *The Negro Soldier*, a film intended for both black and white troops as a means of teaching

the former a reason to fight and the latter a basis for unity across racial
lines. Organised Negroes quickly saw the project as a potential
propaganda weapon to complement White's work in Hollywood.[28]

After January 1944 the film became mandatory viewing for all
soldiers. Black leaders quickly pressed for a civilian version to be
released through OWI as a means of enlarging the audiences exposed
to its message of goodwill and harmony expressed in the various official
slogans. A high moment of the co-operation between liberals, blacks,
OWI and Hollywood, the film reached far beyond earlier pleas for
wartime unity. For example, a year after Pearl Harbor the Department
of Agriculture released Roger Barlow's *Henry Brown, Farmer*, a film
designed to show Southern blacks how to contribute to the war effort.
But like many well-meaning liberal projects, it only whetted Negro
appetites for more forceful statements. Claude Barnett, the black
journalist who had suggested the idea, complained of the 'insipid little
story far from our original purpose', while another critic asked bitterly:
'Is there only one Negro family in the war and is the only thing they
are doing farming?'[29]

The Negro Soldier was a different sort of film. Goaded by Hastie,
Secretary of War Henry L. Stimson approved the project which
revived the liberal coalition in the persons of scriptwriter and 'star'
Carlton Moss, Frank Capra, Stuart Heisler and other Hollywood figures,
Donald Young and Charles Dollard, social scientists with an interest
in race relations propaganda, and General Frederic H. Osborn, himself
a member of the Social Science Research Council. Together they
shaped a film without precedent, a government propaganda message
that spoke for the aspirations of a racial minority. White heard of
it at the time of his UCLA address and immediately saw uses for it
beyond the army's modest goals. 'This film is certain to be an
outstanding contribution to the morale of Negro troops and civilians,
an advance toward a better understanding between the races, and
a telling blow against Japanese race and color propaganda', he
predicted.[30]

The finished film presented the war as a struggle in which blacks
had an investment by drawing an analogy between the war and Joe
Louis's defeat of the German boxer, Max Schmeling, and by having a
Negro preacher read racist passages from *Mein Kampf*. Unfolding from
this premiss came a narrative of black participation in all of America's
wars since the Revolution, as though placing World War II in a great
tradition of black heroism.[31]

Even though the film ignored rampant racial discrimination in

America, black critics leapt at the chance to demand that the government distribute it to civilians. After previewing it for various audiences and cutting it by half, OWI acceded to Negro demands and released it to civilian theatres where, despite a lukewarm reception from leftist critics, *The Negro Soldier* enjoyed a run in several thousand largely Northern urban theatres and the accolades of most critics. Liberal activists attempted 'to rally the public and force the special film, *The Negro Soldier*, to be released in full to audiences of both races', a plea that resulted in yet another audience composed of churches and film societies who projected 16 mm film.[32]

Thus 'the greatest War Department picture ever made', as Harry Cohn of Columbia had dubbed it, became the vehicle that carried the wartime slogans of unity, tolerance and brotherhood to an unprecedented civilian audience. Its success inspired Moss and some of his team to develop a sequel called *Teamwork* that elaborated the message and together with *The Negro Soldier* became staples in the catalogues of the revived postwar 16 mm distributors. Years after the war these narrowly conceived, limited films continued to broadcast their message to conscience-liberals.[33]

Politically alert critics were quick to see such films as vehicles for carrying war-borne liberalism into peacetime for political purposes unintended by the army. 'It will educate every white American who sees it', said one leftist paper. Another reckoned its worth as greater than 'tons of material and volumes of the best anti-fascist speeches'. Moss himself hoped it would inspire white Americans to ask 'What right have we to hold back a people of that calibre?' Writers on the left hoped that, in Virginia Warner's words, it would be 'a pioneer in preparing further steps in the direction of screen reflections of national unity', that is, it would challenge Hollywood to produce a postwar era of conscience-liberal movies.[34]

The army's movies did not disappoint their liberal advocates. In the five years following the war they appeared in many catalogues of film distributors, reaching the same conscience-liberal audiences that were attracted to Sidney Meyers's *The Quiet One* and the many other evocative liberal documentaries which burst upon the documentary scene that had been, with a few exceptions, no more than a jute-mill for dull 'educational films' in the 1930s.

Thus in its way *The Negro Soldier* propagandised and thereby perpetuated the conscience-liberal sentiments generated by World War II. By carrying them to postwar audiences the film extended the life of these social ideas set loose by wartime crisis and allowed them to become part of a peacetime liberal agenda by means unavailable to the conscience-liberals of Reconstruction, the Progressive Era or the Great Depression.[35]

Moreover, *The Negro Soldier* and its impact, unlike conscience-liberal feature films such as *Casablanca* or films like *Tennessee Johnson* that were broken relics of battles fought off-screen, inspired and spoke to the exclusive interests of documentary film makers. Along with other documentary films, many of them supported by government funds or intervention, *The Negro Soldier* provided the political thrust that carried over into the peacetime era and helped create an artistic and political renaissance of 16 mm film in the work of Willard Van Dyke, Helen Lowitt, Janice Loeb, George Stoney and Sidney Meyers.

The line from *The Negro Soldier* to Hollywood's postwar liberal 'message movies' is less clear. Nevertheless, it can be shown that many Hollywood craftsmen who worked on war films cultivated a liberal sensibility that coloured their later work. For example, just after serving as 'script doctor' on *The Negro Soldier*, Jo Swerling wrote scripts for the anti-Nazi and anti-racist films *Crash Dive* (1943) and *Lifeboat* (1944). Darryl F. Zanuck, the NAACP's advocate in Hollywood, made *Pinky* (1949), the model liberal 'message movie'. Army films contributed to Carl Foreman's 'political development' which had grown from college days, to 'B' movies like *Spooks Run Wild* (1941), to Stanley Kramer's *Home of the Brave* (1949) with its black hero named 'Mossy' in small tribute to Carlton Moss. Kramer himself had worked in the army's production centre at Astoria, Long Island. Stuart Heisler, the director of *The Negro Soldier*, followed his military term with *Storm Warning* (1950), a polemic against the Ku Klux Klan.[36]

In the five years following the war Hollywood studios dissolved from a handful of major corporations into lots of independent units, many of which sought to extend the themes of feature films beyond mere entertainment. Supported by Supreme Court decisions that struck down monopolistic practices which had frozen out independents, and decisions that weakened local censor boards, the independents set the tone of Hollywood films by breaking away from sound stages, shooting on location, borrowing documentary style, experimenting with new genres such as *film noir*, seeking funds outside the industry, abandoning the 'star system', and taking up social and political themes. So effectively did their work alter Hollywood that congressional committees investigating alleged Communism in the motion picture industry may have constituted a conservative response to fears that old virtues of Middle America were being subverted by liberals who seemed to have engineered a *coup d'état* in the media of mass communication.

Thus the social forces unleashed by the dislocations of war instigated a scenario for the acceleration of a liberal political trend. Movies mirrored the trend at every stage of its development from the casual shots of Sam, the piano player in *Casablanca*, and other conscience-liberal movies, to the pressure-group power that grew in the years between *Tennessee Johnson* and *Pinky*, and finally to the penetration of a coalition of activists into government agencies which resulted in the making and distribution of *The Negro Soldier*. After the war the trend became self-perpetuating, raised the expectations of the faithful, drew new adherents as to a movement, and blunted most conservative counter-strategies. The movies that reflected the spirit of the times introduced their audiences, often in softly timid terms, to almost every aspect of the sociology of race in America; predictably few of them would be remembered as works of cinema art. The message of the film mattered more than its beauty of imagery. *The Burning Cross* warned against terrorism; *It Happened in Springfield* invited small-town citizens to stand up for conscience-liberalism; *The Boy with the Green Hair* excoriated racism through a clever allegory; *The House I Live In* preached to teenagers; *Crossfire* and *Gentleman's Agreement* attacked anti-Semitism, *Pinky, No Way Out, Lost Boundaries, Stars in My Crown, Intruder in the Dust, Home of the Brave* and others asked their viewers to accept Negroes into American society long before the Supreme Court did. In this sense, the conscience-liberal movies of the 1940s may have been the ideological preconditions of the modern civil rights movement.

Notes

1. In various forms 'conscience-liberalism' surfaced in former times as 'conscience-Whigs' who opposed slavery while lacking the political will to contend with it: President Theodore Roosevelt's characterising the ideals of the Progressive era as a matter of 'fair play'; and the often vaguely stated programmes of the Democratic Party of the twentieth century: The New Freedom, The Square Deal, The New Deal, The Fair Deal, The Great Society and so on.

2. Recent research has been synthesised and bibliographies appended in: Thomas C. Cochran, *The Great Depression and World War II, 1929-1945* (Glenview, Illinois, 1968), pp.104-6, 111-24, 175-88; Richard Polenberg, *War and Society: The United States, 1941-1945* (Philadelphia, 1972), pp.2, 29, 243, 208-9, 194-6; and especially John Morton Blum, *V was for Victory: Politics and American Culture During World War II* (New York, 1976), pp.38-9, 99, 130,

104, 120, and Ch.VI, 'Black America: The Rising Wind'.

3. Richard Dalfiume, 'The "Forgotten Years" of the Negro Revolution', *Journal of American History*, LV (June 1968), pp.90-126; see also his *The Desegregation of the United States Armed Forces: Fighting on Two Fronts, 1939-1953* (Columbia, Mo., 1969), *passim*. See also more specialised accounts in Harvard Sitkoff, 'Racial Militancy and Interracial Violence in the Second World War', *Journal of American History*, LVIII (December 1971), pp.73-89, and August Meier and Elliott Rudwick, 'How CORE Began', *Social Science Quarterly*, XLIX (December 1969), pp.789-99.

4. For a survey of the topic see Thomas Cripps, *Slow Fade to Black: The Negro in American Film, 1900-1942* (New York, 1977), *passim*.

5. Cochran, *The Great Depression and World War II*, pp.76, 103-6, 111-14, 124, 175, 181-8; Blum, *V was for Victory*, Ch.VI.

6. Derived from a survey of the show business trade paper, *Variety*, through the first war year, 1942. *Native Land* (Frontier Films, 1940) may be rented in USA.

7. David O. Selznick to Sidney Howard, 6 January 1937, in Rudy Behlmer (ed.), *Memo from David O. Selznick* (New York, 1972), p.151; see also Margaret Mitchell to Katherine Brown, copy, 6 October 1936, in Margaret Mitchell Papers, University of Georgia, Athens, Georgia; and a film 'treatment' by Sidney Howard, Howard Papers, Bancroft Library, University of California at Berkeley.

8. A broad sample of the press from left to right may be found in: Thomas Cripps, *'Gone with the Wind* in American Race Relations', unpublished paper; Peter Noble, *The Negro in Films* (London, 1948), pp.75-9; John D. Stevens, 'The Black Reaction to *Gone with the Wind*', *Journal of Popular Film*, II (Fall 1973), pp.366-71; and Cripps, *Slow Fade to Black*, pp.363-4 and notes. On the Communist response, see David Platt to Thomas Cripps, n.d. [March 1979].

9. Whitney Stine, with commentary by Bette Davis, *Mother Goddam: The Story of the Career of Bette Davis* (New York, 1974), pp.154, 161; telephone interview, Schary and Cripps, March 1979.

10. Howard Koch, *Casablanca: Script and Legend* (Woodstock, New York, 1973), *passim*.; Howard Koch, 'Notes on the Production of *Casablanca*', typescript in Koch Papers, Theatre Arts Collection, Wisconsin State Historical Society, Madison, Wisconsin; Julius J. Epstein to editors of *New York*, VI (28 May 1973), p.5; Ronald Haver, 'Finally, the Truth About *Casablanca*: It Keeps Playing and Playing – And Here's the Story behind the Story', *American Film*, I (June 1976), pp.10-16; Andrew Sarris, 'Those Wild and Crazy Cult Movies', *Village Voice* (18 December 1978), pp.60ff; John J. Croft, 'Casablanca Revisited: It Has Survived Its Directors', *Classic Film Collector* (Spring 1974), p.43; Mary Beth Crain, 'Casablanca: In Defense of What's-His-Name', *Media Montage*, I, 1, pp.12-17; Mary Beth Crain, 'Casablanca's Unsung Hero: A Conversation with Paul Henreid', *Media Montage*, I, 1, pp.18-25.

11. Political Hollywood can be seen only in fragments; two interviews with John Cromwell (January 1977) and Dore Schary (March 1979) were most useful.

12. Wendell Willkie quoted by Walter White in *A Man Called White* (Bloomington, Indiana, 1970), pp.199-200.

13. 'Race – A Basic Issue in This War', undated MS in box 278; White to Sarah Boynoff, copy, 12 March 1942, box 273; and other White-Boynoff correspondence, calendars, memoranda and minutes of meetings, box 31, 278, NAACP Records, Library of Congress, Washington, DC. On OWI, in addition to correspondence between White and Lowell Mellett and Nelson Poynter, NAACP Records, see Clayton R. Koppes and Gregory D. Black, 'What to Show the World: The Office of War Information and Hollywood, 1942-1945', *Journal of American History*, LXIV (June 1977), pp.87-105.

14. 'Native Land: An Interview with Leo Hurwitz', *Cineaste*, VI, pp.3, 4ff; Leo

Hurwitz, 'One Man's Voyage: Ideas and Films in the 1930s', *Cinema Journal*, XV (Fall 1975), pp.1-15.

15. *Variety* (9 February 1944), p.8; Dalton Trumbo, 'Blackface Hollywood Style', *Crisis*, LII (December 1943), pp.365-7, 378. For another black social usage of film see Lawrence J. Reddick, 'Movies in Harlem: An Experiment', *Library Journal*, LXVIII (1 December, 1943), pp.981-2. HWC, Proceedings, full cite, pp.14-18, 27, 32, 495-501, 629.

16. Georges Sadoul, *Dictionnaire des Cinéastes* (Paris, 1965), pp.76-7; Manny Farber, 'Black Tails and White Lies', *New Republic*, CVII (12 October 1942), p.467; *Amsterdam News* (New York) (15 August, 10 October, 28 November 1942); *Variety* (3 June 1942), p.2; Philip T. Hartung, *Commonweal*, XXXVI (29 June 1942), p.137; *PM* (28 September, 1942) (in Schomburg Collection, New York Public Library); Paul Robeson, *Here I Stand* (London, 1958), p.39; Thomas Cripps, 'Paul Robeson and Black Identity in American Movies', *Massachusetts Review*, XI (Summer 1970), pp.468-85. Cameraman Arthur Miller remembered his work only as 'a Sunday shot of a Negro minstrel band': see Charles Higham, *Hollywood Cameramen: Sources of Light* (Bloomington, Indiana, 1970), p.154. As early as 13 October 1942, the *New York Daily News* labelled Robeson a 'Communist' because of his opinion of the movie.

17. James S. Allen, *Reconstruction: The Battle for Democracy 1865-1876* (New York, 1937); and W.E.B. DuBois, *Black Reconstruction in America, 1860-1880* (New York, 1935, 1964); David Platt to Walter White, 8 August 1942; *Daily Worker* (2 August 1942), in NAACP Records.

18. Holograph notes with page references, n.d.; Dieterle, unlike Balderston, enjoyed a reputation as a liberal, having done Walter Wanger's *Blockade* (1938), an early alarm against impending war. Nelson Poynter to 'Dear Walter', 28 August 1942, in box 276, NAACP Records.

19. Interview, Carlton Moss and Thomas Cripps, telephone, 6 July 1977, in which Moss recalled screenwriter Tony Veiller introducing him to Balderston in order to offer him a sketch for a friendlier treatment of Stevens.

20. Walter White to Louis B. Mayer, copy, 3 August 1942; White to 'Dear Irene' [Selznick], copy, 4 August 1942; Mayer to White, 19 August 1942, agreeing to a 'rough cut' preview; White to Lowell Mellett, OWI, copy, 17, 24 August 1942; White to Mrs Charles E. Russell, copy, 20 August 1942; Lucy Stewart to White, copy, 24 August 1942; White to Nelson Poynter, copy, 26 August 1942; in box 276, NAACP Records.

21. White to Lowell Mellett, copy, 17 August 1942; White to Nelson Poynter, copy, 26 August 1942; Poynter to White, 28 August 1942, in box 276, NAACP Records.

22. Poynter to White, 28 August 1942, in box 276, NAACP Records.

23. [?] Wills, 20 June 1939; memorandum to Mr McKenna, 'confidential', on *The Man on America's Conscience;* John L. Balderston, 'Andrew Johnson: The Man on America's Conscience', 20 May 1942; Balderston to Dieterle, 3 September 1942, in Dieterle Papers, Doheny Library, University of Southern California, Los Angeles; Howard Dietz to Walter White, 16 September, 5 November 1942, in box 276, NAACP Records.

24. Nelson Poynter to White, 3 November 1942; White to William R. Hastie, wire, 20 November 1942; White to Howard Dietz, copy, 27 November 1942; William R. Hastie, 'Memorandum Concerning *Tennessee Johnson*' [27 November 1942]; George B. Murphy, Jr, National Negro Congress, to White, 11 December 1942; Dietz to White, 2 December 1942 (quoting Mellett); MGM press release, n.d.; Ernest E. Johnson, 'Fight on Film *Tennessee Johnson* to be Waged', n.d. (in Barnett Papers, Chicago Historical Society); Release No. 91; *Variety,* (30 December 1942), p.7; *Amsterdam News* (New York) (10 December 1942); H.G. Barbes, Lichtman Theatres, to White, 23 February 1943; E. Franklin

Frazier to Lichtman Theatres, copy, 22 February 1943; *PM* (13 January 1943), in box 276, NAACP Records; *Time*, XLI (11 January 1943), p.88.

25. Thomas Kiernan, *Jane: An Intimate Biography of Jane Fonda* (New York, 1973), p.22; George Bluestone, *Novels into Film* (Baltimore, 1957), Ch.VI; Howard Koch in discussion at Woodrow Wilson International Center for Scholars, Washington, DC, 21 June 1977; Corliss Lamont, National Council of American-Soviet Friendship, to White, wire, 26 May 1943; Herman Shumlin to White, 1 June 1943; White to Walter Wanger, 23 April 1943, in box 274, NAACP Records; John Howard Lawson, *Film: The Creative Process* (New York, 1967), pp.140-2; Sue Lawson to Thomas Cripps, 3 December 1977; press release, 'Columbia Pictures Praised for Ingram Role in *Sahara*', 17 February 1943, box 274, NAACP Records.

26. *Los Angeles Tribune* (15 February 1943); William Grant Still to Walter White, 2 June 1943, in box 279, NAACP Records.

27. Blum, *V was for Victory*, pp.199-207; *Amsterdam News* (New York) (31 July 1944); *Chicago Defender* (31 July 1943); White to Darryl Zanuck, wire, 2 July 1943; Jason S. Joy, 20th Century Fox, to Roy Wilkins, 31 March 1944, in box 273, NAACP Records; White, *A Man Called White*, p.202.

28. A thorough analysis of this project is in Thomas Cripps and David Culbert, '*The Negro Soldier:* Film, Social Science, and Changing Patterns of Race Relations in America During World War II', *American Quarterly*, XXXI (Winter 1979, No.5); a briefer account is in Thomas Cripps, *Black Film as Genre* (Bloomington, Indiana, 1978), Ch.V.

29. Claude A. Barnett, Associated Negro Press, to Victor Roudin, copy 26 March 1953, in Barnett Papers, Chicago Historical Society; William Ashby to Elmer Davis, OWI, box 1431, entry 264, RG 208, National Records Center, Suitland, Maryland.

30. Interviews between Cripps and Frank Capra, 31 December 1976, La Quinta, California, and telephone, 18 January 1977; David Culbert and Donald Young, 13 February 1977; Frank Capra, *Name Above the Title* (New York, 1971), pp.326-8; Writers' Congress, *The Proceedings of the Conference Held in October 1943 under the Sponsorship of the Hollywood Writers' Mobilization and the University of California* (Berkeley, California, 1944).

31. The film is in Motion Picture Section, Archives of the United States, Washington, DC.

32. The complex debate over both mandatory viewing by troops and eventual civilian distribution is reflected in the documentation of Cripps and Culbert, '*The Negro Soldier*'. For critics see *New York Times* (22 April 1944); *Nation* (11 March 1944), p.316; *Time* (27 March 1944), pp.94, 96; *Negro*, II (September 1944), p.94.

33. Cohn quoted in Truman Gibson to Anatole Litvak, 14 April 1944, proj. 6024, 062.2 ocsigo, box 12, A52-248, National Records Center, Suitland, Maryland. The extent of Moss's participation is derived from army correspondence supported by numerous personal interviews.

On the growth of 16 mm film, see: Film Council of America, *Sixty Years of 16 mm Film, 1923-1983: A Symposium* (Evanston, Illinois, 1954), pp.148-59; Dorothy E. Cook and Eva Rahbek-Smith, *Educational Film Guide* (New York, 1945), p.152; [Iris Barry], 'Films from the OWI, Domestic Branch', n.d. [March 1946], central files, Museum of Modern Art, New York. *Teamwork* is in Motion Picture Section, Archives of the United States, Washington, DC.

34. Clippings in Box 277, NAACP Records; Schomburg Collection of New York Public Library; and Carlton Moss Papers, examined through the courtesy of Moss.

35. A brief survey of the era is in Thomas Cripps, 'The Death of Rastus: Negroes in American Films Since 1945', *Phylon*, XXVIII (Fall 1967), pp.267-75.

36. Interviews, Carl Foreman and Cripps, telephone, 12 July, August 1977; Abraham Polonsky and Cripps, telephone, 20 July 1977; Carlton Moss and Cripps, telephone, 6, 8 July 1977; Stanley Kramer and Cripps, telephone, 11 July 1977; and Stuart Heisler and Cripps, telephone, August 1977.

8 HOLLYWOOD FIGHTS ANTI-SEMITISM, 1945-1947

K.R.M. Short

When the United States threw the full force of its industrial and military might into the Second World War, it did so with the idealistic fervour that had motivated its intervention in Europe only a generation before. With war raging in the Pacific, in Europe and in the shipping lanes of the Atlantic, Hollywood made a conscious effort to create a sense of solidarity amongst the nation's racial and ethnic groups (excepting the Japanese-Americans and the blacks) reflecting the composition of America's citizen army of men and women in the factories, on the land and at the battlefronts. At the same time the movie industry sought to minimise the differences which existed between America and its allies, particularly Great Britain (*Mrs Miniver* and *The White Cliffs of Dover*), and, with greater difficulty, the Soviet Union (*Mission to Moscow, North Star, Song of Russia*).[1] Thus mobilised, sacrificing production standards to cuts in manpower and budget to conform to governmental guidelines, the movie studios found themselves accepting a far greater social and political responsibility than that originally contemplated by their production Code of Ethics.

During 1940, films such as Charlie Chaplin's *The Great Dictator* and MGM's *The Mortal Storm* depicted, with varying degrees of success, the Nazi persecution of the Jews. As the war progressed, Warner Brothers and 20th Century Fox added an important dimension when Jews began to appear in their films as recognisable and valued American citizens. *Action in the North Atlantic* (Warner Brothers, 1943) told the story of the heroic crews of Murmansk-bound merchant ships, fighting the weather and the U-boats. Sam Levene, as 'Chips Abrahams', portrayed a sympathetic Jewish merchant seaman. *Air Force* (Warner Brothers, 1943) featured George Tobias as Corporal Weinberg. Tobias was to appear the following year in *Objective Burma* as one of that group of intrepid American paratroopers led by Errol Flynn. While Tobias had become 'one of the guys', William Prince played the now increasingly common Jewish role, promoted in rank, as Lieutenant Jacobs. 20th Century Fox took its social conscience in hand and admitted the existence of American Jews in the film version of Moss Hart's (also Jewish) *Winged Victory*. The cast included such leading Jewish players as Judy Holliday, Lee J. Cobb and Red Buttons. Other

157

films of this sort which recognised the Jewish presence in the American
war effort included 20th Century Fox's *A Walk in the Sun* (1945) and
Guadacanal Diary (1943), with the laurels for the most unusual
portrayal going to *Bataan* (1943). In that film Thomas Mitchell played
his usual Irish iron-man in his portrayal of Corporal Jake Feingold.
According to Henry Popkins, the best role of a Jewish fighting man was
the characterisation by Sam Levene of Lieutenant Wayne Greenbaum
in Darryl F. Zanuck's *The Purple Heart.*

When Zanuck returned to Hollywood after a tour of duty as a
lieutenant colonel with the Signal Corps in the Aleutian Islands, he
thought that Americans generally minimised the Pacific War as being
little more than a sideshow to the European theatre. Hoping to
re-educate public opinion, he decided to make a film about the illegal
trial of eight American airmen captured by the Japanese after General
James Doolittle's famous B-25 bomber raid on Tokyo on 18 April
1942. The eight flyers had been tortured to find out where Doolittle's
16 bombers had come from; the four that survived the torture were
tried as a propaganda exercise claiming American war crimes against
a civilian population (reminiscent of similar incidents during the
Korean War ten years later). Supplied with information by two
newsmen who had been in Tokyo jails at the same time, Zanuck,
writing under the name Melville Crossman (he had started out in movies
as a screenwriter for the highly successful *Rin Tin Tin* series), created a
story which was, according to *The New York Herald Tribune's* (5 March
1944) 'high military authorities', the 'best job of second guessing . . .
that Hollywood has ever done'. That notwithstanding, Zanuck was
refused the official permission which he sought from Washington to film
the story. Gambling that this was only a temporary situation, production
began in late summer 1943 with a total studio information blackout on
the film. By the time shooting was completed the government had
released the detailed reports on the unbelievable suffering of
American prisoners at the hands of the Japanese and Zanuck was
able to release the film almost immediately.

The title, *The Purple Heart*, referred to the award founded by
General George Washington during the American War of Independence.
The opening dedication was to all Americans 'who have given and are
giving, their life's blood for the United States'. Zanuck sought to define
who the Americans were that displayed the small flags in their front
windows indicating men and women in the service: red stars for
those serving and gold stars for those who had already given their lives.
The names of the eight flyers indicate clearly Zanuck's America: Captain

Harvey Ross (Dana Andrews), Lieutenant Angelo Canelli (Richard
Conte), Sergeant Howard Clinton (Farley Granger), Sergeant Jan
Skvoznik (Kevin O'Shea), Sergeant Martin Stoner (John Craver),
Lieutenant Peter Vincent (Donald Barry), Lieutenant Kenneth Bayford
(Charles Russell) and, finally, Lieutenant Wayne Greenbaum (Sam
Levene). These were the men from two of the downed B-25s, men
who represented White Anglo-Saxon America, as well as the immigrant
communities of the Irish, Italians and Poles, and the religious beliefs
of Protestantism, Roman Catholicism and Judaism. Except for a
brief sequence, in which one of the crews parachutes into
Japanese-occupied China, and some domestic flashbacks, the film is
set in the courtroom and the cell. As the Japanese Army and
Navy fought to place the blame on each other for the failure to
prevent the raid, Ross ('the Texan') was the American crew's democratic
leader, while Greenbaum provided both humanity and the voice of the
law. Navigator for one of the two crews, Greenbaum was a graduate
of the City College of New York, that city's subway university for
its aspiring masses of second-generation hypenate Americans.
Greenbaum was not a pampered WASP graduate from Harvard or
Princeton but a New York Jew who took his law degree the hard
way. In the first of the courtroom scenes, Greenbaum challenges
the legality of the court, quoting from memory the entire
prisoner-of-war clause from the Geneva Convention. The flyers
never reveal that strike-base Shangrila was the US Aircraft Carrier
Hornet, nor do they 'confess' to the supposed war crimes. They
are executed.[2]

The reviewers were prepared to acknowledge Zanuck's anti-
Japanese propaganda; of equal significance must be his pro-American
propaganda of an (almost) all-American crew with its Jewish lawyer
defending his tortured comrades against hopeless odds with only
his legal training to sustain him. The movie did not garner either
Academy Awards or nominations. Zanuck received the Irving
G. Thalberg Memorial Award for 'outstanding motion picture
production' in 1944 (he had been the first recipient in 1937 and
received the award again in 1950), a fitting reward, it might seem, for
the courage to make *The Purple Heart* the way he wanted to. The
film was specifically produced as propaganda but its release at the
Roxy Theatre in New York at the beginning of March 1944 provides
a cautionary tale for the aspiring propagandist. The movie was shown
with the usual newsreel, but, in addition, the audience was treated to
the Roxy's stage show — a fact mentioned by most reviewers. The

following quotation comes from Eileen Creelman's review in the *New York Sun* and includes the closing sentence from the film review, carrying on with the stage show (an abbreviated account in comparison with most reviews). The contrast is self-evident.

> ... This is an agonizingly painful story vividly told.
>   The Roxy's vaudeville show features Count Basie and his orchestra, Carol Bruce, the Berry Brothers, James Rushing, Earle Warren, Jo Jones and Thelma Carpenter, Frank Paris, the Ben Yost Singers, the Gae Foster Roxyettes, Zero Mostel, and Paul Ash with the Roxy Theater orchestra.

A curious combination: Japanese atrocities and Zero Mostel's comic impressions of well-known actors; beautiful dancing girls, swing music and GI heroism. Curious, but perhaps in the American mind of 1944 that Roxy stage show may have symbolised a large part of what they were all fighting for.

As the war drew to a close, Jerry Wald at Warner Brothers resolved to have a more forceful treatment of the 'Jewish problem'. The film would show both the heroism of a Jewish Marine in the South Pacific and his own fears that the peace, which he had been fighting to win, would be clouded with the anti-Semitism he had faced in his youth. *Pride of the Marines* was taken from a book by Robert Butterfield, with the adaptation by Marvin Borfield and the script by the Communist screenwriter Albert Maltz. The star was the Jewish actor John Garfield, cast as the rough and tough working-class Al Schmidt. The love interest was supplied by Eleanor Parker (Ruth) whom he convinces that he is really lovable, especially when hunting – his favourite pastime. When Pearl Harbour is attacked, Al decides that it would be 'more fun shooting Japs than bears!' He joins the Marines and finds himself with the rest of his machine gun crew on Guadacanal where intercut newsreel material adds a marginal note of authenticity in a film very short on battle realism. Symbolically the 30 cal. machine gun has a shamrock, the word 'Chief' and the Star of David painted on the side of its breech. When the Jewish crew member, Lee Diamond (Dane Clark) is wounded, Schmidt is forced to fight the gun alone at night against a Japanese counterattack. An exploding hand grenade blinds him but he fights on, repulsing the attack. He and Diamond are to win the Navy Cross for killing 200 Japanese. There is no cool heroism portrayed as Schmidt seemingly goes beserk, while firing the machine gun through the night.

Schmidt and Diamond are sent to a Naval Hospital in California. Here Virginia (Rosemary DeCamp, whose voice was known to millions of radio listeners as Dr Christian's 'nurse'), a Red Cross worker, tries to wrench Schmidt out of his self-pity to face probable permanent blindness. Here director Delmar Davies anticipated the central theme of William Wyler's *The Best Years of Our Lives* (1946) with a sensitive set piece of a dart-game where the recuperating Marines express their doubts as to their ability to return to society. Fears are expressed about their wives, as well as their jobs. 'Irish' from Milwaukee says that he has a street corner all picked out; like his father before him, he expects to be an unemployed veteran selling apples. Al Schmidt offers to join him selling pencils – the usual job for the blind. It is Lee Diamond that breaks in: 'Ah, come on, climb out of your foxholes, what's a matter you guys, don't you think anybody learned anything since 1930? Think everybody's had their eyes shut and brains in cold storage?' The GI Bill of Rights is cited as evidence that they are going to have a shot at a new life and a college education as well as the guarantee of their old jobs; to which one man bitterly replies that his old boss is in a new business and his old job 'just ain't'. Another says that when he gets back to El Centro he will find that a Mexican has got his job. The racial jibe is caught by a wheelchair-bound Mexican-American Marine, Juan. It is Diamond that calls down the racist remark, saying that Juan has spent more time in combat than the other man in the Marine Corps. The bitterness of the group, fearing apples and bonus marches, is not modified by Virginia's plea to trust the people who are their own families and friends. Again Diamond comes in to say that just because they have fought the war they cannot expect a free ride:

> I fought for me, for the right to live in the USA. And when I get back into civilian life if I don't like the way things are going, O.K. it's my country; I'll stand on my own two legs and holler! if there's enough of us hollering we'll go places – Check?

After establishing the need for political involvement to prevent another war, Diamond proceeds to 'wrap it up' with the background music slowly coming up with 'America the beautiful'':

> One happy afternoon when God was feeling good, he sat down and thought of a rich beautiful country and he named it the USA. All of it Al, the hills, the rivers, the lands, the whole works. Don't tell

me we can't make it work in peace like we do in war. Don't tell me
we can't pull together. Don't you see it guys, can't you see it?

Schmidt tries to speak with Ruth because of his blindness, but he is
ordered to the Philadelphia Naval Hospital. As the train approaches
Philadelphia, Diamond compares Al's physical disabilities with those
he has suffered as a Jew. He accuses Al of being 'a hopped up kid
looking for excitement' – not a hero. Diamond says that some had to
die and others be maimed but they were not 'suckers' but 'had lost some
chips in the winning'. Al replies that Lee has no problems to which Lee
replies:

> That's what you think. Sure there will be guys who won't hire you
> even when they know you could handle the job. But there's guys
> who won't hire me because my name is Diamond instead of Jones;
> because I celebrate Passover instead of Easter. Do you see what I
> mean? You and me, we need the same kind of world, a country to
> live in where nobody gets booted around for any reason.

It is Lee who arranges with Ruth for the reconciliation, thus
completing the pivotal role he plays in the film. Al eventually accepts
his blindness, although the realistic edge is considerably blunted by
a partial return of his sight at the end of the film. Al Schmidt is a
hero in the foxhole but the real strength and optimism is that of
Diamond; Lee Diamond is both a Marine hero and a Jew. He is a man
who has known prejudice but almost alone of the wounded Marines
in the hospital holds out the promises of the American dream against
the pessimism of his comrades. The parting words of Schmidt and
Diamond are *Shalom Aleichem* – Hebrew for 'Peace be with you'.
The role of Lee Diamond was without any doubt the most important
Jewish role in the American cinema up to 1945.[3] It would be two more
years before another equally articulate Jewish hero would appear,
and then it would be John Garfield in *Gentleman's Agreement* (1947).
   The Pride of the Marines (although a commercial 'smash') did not
figure in the major Academy Award nominations that year, which
were dominated by Billy Wilder's *The Lost Weekend* (Paramount),
sweeping best picture, best direction and best actor. While *Pride* was
making a straightforward statement on the American Jew, in *The Lost
Weekend* the writer Don Birnam (Ray Milland) staggers down New
York's Third Avenue clutching his typewriter looking for a pawnshop.
In the novel he found out from two Jews in their 'Sunday best' that

all Jewish-owned pawnshops were closed for Yom Kippur and that was all. In the screen version Birnam cries: 'What about Kelly's and Gallagher's [other pawnshops]?' They explain: 'They keep closed on Yom Kippur and we don't open on St Patrick's', which was to say that the Jews at least were no more peculiar than the Irish. At best it was an apologetic approach to the role of the Jew as a despised pawnbroker.

Warners also released *Rhapsody in Blue* in 1945 – the life of the Jewish composer George Gershwin. The Jewishness of his family is made 'vaguely evident by tearfully playing an occasional Jewish melody in the background and by using for comedy purposes a limited number of Jewish attitudes, some of which are pretty funny' (*New Republic*, 23 July 1945). *Time* (2 July 1945) was pleased that the film managed not to wallow in melodrama while picturing a

> warmly devoted, richly accented Jewish family on New York lower East Side without slobberings of sentiment or catalepsies of caricature . . . As card-playing Papa Gershwin, Morris Carnovsky blends humility, humor and awesome respect for his gifted son. ('How nice you write it out, Georgie, such black ink', he says, while examining in incomprehending wonder George's first musical manuscript.)

Ira Gershwin, played by Herbert Rudley, and George's piano teacher, Professor Frank, by Albert Basserman, are both instances of sensitive casting but Rosemary DeCamp was certainly not what one expected for Momma Gershwin. The screenplay by Howard Koch and Elliot Paul had to struggle with the basic requirement of playing as much of Gershwin's marvellous music as possible in the two hours of the film's running time. In a film filled with musical giants such as Al Jolson and Paul Whiteman, the figure of Oscar Levant, playing himself, came across with great strength. Levant's biting self-depreciating humour was the fulfilment of the audience's expectations of the witty Jew in both tone and appearance. All in all, Warner's bio-musical provided a sympathetic picture both of the composer who died at the age of 38, and of his Jewish family and friends, including his Gentile girlfriends, played by Alexis Smith and Joan Leslie.[4]

In the summer of 1946 Dore Schary released *Till the End of Time* (RKO), starring Dorothy McGuire, Guy Madison, Robert Mitchum and Bill Williams; the Edward Dmytryk film was basically about the problems of rehabilitating veterans. Allen Rivkin's screenplay brought the story to its climax in a cheap bar where the ex-Marines Mitchum

and Madison are playing the pinball machine with a Negro soldier.
Madison and Mitchum are approached by members of the
American Patriots' Association, a veterans' organisation. Hoping to
get two new members, they explain that all Americans are eligible
except Jews, Negroes and Catholics. Mitchum is sure that his friend
Maxie Klein would not have liked that; Maxie was his best friend who
had been buried on Guadacanal. Mitchum takes the man by the collar
and says: 'I am going to spit in your eye for him, because we don't
want to have people like you in the USA. There is no place for racial
discrimination here now!' Then comes the big fight.

Universal Pictures lacked the courage of either RKO or Warner
Brothers when Chester Erskin produced *All My Sons*, Arthur Miller's
play about a Jewish war profiteer finally caught up by the truth,
having previously convinced a court of his innocence. Directed by
Irving Reis, it starred the formidable Jewish actor Edward G.
Robinson as Joseph Keller. It was a memorable performance, but
not one that any movie goer would have recognised as any more
Jewish than, say, Little Caesar, thus effectively preventing any
complaints of anti-Semitism. One can understand the desire to
film the play, as well as the frightening prospect of admitting that
Miller's central villain was Jewish. What could be said on the stage
could not be said on the screen; at least that was Hollywood
orthodoxy of the moment.

Towards the end of 1945 Columbia Studios, where the 60-year-old
Al Jolson was employed as a producer, announced that it was going to
do a film of his life. The brainchild of a Hollywood gossip columnist,
Sidney Skolsky, everyone, including Warner Brothers (celebrating
the twentieth anniversary of their introduction of sound), was
convinced it would be a flop. Although Jolson had been a popular
entertainer touring the war fronts, most felt his career was over.
Skolsky had a bonanza, using the look-alike Larry Parks and highly
effective lip-synchronisation while Jolson sang the soundtrack. It
was the *Jazz Singer* all over again.

The film was released in September of the next year. Jolson was
the son of a Washington DC cantor (Ludwig Donath) and his wife,
Mrs Yoelson (Tamara Shayne). The treatment was sensitive, stressing
the importance of his Jewish heritage, although some of the dialogue
of Cantor and Mrs Yoelson, authentic though it might have been,
gives one the feeling of being a bit too close to the old musical
comedy Jews. When Al sends a postcard from Walla Walla his parents
comment that the people must have loved the town so much they

named it twice; also mispronouncing Dubuque (Iowa) as *dybbuk* (Yiddish for demon). Stephen Longstreet's original screenplay may not have been strictly accurate in the story which takes Jolson up to the mid-thirties (Jolson's former wife Ruby Keeler insisted on not being named) but Jolson did not mind, apparently. The story was close enough, especially on the point that, like so many of the Jewish movie heroes of the 1920s and early 1930s, Jolson had married Gentiles. This technicolour combination of biography and backstage musical, which cost $2.8 million to produce and promote, was tremendous entertainment while at the same time presenting a sympathetic picture of perhaps the greatest pre-war Jewish entertainer. The American public needed to appreciate the talents of the Jew as much as to hear Robert Mitchum saying, on the verge of a bar-room brawl, that there was no place for prejudice in America. Within the first year the film grossed $9.2 million and Columbia prepared to film the sequel *Jolson Sings Again* (1949).

The year 1946 was also the 'year of the anachronism' for Bing Crosby Productions (United Artist release) re-made Anne Nichols's *Abie's Irish Rose* with the necessary updating to bring the story to London at the close of World War II. Private Abie Levy (Richard Norris) of the 101st Airborne Division (well remembered for its drop into Europe and heroic stand at the Battle of the Bulge during the bitter Christmas of 1944) meets the lovely Irish-American Rosemary Murphy (Joanne Dru), a member of an armed forces' entertainment troop. They fall in love and are married, for lack of a Rabbi or Roman Catholic priest, by a Protestant chaplain of the 101st. Abie then returns home to New York and his father's department store where he begins to pick up his life without admitting his marriage. His father, Solomon Levy, tries some match making until the lovely 'Rosie Murpheski' arrives from Europe. When asked her father's name, Abie keeps up the charade with the answer, 'Solomon Murpheski' (while Rosie crosses herself!). The story continues predictably with the young couple being married by Dr Jacob Samuels, a conservative Rabbi (this scene did not appear in release, although it does in publicity stills), and, after a heated confrontation between the two fathers, Solomon and Patrick, Rosemary's family priest gets permission (most unlikely) from the Bishop of New York to marry them again. Rosemary then has twins which form part of the great compromise: she names the boy Patrick Joseph after her father and the girl Rebecca after Abie's deceased mother. The three clergymen now act in concert to unite the family split because of religious and ethnic differences. The climax comes when, after another argument between the grandfathers, the baby Patrick swallows the hook of a Christmas tree ornament. The room with its Christmas tree and lighted menorah is then the scene of a united prayer to the one God of them all for the life of the child. The baby is saved and the film collapses into the worst sort of sentimental conclusion with the Irish cop-on-the-beat singing a melodic mixture of Bing Crosby's hit of the previous year 'Tur-a-lur-a-lura, It's an Irish lullaby' and 'Eli-Eli' to the twins.

At times it was a very entertaining movie with a strong strain of traditional ethnic comedy that Universal audiences had come to see again and again in the *Cohens and the Kellys*. Here, however, it was furnished by Michael Chekhov as Solomon and J.M. Kerrigan as Patrick. Vera Gordon played the stereotyped Jewish wife (against George E. Stone's 'Isaac Cohen') like she had on other occasions, but being now sufficiently broad-minded to help Abie and Rosie after their father had rejected them, even to the point of putting the 'ham in the oven', though against her will. There was also a vignette of a Negro role in which the Levy's maid came forward to say that she had known Abie long enough to wish him *Mazel Tov* (good luck) on his wedding. Over all, the plea for tolerance is really a plea for Jewish assimilation. More positively, Solomon Levy, besides being the comic with the funny accent, is portrayed as a businessman who extends unlimited credit to a man out of work because he knows him to be honest, while in a later scene he is found carefully fingering the fabric of his future daughter-in-law's coat, assessing its quality. The film's message (scripted by Anne Nichols herself) was that differences exist in America and only love which surmounts intolerance will produce an equitable society. It is easy to be snobbish about *Abie's Irish Rose* when compared with the heavy anti-prejudice films, but prejudice was not to be conquered by one film; perhaps there was also a place for humour in the anti-Semitic arsenal.

There was, however, a most unexpected effect upon the career of the director of *Abie's Irish Rose*, Edward Sutherland. In a taped interview transcribed and typed by the Oral History Research Office of Columbia University (page 187, February 1959) Sutherland made the following comments:

I think, in signing off, I'd like to say this. For twenty years, I was in Hollywood as a director. For those twenty years, I think I was always in the first twenty or first ten. Then I finally made a picture —

and this was bad judgement on my part — the company was owned
by Mr Bing Crosby and Bing and I tried to do a plea for tolerance
called *Abie's Irish Rose*. Unfortunately, this thing backfired, and it
offended a lot of people, and the picture was boycotted.
Unfortunately, I was boycotted too, I guess. It was finished in
1946, and I kept seeing that I wasn't wanted around there and
finally in 1949 I admitted to myself that the people were right.
I gave it a three year try. No work at all in those years, no office,
no nothing.[5]

While the anachronistic *Abie's Irish Rose* was emerging uneasily from
Hollywood, Richard Brooks's novel *The Brick Foxhole* had been high
on the best-seller lists in 1944. Written in Brooks's spare time during
three years in the Marine Corps, it was about a homosexual who
became 'the target for a sort of military mob violence'. The screen
rights were bought by RKO which changed the victim to a Jew,
presumably because it was 'more' acceptable to Hollywood's
Production Code and potential audiences. Brooks was convinced that
the switch *'did not in any way alter the basic story'* (his emphasis)
because it was: 'The story of unthinking passion, of vicious, hysterical,
violent compulsion toward brutality, which is sometimes engendered
by the militarization of civilians, and which is sometimes unleashed
for trivial reasons on any handy victim.' Brooks recalled working
'closely and constantly' with Dore Schary (the newly appointed
production executive at RKO) and John Paxton on the screenplay;
they saw 'eye to eye' on almost all points.[6] The better part of two
years elapsed between the securing of the property and getting the
film in production because, even without a homosexual victim, the
story (now called *Crossfire*) was considered too risky for a box office
success. Producer Adrian Scott had kept the story from vanishing
altogether and, with director Edward Dmytryk, gained the full support
of the 42-year-old Schary. Although Schary could override the internal
opposition he also had to face a delegation from the American Jewish
Committee.

The American Jewish Committee's representatives came to Schary's
offices at RKO to ask that he cancel production of the film because
of their fear that such an amateurish attempt to improve the problems
of race relations could have the opposite effect; *Crossfire* might
boomerang, as the popular jargon had it. It is possible to reconstruct
the main points of the case that was put to Schary, probably by
Samuel H. Flowerman, the director of the Department of Scientific

Research for the American Jewish Committee. Flowerman and his staff, working with the Bureau of Applied Social Research at Columbia University, which carried out specific projects for the AJC, had been researching the use of mass propaganda techniques in the war against bigotry. The research findings on various aspects of the problem were currently appearing in such journals as the *Journal of Psychology* and *The Journal of Abnormal and Social Psychology*, in addition to the AJC's house organ, *Commentary*. Armed with what research had thus far suggested was possible, the AJC tried to get Schary to recognise that not enough was known of the use of movies to justify the tremendous risk they felt he was taking. To do the job properly, they argued, would take a concerted campaign using all of the media and vast sums of money. Even then, for the 'protolerance' propaganda to have the desired effect, everyone would have to hear or see the sum total, the whole of the nation's 140,000,000 people. There was a well-documented tendency for those to whom such a message was especially addressed to avoid seeing or hearing it. Even if the bigots got the message, there was substantial evidence to show that propaganda generally tended to be rejected by antagonists. The message, even when it reached the bigot, was invalidated by his accepting the message in general but not in the particular. The example cited in an article by Eunice Cooper and Marie Jahoda of the AJC's Research Department was of prejudiced persons agreeing with the Golden Rule, 'live and let live', but adding 'it's the Jews that don't let you live; they put themselves outside the rule.'

The other tendency was to accept the isolated tale presented in propaganda as 'just a story'. CBS's radio series *We, The People* presented the dramatisation of 'The Belgian Village' in which a Jewish couple are saved from the Gestapo by the loyal support of the villagers. This was followed by Kate Smith making a direct appeal for sympathy and tolerance towards the Jews. Significantly, more of the apparently prejudiced members than of the others in the test audiences refused to admit the application of analogous behaviour in other situations. Flowerman also cited current protolerance slogans such as 'Don't be a sucker, Americans all — immigrants all' and 'All races and all creeds working and living together', but even here the effect was uncertain. The position taken by the committee was not that mass protolerance propaganda was in principle wrong, but that the current attempts, including what they knew about the story of *Crossfire* were 'deficient in content . . . doomed to ineffectiveness because generally the conditions for successful mass persuasion were absent'.[7]

A point that they particularly took exception to was the use of Brooks's widely read novel, changing the victim from a homosexual to a Jew. It was a device which seemed fraught with potential misunderstanding. Faced with Schary's intransigence, it was suggested that he go ahead with the film but please make the victim a Negro — keep the Jews out of this! Schary refused even this — or especially this — for he was personally convinced, along with Adrian Scott, Edward Dmytryk, John Paxton and Richard Brooks that the film (even if made from a re-treated novel) was going to be an effective protolerance statement, no matter what the self-appointed academic experts predicted. As a Jew he had a personal stake in its success even though he was taking a great professional risk in crossing the line which had separated Hollywood from the reality of anti-Semitism. Possibly as a parting threat or simply within the context of the discussions, the American Jewish Committee's representatives promised to use the press against the project. Schary was unimpressed by that kind of pressure, as he was by Warner Brothers' subsequent threat not to distribute *Crossfire* in their theatres.

Production went ahead with a release date set for the early summer of 1947. The low-budget ($550,000) film was quickly shot but Schary was not going to depend solely on his own judgement where the results were concerned. Thus he arranged a screening with B'nai B'rith's Anti-Defamation League, which was just taking over responsibility for 'Hollywood watching' from the parent organisation, an aspect of B'nai B'rith's work since the widespread Jewish criticism of DeMille's *King of Kings* in 1927. Some 50 psychologists, psychiatrists, educators and film industry people saw the film. A majority report suggested that one or two films were not going to cure anti-Semitism; neither did the author of the report feel that *Crossfire* could aggravate anti-Semitism (the basic fear of the American Jewish Committee). Recommendations were made by the preview group which led to the setting up of preview groups in Boston (30 June), in Denver (7 July) and at an Ohio high school to see if the viewing of *Crossfire* could positively alter such deep-seated attitudes of prejudice as anti-Semitism.[8]

The film which the preview group saw was an extremely well-made crime film. It opens with the shadowy, apparently motiveless, beating to death of a Joseph Samuels (Sam Levene) in his Washington DC apartment. The police detective, Captain Finlay (Robert Young), finds an army cap and wallet in the apartment which leads him to a group of Signal Corpmen waiting for their release from the army, housed in a hotel. The disillusionment of these soldiers is played out in the background as the hunt for the murderer(s) continues with flashbacks establishing from various viewpoints what has actually happened. The first man to make an appearance at the apartment after Samuels's death is a 'demobbed' Sergeant Montgomery (played by an ex-Marine acquaintance of Richard Brooks, Robert Ryan). Montgomery's anti-Semitic opinions emerge at the very beginning of the investigation when Captain Finlay asks if he has ever seen Samuels before. The answer is an unequivocal 'No . . . of course I've seen a lot of guys like him'.

Finlay: Like what?
Montgomery: Ah, you know. Guys that played it safe during the war.
               Scrounged around keeping themselves in civies, got
               swell apartments, swell dames, you know that kind?
Finlay: I'm not sure that I do, just what kind?
Montgomery: You know, some of them are named Samuels, some of
               them have funnier names.

Finlay does not pursue the conversation with Montgomery but, after he leaves, Sergeant Keeley (Robert Mitchum) turns to Finlay and says: 'He ought to look at the casualty list some time. There are a lot of funny names there too.' Samuels had himself been wounded on Guadacanal and the script made him as assimilated as possible without changing his name to hide his race; he had a Gentile girlfriend, worked on a newspaper and liked baseball. Sam Levene was not allowed fully to develop the character but that in itself supported the theme that Samuels was killed simply because of hatred and intolerance. Montgomery, fired by alcohol, had chosen him as a target simply because his name was 'Sammy' Samuels. Detective Finlay comments:

This business of hating Jews comes in a lot of different sizes. There's the, 'ah, you can't join our countryclub kind'; and 'you can't live around here kind', yes, and the 'you can't work here kind'. Because we stand for these we get Monty's kind. He's just one guy, we don't get him very often but he grows out of all the rest.

There was no mistaking that Montgomery was an unusual type of anti-Semite and no attempt at generalising from his experience was in the mind of RKO's production team. Rather, it showed how hate, mixed with postwar depression about the future and alcohol, could provide the irrational motive for an equally irrational and brutal

violence culminating in a brave and humane man's death — his only
crime lay in being a Jew. Prejudice against Jews is mirrored against
historical prejudice against Irish Roman Catholics and other American
minority groups. The plot of this *film noir* demanded that the killer
be himself killed judicially and surgically with two shots from the
detective's gun high above the darkened street, along which the
bigoted murderer sought to escape. It was a film *genre* that the American
public knew well: darkened heavily shadowed sets, police offices with
President Roosevelt's portrait on the wall, poker games in hotel rooms,
sleezy dance halls, plush apartments and the crime unfolding in the
detective's investigation. What marked it out from other films of this
type was that the motive for the murder was not lust, revenge or
money. The motive was prejudice of a very special form. After the
nation-wide previews, Dore Schary and his production team thought
they had an honest but hard-hitting movie against prejudice,
which would also commercially justify their investment.

The 86-minute film was premiered at New York's Rivoli Theatre
on 22 July 1947. It was to make money at the box office and find the
newspaper critics more than receptive. Bosley Crowther of the *New
York Times* saw the film deserving of an 'unqualified *A* for effort
in bringing to the screen a frank and immediate demonstration of the
brutality of religious bigotry as it festers and fires ferocity in certain
seemingly normal American minds'. Robert Mitchum (nominated for
best supporting actor in *The Story of G.I. Joe*, 1945), Gloria Grahame,
as a dance hall girl, and Robert Ryan were all praised for first-rate
performances, as was Dmytryk's direction and Paxton's screenplay.
Such criticism that did emerge was concerned with a rather heavy-
handed restatement for the 'hypothetical eight-year-old minds' that
Hollywood movies were supposed to be written for when the point
had already been dramatically made.[9]

The threatened criticism by the American Jewish Committee had
yet to come and when it did it was in an open nine-page *Letter to the
Movie-Makers: The Film Drama as a Social Force* by Elliot E. Cohen.
Cohen, the editor of the American Jewish Committee's journal
Commentary had his answer to *Crossfire* in the August issue of
Commentary (vol.4, no.2) looking, as it were, the gift-horse in the mouth.
He provided a cogent rehearsal of the plot for his readers, stressing
that two of America's best-liked and respected movie personalities,
Robert Young and Robert Mitchum, speaking as a Catholic and as a
Protestant respectively, condemned anti-Semitism, and that in the
end the bigot dies, 'a capital punishment for a capital crime'. Cohen

found the film without merit as an attack on anti-Semitism, because he could not imagine it converting a rabid anti-Semite. He feared that because of its ambiguity the story might 'boomerang' to the point of evoking sympathy for the expertly played ex-Sergeant Montgomery. In the context of his general diatribe against Hollywood films, Cohen challenged the movies, seemingly prepared to embark upon high-minded aims, to make 'their medium a conscious social force, to lend their art to the purposes of enlightenment and progress', to improve knowledge, to use scientific testing, *and* to produce real art.

Dore Schary answered Cohen's criticism. He was substantially briefer but fired with as much bitterness; it was an extraordinary exchange between two leading American Jews publicly fighting it out over how to fight anti-Semitism. Schary rightly rejected the dismissive tone of Cohen's letter as well as his sarcasm. Schary claimed that they did not intend *Crossfire* to convert the violent anti-Semite: 'It was intended to insulate people against violent and virulent anti-Semitism.' Although the movie might only move 'slightly anti-Semitic' people into the liberal camp, this was in itself worth while and in no way was the film going to be enjoyed by violent unreasoning anti-Semites. Schary cited some of the evidence which was gleaned at the previews, seeking to evaluate reactions to certain problematic aspects of the plot. The questionnaires suggested that almost 92 per cent approved of the ending of the film (the trap) and understood LeRoy's motive in co-operating. The remaining 8 per cent were divided as to whether Monty should have been tried, jailed and reformed. Schary felt that in the context of the Western idiom 'the adolescents particularly . . . understood and enjoyed the villain getting knocked off by expert gun play executed by a right guy wearing the equivalent of a Sheriff's badge'. Sergeant Montgomery could not evoke sympathy in an American audience; the screenplay carefully covered that possibility by making him a coward (he runs), a double-crosser (he kills his best friend), and a hater of 'civilian' soldiers (94 per cent or so of the American armed forces). Most interestingly, Schary pointed out that 'he is sweaty and slop'py (no bobby-soxer virtue for heroes)'.

Schary also rejected the criticism of the portrayal of Sammy Samuels, for there was no characterisation which could guarantee sympathy. The following is a part of Schary's perceptive list.

If the Jew is poor, they are all Communists. If the Jew is rich, they are all dirty bankers. If the Jew is happily married, they're clannish, selfish, and, anyway, they have Gentile mistresses. If the Jew is single or divorced, they are all libertines or homosexuals. If the Jew was in the army, he was goldbricking — if he wasn't, he's a slacker. If he was an officer, he bought his commission — if a private, he avoided doing his job.

This letter did not convince Cohen, but it is particularly revealing about some of the perceptions which were to give the film shape. One interesting question in this line is whether the soldiers involved were designated as members of the Signal Corps not only so that one could justify their presence in Washington (the home of American liberties) but also because in theory they had not been forced by war to kill as infantrymen, thus removing another psychological rationale for Montgomery's behaviour. Cohen's reply to Schary came closer to the constructive dialogue for which one hoped, pointing out that the 'out of his head or crazy' characterisation of Montgomery could have the effect of creating virulent anti-Semitism beyond the experience and comprehension of the smug Gentiles[10] who practised the normal mechanics of prejudice which are referred to in Finlay's brief speech about Jews and country clubs, jobs and certain neighbourhoods.

'There is a good chance that, instead of achieving Mr Schary's aim of insulating the mildly anti-Semitic against anti-Semitism, *Crossfire* might insulate them against personally facing the problem of anti-Semitism.' Cohen argued that anti-Semitism was still a force to be contended with, citing the latest *Fortune Magazine* Roper Poll which had found that 36 per cent of their national cross-section (America's movie audience) believed that American Jews had too much economic power and 21 per cent that they were getting too much control over government. Cohen also made reference to Schary's opinion polls on *Crossfire*, dismissing them as 'superficial, low-standard and unreliable'. Nor did they prove people understood the film: in Boston and Denver, out of 1,200 people between 20 per cent and 30 per cent liked Montgomery and, of a thousand people asked if Montgomery ought to have a better reason for killing Samuels, they split, between yes and no, almost 50-50. Cohen argued that a movie needed a normal anti-Semite and a normal Jew[11] in order to combat anti-Semitism in America. His appeal was:

(1) study by the movie-makers of available knowledge on the causes

and mechanisms of anti-Semitism; (2) scientific testing of the effect
of film dramas on the social attitudes of audiences; and (3) the
development of a more sensitive, mature film art to deal more
adequately with such complex human issues as race hatred'.

Cohen did not condemn *Crossfire* 'out of hand' but he was not prepared
to accept Schary's personal certainty that it would be helpful.

While the mixed reviews of *Crossfire* were provoking wide discussion
amongst the liberals and the Jewish community, the production of
Gentleman's Agreement went ahead at 20th Century Fox. Darryl F.
Zanuck, head of production, had announced that he was going
personally to produce the film at about the same time as Dore Schary
got *Crossfire* into production. The Laura Z. Hobson best seller was to
be directed by Elia Kazan and the Jewish playwright and Pulitzer
Prize winner Moss Hart was hired to do his first screenplay. In contrast
to RKO's limited financial commitments, Zanuck, a Gentile, was
committed to a prestige production with a budget of $2,000,000
(4 times that of *Crossfire*). Zanuck was to run into opposition similar
to that faced by Schary but it was a group of the wealthy Hollywood
Jewish elite who met in his offices to convince him that anti-
Semitism would be fanned into life by raising the issue in a film.
A scene in the film in which such advice is given (discussed later)
was written in by Hart and was probably based on this meeting.
One reviewer's comparison rather neatly did the job: '*Crossfire* took
care of ignorant violent haters who don't know any better.
Gentleman's Agreement covers society people, commuters,
fashionable resorts, anti-Semitic Jews, and, most subtle of all,
the prejudice that surprises people who think they have none.'[12]
When the two-hour-long *Gentleman's Agreement* opened at New
York's Mayfair on 11 November it was acclaimed an artistic
success, as well as a crusading film. The story was shot by Kazan in
a straightforward way that gives one the feeling that one is
watching a play rather than a movie filled with the tricks of the
trade which feature so prominently in Dymytryk's *Crossfire*.

In *Gentleman's Agreement* the central character is an investigative
magazine writer who moves to New York with his eleven-year-old
son Tommy (Dean Stockwell) and his mother (Anne Revere) to begin a
new assignment for *Smith's Weekly*. Phil Green (Gregory Peck) initially
resists doing the series of articles on anti-Semitism until he decides
to become Phil Greenberg and personally experience the problem
in daily life. Introduced to the magazine staff as Jewish, he finds

that his secretary has changed her name, a Jewish one, in order to get
a job. 'Phil finds prejudices cropping up fast — flicks here and flicks
there of insult that tap constantly on the nerves. No yellow armbands,
no marked park benches, no Gestapo, no torture chambers — just
a flick here and a flick there.'[13] His son is beaten up and insulted at
school; the family doctor reacts negatively when he suggests a
Jewish heart specialist for his mother; he is refused a room in an upstate
resort hotel with 'restrictive' rules; his janitor suggests that Green is a
better name on the mailbox than Greenberg and so on. In the meantime
Phil, a widower, has fallen in love with Cathy (divorced) but the
relationship flounders on his remaining Jewish until the series is completed.
Cathy (Dorothy McGuire), who initially suggests the series to her uncle,
the editor of *Smith's Weekly*, wants to tell her Connecticut family the
truth, thus revealing the limits of her own liberalism. At this point
an old friend and a real Jew, Captain Dave Goldman (John Garfield),
arrives back from Europe. He and Phil discuss the difference between
the ways they react to anti-Semitism. Through Dave's help Cathy
sees how individuals must fight the social cancer. The articles are
successfully published and Cathy and Phil are reunited.

Moss Hart developed the key issues of American middle-class
anti-Semitism in a series of set pieces of which the most important
were: Phil Green's initial attempt to explain to his son what a Jew is;
the conservative Jewish opinion on ignoring anti-Semitism put
forth by Professor Liebermann (Sam Jaffa) and the Minify-Weismann
dialogue on the magazine series; Dave Golden's statements on being
the object of anti-Semitism (the thesis was that the key to defeating
prejudice lay in the fair-minded liberals who refused to speak out,
thus allowing prejudice to continue to fester in American life);
and finally the optimistic summary statement made by Mrs Green
at the end of the film. Early in the film, shortly after being asked
to do the magazine series, Phil Green is asked by his young son
Tommy at breakfast to explain what anti-Semitism is, and the
following dialogue is the answer.

Tommy:	What's anti-Semitism?
Phil:	Hm?
Tommy:	What's anti-Semitism?
Phil:	Oh, that's where some people don't like other people just because they're Jews.
Tommy:	Oh, why? Are they bad?
Phil:	Some are, some aren't, it's like everybody else.

Tommy: What are Jews, anyway? I mean exactly.

Phil: Well, remember last week when you asked me about that
            big church (Tommy: 'sure') and I told you there were lots
            of different churches (Tommy: 'yeh')? Well there are people
            who go to that particular church and they are called Catholics,
            then there are people who go to other churches and they are
            called protestants, then there are others who go to still
            different ones and they are called Jews; only they call their
            churches synagogues or temples.

Tommy: And why don't some people like those?

Phil: Well that's kind of a tough one to explain, Tom. Some
            people hate Catholics and some hate Jews.

Tommy: And no one hates us because we are Americans?

Phil: (clears throat) Well, no, that's another thing again because
            you can be an American and a Catholic or an American and
            a Protestant and an American and a Jew. But look Tom, like
            this: one thing's your country, see like America, or France
            or Germany or Russia, all the countries, the flag is different,
            and the uniform is different, and the language is different.

Tommy: And the airplanes are marked different.

Phil: Different, that's right. But the other thing is religion, like the
            Jewish or the Catholic or the Protestant religions, see, that
            doesn't have anything to do with the flag or the uniform or
            the airplane. You got it? (Tommy: 'Yep') Now don't ever
            get mixed up on it. (Tommy: 'I got it!') Some people are
            mixed up.

Tommy: Why?

Mrs Green: It's eight-thirty Tommy, you better get going to school.

Phil: Yeh, yeh, you'll be late.

Although the definition of a Jew was wholly inadequate, it served to
illustrate how little Phil himself knew about the issue, not merely that
he was trying to couch the answer in terms that his young son could
understand. Yet for the story's purpose his son's confusion provides
the motivation for Green to accept the assignment to do the
magazine series. A second shot at the problem takes place at a party
given by the magazine's fashion editor Anne (Celeste Holm). Here
Sam Jaffe as Professor Liebermann delivers a high-speed analysis of
the Jewish problem as a humorous sort of monologue:

Phil: I'm doing a series on anti-Semitism.

Liebermann: For or against?

Phil: Well he [Minify] thought we might hash over some ideas.

Liebermann: What sort of ideas?

Phil: Palestine for instance, Zionism. . .

Liebermann: Which? Palestine as a refuge or Zionism as a movement for
            a Jewish state?

Phil: The confusion between the two more than anything.

Liebermann: If we agree there is confusion, we can talk. We scientists love
            confusion. But right now I am starting a new crusade of my
            own. You see my young friend I have no religion and I am
            not Jewish by religion. I am a scientist so I must rely on
            science which tells me I'm not Jewish by race. Since there's
            no such thing as a distinct Jewish race, there's not even
            such a thing as a Jewish type. Well, my crusade will have a
            certain charm, I'll simply go forth and state flatly I'm
            not a Jew. Well with my face that becomes not an evasion
            but a new principle, a scientific principle.

Phil: (laughing) For a scientific age.

Liebermann: Precisely. There must be millions of people now-a-days who
            are religious only in the vaguest sense. I've often wondered
            why the Jewish ones among them still go on calling
            themselves Jews. Can you guess why, Mr Green? (Phil:
            'No, but I'd like to know.') Because the world still makes it
            an advantage not to be one, thus for many of us it becomes
            a matter of pride to go on calling ourselves Jews. So you
            see I have to abandon my crusade before it begins. Only if
            there were no anti-Semites could I go on with it. And now
            I would like to try another little scientific experiment. I
            wonder if you would leave me alone with your very
            beautiful fiancée [Cathy] while you went out and got me a
            plate of food.

Even as Dore Schary had responded to the American Jewish Committee
attack on the *Crossfire* project by seeking the stamp of approval for the
finished film by the Anti-Defamation League of B'nai B'rith, Zanuck
took his experience with Hollywood's unnamed Jewish elite and put
their opinions into *Gentleman's Agreement*. This scene was not in the
Hobson novel and Moss Hart gave the 'keep your heads down' view
prominence in the developing plot. This key scene was a luncheon in
the staff dining room of *Smith's Weekly* where Phil Green was introduced
and identified as the individual responsible for a series on anti-Semitism

to Mr Irving Weismann, a leading industrialist.

Minify:	Mr Green is going to do a series on anti-Semitism for us.
Weismann:	Really, again?
Minify:	Not again, for the first time. We are going to split it wide open.
Weismann:	Do you mind my saying as an old friend, that I think it a very bad idea, John? The worst, the most harmful thing you can possibly do now.
Minify:	Not at all, why is it a harmful idea?
Weismann:	Because it will only stir it up more. Let it alone. We'll handle it in our own way.
Minify:	The hush-hush way?
Weismann:	I don't care what you call it. Let it alone. You can't write it out of existence. We've been fighting it for years and we know from experience the less talk there is about it the better.
Minify:	Sure, pretend it doesn't exist and add to the conspiracy of silence. I should say not. Keep silent and let Bilbo and Gerald L.K. Smith[14] do all the talking. No Sir! Irving, you and your 'let's be quiet about it committees' have got just about no place. We're going to call a spade a dirty spade. And I think it's high time and a fine idea.

Furthermore, Darryl F. Zanuck, the 'Minify' at 20th Century Fox, rejected the advice of the 'Weismanns' who attempted to get him to abandon the film. Here we have, however, a dramatisation of his own confrontation, the essence of the advice given; and his own answer is a unique bit of historical film reconstruction which provides insight into the character not of the anti-Semite but the Jews themselves as they faced persecution American-style.

The 'liberal' problem of keeping silent in the face of anti-Semitism is placed in the context of Phil's relationship with Cathy, who first suggested the series. During their engagement she has become increasingly frustrated by the strain of Phil's being 'Jewish', whether it has to do with going to a party of her sister's in Connecticut (Darien and New Caanan are mentioned as characteristic of restricted housing with New Caanan singled out as the town where there is a *gentlemen's agreement* not to sell to Jews), or with helping Dave out by loaning him her house in Gentile Connecticut. Such strains lead Cathy to tell Phil that he considers her to be an anti-Semite and the engagement flounders. Two important scenes then develop her problem, that of liberal America: in the first scene Anne criticises Cathy for her insipid do-nothing liberalism in an attempt to get Phil to marry her; and in the second Cathy meets Dave and tries to get him to assure her that she is not what Phil thinks her to be — prejudiced against Jews. Cathy recalls for Dave a man telling 'a vicious little story' filling her with rage and shame. Dave presses her to explain. 'Kike and coon' figure in the story. Cathy says: 'I wanted to yell at him, get up and leave, I wanted to say to everyone at that table: Why do we sit here and take it when he is attacking everything that we believe in? Why don't we call him on it?' She admits she merely sat there and felt ashamed. Dave tells her she would feel better if she had fought: 'There's a funny kind of elation about socking back!'[15] Behind that joke and their like lay the whole bitter experience of prejudice, which had been graphically illustrated in the film. The trouble lay with the nice people refusing to fight for the American principles of the Constitution and the Bill of Rights for which the war had been fought; prejudice was as real an enemy as the Nazis. This self-revelation leads Cathy to defend her beliefs and, as Phil's articles go to press, they are reunited. Phil's central experience is the refusal by the Flume Inn to honour their honeymoon reservations because he is a Jew. The only part of his 'articles' that appears in the movie is read by his mother.

Mrs Green (reading):

Driving away from the inn, I knew all about every man or woman who'd been told the job was filled when it wasn't, every youngster who'd ever been turned down by a college or a summer camp. I knew the rage that pitches through you, when you see your own child shaken and dazed. From that moment I saw an unending attack by adults on kids of seven and eight and ten and twelve, on adolescent boys and girls trying to get a job or an education or into medical school, and I knew that they had somehow known it, too — they, those patient, stubborn men who argued and wrote and fought and came up with the Constitution and the Bill of Rights. They know that the tree is known by its fruit and that injustice corrupts a tree; that its fruit withers and shrivels and falls at last to that dark ground of history where other great hopes have rotted and died. For equality and freedom remain still the only choice for wholeness and soundness in a man or in a nation ... your father would have liked to have you say that, Phil.

The final word of the film's central theme is then spoken by Mrs Green: a word of optimism and confidence in the principles upon which America was founded and the people who make up her population:

> Wouldn't it be wonderful Phil if it turned out to be everybody's century, when people all over the world, free people, found a way to live together? I'd like to be around to see some of that, even a beginning. I may stick around for quite a while.

The movie industry, through the Academy of Motion Picture Arts and Sciences, responded to *Gentleman's Agreement, Crossfire* and *Body and Soul*, with its muted Jewish theme, with Oscar nominations for 1947. Amongst the major nominations, *Crossfire* and *Gentleman's Agreement* were selected for best picture, John Garfield (*Body and Soul*) and Gregory Peck for best actor, Dorothy McGuire for best actress, Robert Ryan for best supporting actor and Gloria Grahame for best supporting actress from *Crossfire*. Celeste Holm was nominated for the latter category. Edward Dmytryk and Elia Kazan were both nominated for best director. When the votes were finally counted *Crossfire*, with a total of five nominations, undeservedly did not have an Oscar; *Gentleman's Agreement* took best film, best direction and best supporting actress.[16]

Crossfire's failure to achieve even one Oscar may well have been a side effect of the House Un-American Activities Committee hearings that opened like a gala premiere in Hollywood on 20 October, shortly before *Gentleman's Agreement* opened in New York. Many of the industry's leading writers, directors and producers were to appear, including 19 'unfriendly witnesses': twelve writers, five directors, one producer and one actor. Chaired by J. Parnell Thomas, the witnesses were asked whether they had been or were members of the Communist Party. Among the 19 were ten who took the first amendment refusing to testify: writers Albert Maltz, who wrote *Pride of the Marines*, Dalton Trumbo, John Howard Lawson, Alva Bessie, Samuel Ornitz, Ring Lardner, Jr and Lester Cole, directors Herbert J. Biberman and Edward Dmytryk of *Crossfire*, and his producer Adrian Scott.[17] Eight of these men were subsequently convicted of contempt of Congress, fined $1,000 and sentenced to one year in jail; Biberman and Dmytryk were fined $1,000 and given six months in jail.

Adrian Scott at the time was producing *The Boy with Green Hair* (1948) for Dore Schary. It was an allegory about racism: 'a boy

discriminated against because he looked different'. The film was
temporarily put on ice. Scott was not to return to the project
although Joseph Losey, the director, resumed the picture shortly
before Howard Hughes gained control of RKO (which led to Schary's
resignation).

Under pressure from New York financial interests, 50 leading
motion picture executives met in New York at the Waldorf Astoria
in November, and decided to 'discharge' or suspend without
compensation the Hollywood ten. Schary, who had fought the move,
headed the three-man delegation that took the news to the
Screen Writers Guild. Shortly after that meeting a reputable
Philadelphia organisation invited Schary to accept an award for
Crossfire. He declined but Eric Johnson, president and spokesman for
the Motion Picture Producers Association, went in his stead to the
'City of Brotherly Love' armed with an acceptance speech on the
virtues of tolerance. Interestingly enough, in 1952, long after he had
won his Oscar for directing *Gentleman's Agreement*, Elia Kazan admitted
to HUAC in executive session that he had been a Communist Party
member for almost two years in the 1930s, but his public prostration
was enough to keep him in Hollywood, not unlike Edward G. Robinson's
tale of having been used unknowingly by a Communist front
organisation.

John Garfield had played three important Jewish roles in 1947: the
supporting role of the Army Engineer Captain Dave Golden in
Gentleman's Agreement, and the star roles of Charlie Davis in *Body
and Soul* and Paul Boray in the Warner Brothers re-make of Fannie
Hurst's *Humoresque. Humoresque*, written by Clifford Odets and
Zachary Gold, was an excellent example of the ordinary low profile
of the Jewish character in films of this period.[18] Boray's parents on
the East Side of New York, Rudy (J. Carrol Naish) and Esther (Ruth
Nelson), could have been from any immigrant community, and
perhaps only the overtly Jewish Oscar Levant as Sid Jeffers, Paul's
old friend and accompanist, makes the tenuous point; a point made
by association.

The third major Garfield role was the boxer Charlie Davis in *Body
and Soul* in which, despite the non-Jewish surname, his Jewish family
and friends emerge unambiguously midway through the film. The
vehicle was Garfield's own choice. He felt badly used by Warner
Brothers, so he became his own producer through Roberts
Productions of which he was the sole asset, the principle stockholder
and an employee. The film was written by Abe Polansky and directed

by Robert Rossen.[19] There are two major points in the film which are directly related to Jewishness. The first brief but important reference is dramatised when Garfield, whose father has earlier been killed when a nearby 'speakeasy' was bombed, finds his mother (Anne Revere) applying for a loan from a New York welfare agency. During the interview with the social worker, Anna Davis's personal details are set forth as 'race, *white*; religion, *Jewish*; nationality, *American*'. (Was this a mixed marriage which explained the surname Davis?) The social worker is told to leave, for Garfield has resolved to make money in the ring despite his mother's vigorous objections. The most important reference comes when Garfield has returned to New York as the welterweight champion, having agreed to throw the fight because of the debts he owes the corrupt promoter that 'owns' him. In the kitchen of his mother's East Side apartment over the candy shop, he hears an old friend of the family, Schimmon, tell of the neighbourhood's pride in his accomplishments and how they will be betting on him, not for the money, but as an expression of Jewish solidarity.

> Charlie, everybody's betting on you, the whole neighbourhood like you was the Irish sweepstakes . . . it isn't the money it's a way of showing. Over in Europe Nazis are killing people like us just because of their religion, but here Charlie Davis is champean (sic). So you win, and you retire champean, and we are proud.

Charlie is typical of the assimilated East Side Jew whose girlfriend Peg (Lilli Palmer) is a well-travelled Gentile, but nothing is thought of it and, when Charlie's ambition overrides all, she is supported emotionally by his mother. The social message of the film is directed against the inhumane control of the fight racket by gangsters and the way in which the fighters are used, not always against their will. This is certainly not the first film to show the Jew out of stereotype as a boxer. The vigorous Polansky script characterises the black former champion Ben Chaplin (who almost dies fighting Davis because he has a blood clot on the brain), played by Canada Lee, as a strong, brave, honest and increasingly sympathic character. He is initially befriended by Davis out of guilt but gives him total loyalty. There is no deferential black man here, but one who eventually dies having confronted those gangsters who have used him. He falls backwards over the ropes in the ring of the Davis training camp, goes beserk and dies in the ring fighting spectres. Davis finds himself sold out like Ben as he is slowly beaten to a pulp in what is supposed to be an easy decision. Charlie musters all of his anger to defeat the challenger. It is not an intellectual decision for honesty, but a decision not to be betrayed. He emerges from the ring, still champion, to face the wrath of the mobster; yet he has vindicated Peg's faith in him and the film ends with their reconciliation. This was an impressive movie which is remembered for the haunting theme song 'Body and Soul', as well as for James Wong Howe's superb camera work in the fight sequences done with a hand-held camera as he was being pushed around the ring on roller skates.

The year 1947 proved to be a year of importance for the slowly emerging honesty with which America faced the reality that, in the land of the free and home of the brave, anti-Semitic prejudice existed. The movie industry began slowly to emerge from its self-imposed protective shell to meet it. The Jewish John Garfield identified himself as a Jew in three major films in the space of two years, only to be virtually blacklisted in the aftermath of the HUAC hearings for his activity as a so-called 'fellow traveller'. He was to die of a heart attack in 1952, while preparing to star in the revival of Clifford Odets's *The Golden Boy* on Broadway, which was where he had begun his acting career. Ominously, several of the leading figures in *Crossfire* and Garfield in *Gentleman's Agreement* (Kazan's CP membership did not emerge until later) were tarred with the Communistic brush and Hollywood was forced into a more cautious stance in the interests of political self-preservation. This was only a few years before it would face the all-out economic assault of television which would destroy the studio system and stimulate the dispersal of movie production throughout the world.

There was still the question of whether a film like *Crossfire* or *Gentleman's Agreement* had a positive effect in combating anti-Semitism. The *Journal of Psychology* (vol.26, 1948, pp.525-36) carried the report of an experiment carried out at the University of Pittsburg by Professor Irwin C. Rosen of its Department of Psychology. Students were given the odd-numbered items of the Levinson-Sanford *Questionnaire on Anti-Semitism* on 17 March 1948 and half of them (the experimental group) were then given tickets for *Gentleman's Agreement* for Sunday 21 March. The even-numbered questions from the *Questionnaire* were given on 22 March to the entire group. Two days later both groups were given the first half of the test again to test the three-day effects of the film. During the same class session the experimental group was asked the following questions:

1. *Gentleman's Agreement* was selected as the outstanding picture of the year by the Academy of Motion Picture Arts and Sciences. Do you feel that the picture merits the Academy Award? Please underline: Yes, or No. Give below the reasons for your opinion.
2. Did you learn anything from seeing the picture? Answer: Yes, No. If your answer is yes, indicate briefly what you learned.
3. Did the picture change your attitude toward Jews? Answer: Yes, No. Tell why the picture affected or did not affect, your attitudes.
4. There has been criticism of *Gentleman's Agreement* on the grounds that it is propaganda. Please express your opinions on this point.
5. Do you favour the production of more pictures dealing with the treatment of minority groups? Answer: Yes, No. Please comment.

The control group in the meantime was being given tickets to see the film. The experimental group excluded students who did not see the film, people who had read the book, Jews, or students who missed one of the sessions, leaving a group of 50 as compared to the control group of 90. Of the experimental group 73 per cent showed a change in attitude more favourable towards Jews, 26 per cent more prejudiced and 1 per cent no change, comparing scores before and after seeing the film. During the same period of time 47 per cent of the control group showed a more favourable attitude towards Jews, 52 per cent less favourable and again 1 per cent no change.

Interestingly enough, Professor Rosen suggested that the answers to the essay-style questionnaire actually reflected the students' change of attitude best in the way in which they predicted the public would receive future films like *Gentleman's Agreement*. It was, as Rosen points out, a very small sample to generalise from and a class of Pittsburg university students in 1948 was hardly representative of America's movie-going public. Nevertheless, of the students, 67 per cent felt that the movie deserved its Oscar as against 33 per cent who did not; 61 per cent learned something from the picture against 39 per cent who did not (the most frequent learning experienced was 'how it felt to be a Jew'); but 81 per cent claimed that the picture did not change their attitudes towards Jews, while 19 per cent claimed that it did. On the fourth question regarding propaganda 44 per cent said simply 'propaganda'; 29 per cent propaganda — but good; and 27 per cent denied it was propaganda because it reflected reality. Finally, 81 per cent of the students (the 50) felt that more pictures on minority groups were desirable to educate the public; and 19 per cent said such movies could boomerang and turn the viewers against the minority group.

In 1960 an experimental group at Florida State University saw the film and only 15 per cent of them identified the specific theme that passive, intelligent, decent people are largely to blame for the continuance of anti-Semitic prejudice. Of the group, 82 per cent recognised the general theme of Jewish suffering because of prejudice and 3 per cent remained oblivious to the message either specifically or generally! Again, this experiment indicated the positive effects of the film in this second generation of film audiences. Its lasting effect was questionable because, as Professor Russell Middleton says, 'rather than a real change in the attitudes and sentiments of the subjects towards Jews, they may have been simply manifesting embarrassement in admitting to anti-Semitic attitudes'.[20]

Gentleman's Agreement was banned in Spain by order of the ecclesiastical member of the Film Censorship Board on moral grounds. These grounds make fascinating reading, reflecting as they do the extreme Roman Catholic position on Jews. The film was criticised for 'the theological errors' (according to Paul P. Kennedy of the *New York Times*) firstly, of portraying Cathy openly as a divorced person. Furthermore, the film was unacceptable for the following reasons: it stated that there was no real difference between Christians and Jews when Christians *are* superior to Jews; it was a grevious sin for Phil to masquerade as a Jew for even eight weeks; it condoned the idea of the suppression of religion (this vague statement was undeveloped); and it declared that for many Jews it is a matter of pride to be called Jews. The censor asked: 'Pride of what? The pride of being the people who put God to death? Of being perfidious, as they are called in Holy Scripture?' The Roman Catholic censor had, from the security and sanctity of his Church's dogmatic position, clearly seen all of the points which *Gentleman's Agreement* had to make and simply rejected them, confident that his 'anti-Semitism' was justifiable. The same unofficial source 'close to the board' said that it was a Christian duty to 'stimulate love among individuals, societies, nations, and people' but it should not be extended to Jews — the Church could not consent to that which was wrong. The enemies of Christ's holy church, including the Jews, must be humiliated. 20th Century Fox, in seeking to distribute the film in Spain, was clearly meeting rabid and institutionalised anti-Semitism head on. What its effect would have been upon the Spanish people can only be a matter of speculation.

Gentleman's Agreement was not expected to do very well at the box office south of the Mason Dixon line, where comparatively few Jews lived; the area had always been notoriously weak for social problem or 'message' pix. Surprisingly, the film became 20th Century Fox's second-largest all-time grosser in the south, exceeded only by *Leave Her to Heaven* (1945). It also did extremely well on the east and west coasts. A very cool reception was given, however, in the midwest, which reportedly cut the expected gross in 1948 from $5,000,000 to $3,900,000. The sales department blamed the anti-Semitic theme for the film's failure to achieve the 17,000 booking dates normally expected of such a prestige film. The picture was, however, an economic success.

The appearance of *Crossfire* and *Gentleman's Agreement* in late 1947 had led to the fear that 'quickie producers would get into the field with sensational, catchpenny melodrama, debating and distorting the work begun by thoughtful moviemakers' (*New York World*, 7 February 1948). What had not been expected was that an anti-prejudice 'B' film would be in the local theatres at the beginning of 1948. 'B' film producers had on occasion taken vacations from cattle rustlers and jewel thieves to take advantage of momentary interest in such social problems as prohibition and labour troubles, but only to exploit the themes, not to offer criticism or solutions. Frank Satenstein of Marathon Pictures claimed that *Open Secret* had been in production before the release of *Crossfire* and *Gentleman's Agreement*, but that did nothing to convince the critics that his film was not a travesty on the theme of anti-Semitism. Released on 14 February, the film starred John Ireland and Jane Randolph. The story revolves around the disappearance and murder of an old army friend of Ireland. Ireland and his bride, Randolph, find that their friend's apartment has been rifled and that he has been murdered. George Tyne played a Jewish camera shopowner, who is being terrorised by a gang of local bigots. The well-known Jewish actor Sheldon Leonard played the part of an Italian-American police lieutenant. The anti-Semitism in the film is limited to a child being anti-Semitic, a dowdy woman complaining about a Jewish shopkeeper, the gang's obscenities, and the photographs which the murdered man has secretly taken of the gang's attack on local Jewish business establishments. Although Marathon Pictures thought that it was conducting a 'Fight Against Hate', as the publicity blurb put it, the critics were unanimous in their criticism of poor direction, poor acting and a generally substandard product characteristic of 'B' films. They also agreed that such a film could do more harm than good. Alton Cook in the *World Telegram* produced the best epithet for *Open Secret*: 'The next step is Roy Rogers and Gene Autry driving out the cattle-rustlers who hate Jews'; Cecelia Ager in *PM* stated: 'Children should not be allowed to play with movie cameras.'[21]

Did *Open Secret* hurt efforts to combat American anti-Semitism; did *Crossfire, Gentleman's Agreement, The Pride of the Marines* make a positive contribution to the destruction of that cancer of society? Whatever the effect, these were the first hesitant but significant steps in an important battle. Significantly, the American Jewish community was not going to sit quietly by while the battle was being fought. The first indication of this, in a negative sense, was the criticism levelled at both Zanuck and Dore Schary when they began production on their two films. A group of national Jewish organisations responded to the new climate in Hollywood by forming the Motion Picture Project headed by former film producer John Stone. The initiative was stimulated by Bing Crosby's *Abie's Irish Rose* and the project was to try over the next years to 'tone down' such films, to remove dialogue and attitudes which were unfriendly to the Jewish character in particular and American Jewry in general.[22] Hollywood's producers, both Jewish and Gentile, could not be censored; they could only be persuaded to make the changes that Stone and his advisers thought were appropriate. The year 1947 marks an important stage in the development of the presentation of a positive Jewish image in American movies. It was a development that originally owed its existence to men like Zanuck and Schary, in addition to their screenwriters (it is estimated that 85 per cent of them were Jewish). They were to be assisted in their efforts by the gentle persuasion of the Motion Picture Project. The humanisation of the Jew was in the offing.

Notes

1. For a stimulating discussion of the film *Mission to Moscow* see David Culbert's 'Our Awkward Ally: Mission to Moscow (1943)', in J.E. O'Connor and M.A. Jackson (eds.) *American History/American Film* (New York, 1979), pp.121-45.

2. Shangrila was the Tibetan utopia of James Hilton's famous novel *Lost Horizons* (1933) which was filmed by Frank Capra, starring Ronald Coleman, four years later. The script of *The Purple Heart* appears in J. Gassner and D. Nichols (eds.) *Best Film Plays of 1943-44* (New York, 1945), pp.89-148.

The script also indicates a balance amongst the flyers geographically and culturally. One aspect of Greenbaum's character, which was lost in the film, was that he was an aspiring composer who wrote music on the backs of his navigation charts.

3. Larry Swindell claims in *Body and Soul, The Story of John Garfield* (New York, 1975), pp.189-93, 197, that the film was largely Garfield's idea and one of his favourite projects. He had read a magazine story about a blinded Marine, Al Schmid, and encouraged Maltz, an old friend, to produce the treatment upon which the film was eventually based. Garfield spent some time with the Schmid family in Philadelphia, prior to shooting, to build up his understanding of how the blinded man coped with his surroundings. All quotes are soundtrack transcriptions.

4. Two further examples of 'Jewish' characters in show business films are Phil Silvers in *Cover Girl* (1944) and S.Z. Sakall in *The Dolly Sisters* (1945). In *Cover Girl* the friendly bartender calls someone a 'schlomiel'; Silvers immediately corrects him, saying 'schlemiel, schlemiel'. The Yiddish word indicates a person for whom nothing ever turns out right.

5. I am grateful to Kevin Brownlow for this reference.

6. Quoted in R. Koszarski, *Hollywood Directors, 1941-76* (New York, 1978), pp.184f.

7. E. Cooper and M. Jahoda, 'The Evasion of Propaganda: How Prejudiced People Respond to Anti-Prejudice Propaganda', *Journal of Psychology* 23 (January 1947), pp.15-25; S.H. Flowerman, 'Mass Propaganda in the War Against Bigotry', *Journal of Abnormal and Social Psychology*, 42 (October 1947), pp.429-39; S.H. Flowerman and M. Jahoda, 'The Study of Man – Can Prejudice be Fought Scientifically?' *Commentary*, 3 (December 1946).

8. L.E. Raths and F.N. Trager, 'Public Opinion and *Crossfire*', *Journal of Educational Sociology*, 21 (February 1948), pp.345-68.

9. Later criticism, with some justification, complained that the appeal to self-interest (if you allow prejudice to harm others, it could happen to you as well) was hardly a principled reason. The film makers could argue that their reason was a more practical one. The pre-release research suggested little more than that the film did not contribute to anti-Semitism. Dialogue is soundtrack transcription.

10. This is an even more telling criticism of the Sidney Poitier film *Pressure Point* (1961), in which the anti-Semitic character (Bobby Darien's convincing role) was an institutionalised psychopath.

11. Henry Popkin argued in 1952 (*Commentary*, 14, pp.46-55) that Samuels was not endowed with any specific traits other than a vague benevolence so as to enlist everybody's sympathy. Also, Popkin was convinced that Sam Levene was unable to give his 'typical performance' because RKO did not want it saying that 'he was too Jewish'.

12. Archer Winsten in the *New York Post* (undated, Museum of Modern Art, New York (MoMA), Clippings File). There was a clause in Moss Hart's contract to prevent tinkering with the script after he had completed it. Zanuck wrote to Hart assuring him that any changes would be in keeping with their agreed emphasis (in M. Gussow, *Don't Say Yes Until I Finish Talking* (New York, 1971), pp.149f. Zanuck described the film as 80 per cent talk and 20 per cent action so that 'we must not make a dull picture even though it be significant and important'. Gussow feels that the film is a definitive Zanuck film of this period 'in terms of subject matter (anti-Semitism), source (a best-selling novel), approach (a social situation studied through a human relationship), timeliness, controversy, and quality packaging'. All dialogue is soundtrack transcription.

13. 20th Century Fox Release Synopsis in MoMA Clippings File.

14. The Reverend Smith, a close associate of Senator Huey Long of Louisiana, and Theodore G. Bilbo, former Governor of Mississippi, were famous for their public intolerance of anything which was not White Anglo Saxon Protestant.

15. This is consistent with Dave's almost hitting a drunk who calls him a Jew in a restaurant scene earlier in the film. Garfield's role was limited to a few scenes and about twenty minutes of screen time but it was of great importance to the over-all impact of the story. According to Swindell (*Body and Soul*, p.211), Julie Garfield said: 'I'm doing it for Gadge (Kazan) because the picture says something I believe, and it needs to be said.' Elliot Cohen said that the film was a 'moving, thought-provoking film, which dramatically brings home the question of anti-Semitism to precisely those people whose insight is most needed — decent, average Americans'. (*Commentary*, 5 (January 1948), pp.51-6). Cohen, however felt Dave Goldman 'a little too stereotyped' and the supporting figures like Minify, Liebermann, Weismann etc. too thin to be real.

16. Ronald Coleman was awarded the Oscar for best actor (*A Double Life*), while Loretta Young was best actress (*The Farmer's Daughter*). Edmund Gwenn's role in *Miracle on 34th Street* won him the award as best supporting actor.

17. Dmytryk had been a fringe CP member for only a few months, largely through his sympathy for the American black during the US-Soviet wartime alliance. Along with Scott, he left the party in 1946. They had been advised by their attorney to testify but chose to follow the line laid down by Lawson.

18. The traditional Hollywood inclination totally to obscure a central character's Jewishness was found in *Till the Clouds Roll By* from MGM in 1946. A glossy colour biography of composer Jerome Kern (played by Robert Walker), the film gave no hint that Kern was Jewish. But, then, perhaps it was not important.

19. Swindell, *Body and Soul*, pp.207-11. Enterprise underwrote *Body and Soul* and it was released by United Artists. Rossen was Garfield's favourite writer from his early film-making days. Bob Roberts, a close friend and associate of Garfield, headed Roberts Productions.

20. Middleton found reason to believe that the reduction in anti-Jewish prejudice was accompanied by a reduction in the expression of anti-Negro sentiments. See Russell Middleton, 'Ethnic Prejudice and Susceptibility to Persuasion', *American Sociological Review*, 25, no.5 (October 1960).

21. MoMA Clippings File, various dates.

22. For a brief description of the later work of the Motion Picture Project see the interview with Allen Rivkin in 'Introducing: The Jewish Film Advisory Committee, the Official Jewish Presence in Hollywood', *Davka Magazine* (Fall 1975), p.43.

THE CONTRIBUTORS

Tony Aldgate is Lecturer in History at the Open University.

Thomas Cripps is Professor of History at Morgan State University, Baltimore, Maryland.

Paul Monaco is Associate Professor of History at the University of Texas at Dallas.

Nicholas Pronay is Senior Lecturer in History at the University of Leeds.

K.R.M. Short is Senior Lecturer in History at Westminster College.

Elizabeth Grottle Strebel is a Lecturer in the Department of Cinema, State University of New York, Binghamton.

D.J. Wenden is Fellow and Bursar of All Souls College, Oxford.

INDEX